The Turbulent History
of a
Cotswold Valley

To my family
and
all who love these
valleys

The Turbulent History
of a
Cotswold Valley

The Upper Slad Valley and The Scrubs

Patricia M. Hopf

NONSUCH

First published 2006

Nonsuch Publishing Limited
The Mill, Brimscombe Port, Stroud, Gloucestershire, GL5 2QG
www.nonsuch-publishing.com

Nonsuch Publishing is an imprint of Tempus Publishing Group

British Library Cataloguing in Publication Data.
A catalogue record for this book is available from the British Library.

ISBN 1-84588-116-8
ISBN-13 (from January 2007) 978-1-84588-116-0

Typesetting and origination by Nonsuch Publishing Limited
Printed in Great Britain by Oaklands Book Services Limited

Contents

List of Maps

*Based on tithe maps in the Gloucester Record Office, to whom thanks are due for permission to publish

List of Illustrations

KEY FOR SOURCES OF PHOTOS

AL	Alan Lloyd
AP	Ann Parnell
APh	April Phillips
BJ	The late Commander Brian Jones
DN	Dinah Naylor
DS	David Smith
EM	Evangelical Magazine Vol. XI, Dec 1803
ES	The late Ernst Sommerfeld (photographer)
FM	The late Fred Major (photographer)
GM	Gloucester City Museum and Art Gallery who have provided the photos and given permission to publish them
GP	Gloria Peyton
HB	Howard Beard
JD	Jim Dickenson
JG	Jill Gyde
JS	Juliet Shipman
JXB	Jo Xuereb Brennan
LT	The late Lizzie Timbrell
NR	Neil Rees
PA	Peter Anson (1964)
PH	Patricia Hopf
WM	Wilf Merrett

Author's Note

Several histories have been written of the towns and villages in the area but very little has been documented of the lives of those in the countryside. This history considers in detail the Slad Valley from Steanbridge to Dillay Bottom, and its tributary valley going up to The Scrubs as shown in Map 1. In many respects it may be regarded as a microcosm of the valleys in the Frome River area. They have in common a dependence on agriculture and the production of cloth, first in cottages and later in mills. Moreover, the ups and downs of the inhabitants and their businesses are caused in the whole area by the same national and local events. The latter part of the story is of depopulation and nearly final decay of the buildings, reprieved in the second half of the twentieth century by an affluent society wanting to enjoy the privilege of country life. Inevitably such a study must reflect the background and interests of the author. In this case these include an economic slant, an interest in agriculture, an interest in the history of buildings and a curiosity to know what makes people behave as they do. It is hoped the valleys come to life in these terms in the pages which follow.

Principal written sources are old deeds and other records found in the Gloucestershire Record Office (GRO), and in private hands; data from the National Monuments Record (NMR) and publications, particularly on the woollen industry and agriculture as referred to in the notes and references. I am indebted to the excellent collections of the Gloucestershire Record Office, and the Local Studies Library (Gloucestershire Collection). I should particularly like to thank Paul Evans, John Putley, Mick Heath and Jenny Rebbec of the Record Office for their help and patience in finding relevant documents. I have also been able to use Stroud Library, Reading University Library and, for information on the Bishop of Mercia, Lambeth Palace Library. Some of the early documents have been difficult to decipher. It is believed that the interpretation is as accurate as possible.

The tithe maps and apportionments of around 1840 for the parishes of Bisley, Painswick and Miserden have provided a picture of ownership and tenancies as well as the number of dwellings at a moment in time. The Tithe Commission was set up in 1836 to replace the ancient tithe system. As part of its work surveyors were appointed to make large-scale maps and schedules, known as apportionments. The parish boundaries at that time were different from the present boundaries, Miserden Parish was responsible, in addition to its main area, for a tongue of land going into the Slad valley. Change took place in 1958 when most of this narrow strip of land was assigned to Painswick Parish but a few parcels were included in Bisley Parish. Because most of the information about properties relates to years prior to 1958, the original parishes have been used for identification purposes. The tithe maps and apportionments for these parishes were prepared from 1838 to 1842 and give information on landlords and tenants and their houses and fields. They also indicate for each field its size and usage. Not all maps are entirely accurate and some properties seem to have been omitted, but they constitute the most detailed source of information available for that date. As the tithe maps and apportionments are not always of the same dates, they are quoted in the text as 1840 unless the precise date is of special significance. The dates for each parish are as follows:

> Bisley, Apportionments 1841, Map 1842
> Miserden, Apportionments 1838, Map 1839
> Painswick, Apportionments 1839, Map 1839

The censuses from 1841 to 1901 give valuable information on the population, the number of houses, size of family, occupations and movements of population. They are, however, disappointing in that the designation of areas varies greatly from one census to another so that it is rarely possible to obtain comparative statistical data or to trace the history of occupation of individual dwellings. Large named houses, especially farm-houses, are exceptions, though occasionally even they are omitted altogether. Unexpectedly, the 1851 census is the most carefully conducted and the information is good and detailed on, for example, occupations. The 1841 census is also good and, used in tandem with the tithe maps and apportionments, enables many of the dwellings in the census to be located. The 1861 census is also of value. The amount of detail of the 1871 and 1881 censuses is much less, so that it is not possible to determine with any degree of certainty, which of the cottages listed with no identification are in the area of the study, let alone exactly where they are. The 1891 and 1901 censuses redeem themselves in this respect to some extent, but they seem to omit several cottages. The 1891 census has, for the first time, some information on the number of rooms, if under five, in each dwelling.

For some purposes it is necessary to discuss specific areas within the valleys rather than individual properties. The divisions used and the names given to them are shown in Map 1. The names for the two areas of Driftcombe and The Scrubs, which are now usually both called The Scrubs, are the names used in the censuses in the mid-nineteenth century as described in Appendix 2 on Place Names.

Information for the book has been gathered over a long period of time starting with talks with Mrs Lizzie Timbrell at Down Court and later at Stonehouse nearly forty years ago. She would have been 117 years of age had she been alive in 2005. There were many notes of conversations and written sources but writing the book did not begin until about five years ago. In the search to understand the valley I have had great assistance from residents and former residents of the valleys, from experts in particular subject areas, from librarians and curators and many more. Several persons have lent photographs of the area and others have tramped with me over the terrain giving a commentary of their knowledge as we went.

The book is arranged chronologically except for chapters on the Primitive Methodist Chapel, The Townsend Family and the Bishop of Mercia. In the course of gathering data a considerable amount of detailed information has been gleaned about individual properties, their owners and occupants. This has been drawn together in the Gazetteer. The latest information is that of December 2005. References to the sources of much of the material are listed, chapter by chapter, at the end of the book.

Sadly it has been possible to publish only a selection of the many photos given to me. I am grateful for all of them because even if there was not space for them all, they have often informed on some point in the text. The source of the each photograph can be found in the list of illustrations.

The photos originally come from a number of sources, some of them very illuminating. Many of the early ones of Down Farm were sent to Jim Dickenson's father while he was serving abroad in the First World War. The envelope still has a date of 1918. Others are from the photo and postcard collections of Howard Beard and Wilf Merrett. Many of the photos were produced by the Bisley photographer Fred Major about 1910.[1] I am indebted to Peter Baker of Bovis Homes for allowing me to take photos of the murals of Steanbridge House at his offices situated in the Old Rectory at Bishops Cleeve. Andrew Phillips helped me to understand the complexities of storing photos on the computer and my son Robert patiently prepared the photos for publication.

Thanks are due to the Gloucester City Museum and Art Gallery for permission to publish the photos of the Roman votive tablets and to the Gloucestershire Record Office for permission to publish parts of the tithe maps from their collection. I am also indebted to PFD on behalf of the Laurie Lee estate for permission to publish an extract from *Cider with Rosie* by Laurie Lee.

One of the pleasures of writing this book has been the discussions and correspondence I have enjoyed with my neighbours in the valley and in the nearby villages. Although I have generally mentioned only one name for each household, often whole families were involved. I have also had the privilege of discussions with a number of experts in their respective fields. I am indebted to Rupert Barrington of Dillay; Peter Barton of Sydenhams; Marian Beales, formerly of Steanbridge Mill; Harold Berkeley of Bisley; the late Daisy Bevan of Driftcombe; Jinny Cummins of Driftcombe; Ashley Dickenson, particularly on the flint arrow heads and Roman coins found at Stancombe; Jim Dickenson, son and grandson of farmers at Down Farm who knows the valley so well; Stefanie D'Orey of Driftcombe; the late Jack Eyres of Slad, a mine of information; Drucilla Fairgrieve of Steanbridge Mill; Ursula Falconer, formerly of Steanbridge House; Jim Fern who loves the valley and tells so many walkers of its history; Ivor Gardener of Camp whose family was a part of the valley for generations; John George of Down Farm; Jill Gyde, granddaughter of Lizzie Timbrell; William Hancock formerly of the Dillay; Roger Harding of the Scrubs; Mavis Hartwell, formerly of Sydenhams Farm House; Paul Heatlie of Down Cottage; Philip Holford of Sheepscombe, who lived as a boy at Greencourt and was the son of Charlie Holford who lived and worked in the Valley; Eileen Hooper, formerly of what is now August Cottage; Alf James who once lived at Scrubs Bottom; the late Commander Brian Jones of Slad, great nephew of the Squire at Steanbridge House; Quentin Letts of the former Primitive Methodist Chapel; Alan Lloyd formerly of St Benedicts; Ian Mackintosh, Director of the Stroudwater Textile Trust who helped me to understand the woollen industry; Kim McCrodden of St Benedicts; Wilf Merrett of Stroud, local historian and collector of photos and postcards; Dinah Naylor, formerly of Steanbridge House; Jane Newiss of Steanbridge House; Hugh Padgham of Trillgate Farm and formerly of St Benedicts; Ann Parnell, née Mansell, niece of Mrs Lizzie Timbrell; Gloria Peyton, formerly of Mullions; April Phillips of The Scrubs; Sally Rees of Driftcombe, third generation in the valley; Hilda Ruther who once lived at Yew Tree Cottage; Juliet Shipman of Eastcombe, author, including of *Bisley; a Cotswold Village Remembered*; Elizabeth Skinner of Sheepscombe, working on a local history; Dave Smith, son-in-law of the late Kathleen Taylor who lived as a girl at Woodedge; the late Duncan Smith of Driftcombe; the late Rodney Smith of Driftcombe; Maureen Stephenson of Sheepscombe, born at Timbercombe Cottage and granddaughter of Albert Hopkins, farmer at Dillay; the late Lizzie Timbrell formerly of Highwood, St Benedicts, Down Cottage and Down Court and an inspiration for this book; Bill Tombs formerly of Timbercombe Cottage; Adrian Underwood of Steanbridge Cottage; Lionel Walrond, former Curator of the Stroud Museum; Basil Weaving of Bisley who knew the valley and its inhabitants, Meg Weston-Smith of Sydenhams Farmhouse; Carolyn White of Stroud, who loves to paint the valley and has helped with research; the late Norman Williams, following his grandparents and father and farming all his life at Sydenhams; Roland Williams, son of Norman and carrying on the long farming tradition; Sarah Woolley who once lived at Down Cottage; John Workman of Ebworth, Forestry Adviser to the National Trust, bringing compromise between conservation and economics in forestry; the late John Wright of The Scrubs; Jo Xuereb Brennan of Woodedge and Michael Zajac, formerly of Steanbridge Mill.

Many of these have let me have sight of documents and family papers. A particularly important find was the deeds for the purchase of the land for the Primitive Methodist Chapel in 1840 in the possession of Quentin and Lois Letts. Many of those mentioned above have read parts of one of the drafts of the book and some valiant friends: Jean Bouckley, Jo Xuereb Brennan, Jinny Cummins, Jim Dickenson, Brenda Hague, Ian Mackintosh, Ted O'Neil, Carolyn White and my son John Hopf have read a whole draft, in some cases more than once. Very special thanks are due to Leo Cooper who made sure the book would be published. My family has helped in a number of ways—being dragged off to look at ruins, criticising the text and taking and organising the photos.

I have tried to make this history accurate, but it would be over-optimistic to assume that there are not several errors and many omissions. I would welcome any additions, comments or corrections which my readers are able to make.

1.   Merrett, Wilf (1987) 'A Village Photographer,' *Gloucestershire Family History Society Journal*, Manch, p.11

I

Introduction

This book describes the intricate and often traumatic history of the upper part of the Slad valley and its subsidiary valley, now known as The Scrubs (see Map 1). It spans a period from before the Romans invaded to the present, obviously with increasing detail as the centuries pass and more information becomes available. There are four main threads running through the book: agriculture, the woollen industry, the related houses, cottages and mills and, most importantly, the lives of those who dwelt and worked here. These themes are enlivened by vignettes of particular local characters and of dramatic domestic events. Much of the history of agriculture and the woollen industry, as well as the events taking place in England and the rest of the world affected, not just these valleys but the whole Stroudwater area and much of Gloucestershire. This history may be regarded as a case study of the larger area.

A favourite way to approach the Slad valley is through the Scrubs and Driftcombe. Following the road from Stancombe to Sydenhams and the Scrubs, one can glimpse two of the most beautiful and least spoilt valleys in the whole Cotswolds, both well hidden from the outside world. Persons living just three or four miles away in Stroud or Painswick, or even in Bisley, may not even imagine that they are there. At the high vantage point, it is possible to see the top of the spire of Painswick church, only about four miles away, but with two hills and valleys, clad in myriad shades of green, in between. In the Slad valley, Down Court and Down Farm can both be identified. Far away in reasonable weather May Hill can be seen with its unmistakable crown of trees and, in clear weather, the Welsh hills on the horizon. This distant view is an amazing contrast with the cosy, contained feeling in the valley bottom where existence is confined to wooded hills and burbling streams, amongst which are sprinkled a few ancient stone cottages and old manor houses. The valley is shared by the human inhabitants and a profusion of animal wildlife with a tapestry of wild flowers through the seasons.

History shows itself at every step, in old mills of the woollen industry, in the old farm buildings, one-time weavers' or farm labourers'

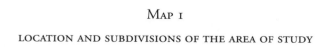

MAP 1

LOCATION AND SUBDIVISIONS OF THE AREA OF STUDY

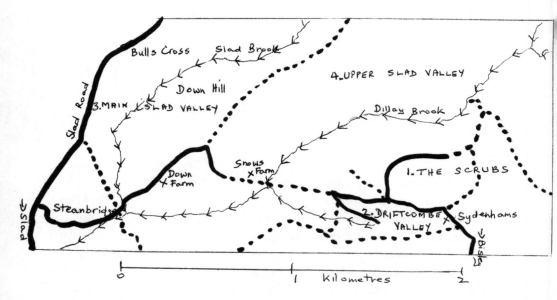

X	EXISTING HOUSES
▬	EXISTING ROADS
●●●●	SELECTED EXISTING TRACKS
→→→	STREAMS

cottages and an old chapel. The residents of the twenty-first century have used it to the full. As you dip down and turn the corner there is Sydenhams, the beautiful old house on the left, partly mediæval, now no longer a farm, but a lovely house with barns and farm buildings looking much as they were built, though well used for modern living. Further along there are arable fields on what was, several hundred years ago, the Common. Before the road plunges steeply down into the valley, there are tracks to old cottages, used mainly by agricultural workers when they were built in the nineteenth century, but now lived in, extended and well maintained by people with no connection with farming. Going down through the woods, the houses, or at least the original parts of them, are older, many of them going back to the 1600s. Here the traditional Cotswold stone positively glows after hundreds of years of weather and use. Many of these were weavers' cottages of one-down, one-up style but now all have been extended.

There is no road to the main Slad valley, though the footpath takes you down to the Roman Bridge over the stream and up again by an old Roman road to Snows Farm. Then, picking up a modern road again, it goes down the valley to Down

Farm and eventually to the old Steanbridge Mill and Steanbridge House, nestling below Slad. This was the home of the Townsend family who owned most of this part of the Slad valley for generations. Steanbridge is as far down the valley as the journey in this book goes. Up the valley from Snows Farm there are no roads; only beautiful footpaths and old tracks with some ruins along the way and Dillay Farm. In this part of the valley time has stood still and nature still manages to hold sway over man's intrusions.

The valleys are no strangers to change. Throughout the ages there have been periods of poverty, even starvation, interspersed with times of relative prosperity. Even in the good years life was constantly subject to the fear of future crop failures and disease. That was made worse by the extreme cold at various periods when the River Thames would freeze over. The history described in these chapters shows that there has been change in levels of prosperity with extraordinary frequency, due to the ups and downs in agriculture and in the woollen industry which dominated the valleys for some four or five centuries. Yet agriculture, in spite of variations due to major changes in climate, as well as the inevitable good and bad years for crops and animals, gradually improved. The yield of wheat provides an example. In the Middle Ages it was as little as two to three cwts an acre, increasing to say six to ten after enclosure, to twenty-five in the 1950s, fifty in the 1970s and 1980s and seventy cwts an acre by 2000. Changes in the technology of farming have speeded up over the centuries but commercial factors, as well as regulation by government and the European Union have sometimes counterbalanced the improvements in technology. This is not new. There has been interference by government for centuries. In the last few years regulation has been damaging to British farming and agriculture is in a period of decline. The reduction in the amount of arable land and the fall in the numbers of sheep and cattle are changing the landscape. In some fields in the Driftcombe valley stinging nettles and bracken dominate where there was once good pasture, and trees are growing up. Unless action is taken this one-time pasture will become woods within the lifetime of the young generation.

The development of the woollen industry on commercial lines, which gathered pace throughout the fifteenth and sixteenth centuries, affected the way of life in these valleys, bringing intermittent prosperity to the home weavers, in spite of their constant battles with the clothiers. Then came the introduction of factory working taking the workers away from home into the fulling mills and later to mills carrying out all stages of production. All this time the workers had been at the mercy of the fluctuations in the fortunes of the industry, affected by national and international politics as well as by the levels of demand and of competition. The woollen industry saga in these valleys came to an end towards the end of the nineteenth century causing degradation of the former woollen workers and a disaster for the valleys.

Superimposed on the relatively gradual changes, there have been traumatic events emanating from outside which, permanently or temporarily, ruined any prospect of gradual evolution. Little is known of the effects of invasions in prehistoric and early times but the coming of the Romans transformed the way of life of the people in these valleys. When they left the pattern of life probably returned to nearer that of pre-Roman times only to be turned upside down by the Normans and their strong government. There is little evidence that the area was badly affected by the Black Death though the effect it had on the feudal system was universal. There is, on the other hand, plenty of evidence of the effect of the Civil War, in the form of the Royalist armies which drove right through the valley with their reputation for rape and looting. They confiscated all the cloth they could find, and this was legally done!

The effects of the Napoleonic wars were economic rather than physically directly disruptive. The twentieth century was more affected by war from 1914–18 and again from 1939–45. Many inhabitants in both World Wars had to go and fight, and for those left it was a period of controls by government and particularly strong regulation of the actual day to day farming operations. Moreover, prior to the First World War agriculture in these valleys was in desperate straits due to the serious depression and, at the beginning of the Second World War, farmers were severely weakened by the 1930s depression and many commenced the war years with debts.

The development of agriculture and the growth and collapse of the woollen industry had taken place over centuries. All that time the people who lived in the valleys were, on the one hand clothiers and landowners and, on the other hand, the working class of agricultural labourer and artisan. The latter lived in the valleys generation after generation or, if they moved, they did so to go to a nearby parish. By the end of the nineteenth century, there was little work in the valleys and, such as there was, was poorly paid so that there was a very low standard of living. Slowly in the first half of the twentieth century people moved out, cottages fell down or became derelict. A few newcomers moved in. Some were refugees from the bombs of London or other large cities, some the lower level of society finding somewhere to live, and at least one a visionary seeking to make his mark. But the situation was still so bad that the valley was described as 'the last stop before the workhouse'.

Then in the late 1950s and 1960s all changed. Prosperity came to the valleys. Professional people from London wanted cottages in the country. They had enough money to be able to do essential repairs and were prepared to wait for greater comfort. But then the trickle became a flood. Houses were bought, modernized and extended and prices rose to what would have been astronomical levels only twenty years before. How did it happen? There seem to be four conditions which were suddenly realized: transport, higher earnings, disillusionment with life in a big city and the information technology revolution. None of this would have been possible until the motor car (or two) became commonplace. It would not have happened without a generally increased standard of living amongst the middle classes and it would not have happened had it been possible to buy a pleasant house and large garden in the towns. Lastly the new residents had to be able to continue to finance their lives and care for their families and that meant staying in constant contact with the source of work while in the country. The speed of its happening is nevertheless remarkable!

In this rural haven, enjoyed to a large extent by those from or connected with cities, are around twenty-five houses, compared with about fifty some 150 years ago. They are built mainly of Cotswold stone which develops a patina with age so that old houses enhance, rather than spoil the natural environment. Also here are about the same number of ruins where only the foundations remain, all the other stone having been reused in the cottages or in the walls of the fields. Indeed in the last 150 years whole small communities have been lost, notably at Detcombe and at Timbercombe. Many of the existing cottages are three or four hundred years old. Indeed it is the solid older houses which have survived, often once farm houses and partly the remains of the cloth industry in the shape of former mills and weavers' cottages.

The population of the area is about forty living in the valleys most of the time and another fifteen or so using the houses as a base for weekends and holidays. The population in 1851 is estimated at about 200. Thus, the number of dwellings has halved and the population is about a quarter of that of 150 years ago. This is in spite of the size of many of the dwellings having increased several fold so that the space per person is probably four or five times as much.

There are disturbing aspects in the present situation. Most of the residents in the valleys make their contribution to the wider economy elsewhere, in the city or in the media, for example. Farming is in decline and the woollen industry no longer exists. At one time the valley produced what it consumed directly or indirectly. Now most of the valley occupants produce almost nothing in the immediate locality. Its role for them is provide a pleasant environment to be enjoyed by the persons privileged to live there and also by the many ramblers who pass through. Yet maybe it is the very tranquillity of the valley which enables the residents to be creative and productive. Their output may be consumed elsewhere, but it is the people of the valley who make it. They must try and ensure that, in enjoying the environment, they do not damage it for whatever role it is called upon to play in the next millennium.

2

Subsistence, Civilisation and Struggle: Before 1066

EARLY HISTORY

People were living in the area round Bisley and Painswick over 6000 years ago and in these valleys at least from the Neolithic period (3500–2500 BC). By this time the inhabitants were beginning to farm. They, or those from nearby villages, buried their dead in long barrows near Holbrook Farm on the Bisley-Camp road and near to Camp itself.[1] There is evidence of everyday life in the form of tools and artefacts. Flint arrow heads have been found at Down Hill and Scrubs Common and nearby at Stancombe. The nearest source of flint is 50 miles away on the Wiltshire chalk downs so that either the flint or the ready-made arrow heads were brought by traders. At least some arrow heads were made locally because Ashley Dickenson, while farming at Stancombe, has found cores, that is, pieces of flint from which slivers have been taken.

Some evidence of Bronze Age (2000–700 BC) settlements has been found near Painswick, at Waterlane and at Miserden and of Iron Age (c. 700–0 BC) occupation near to Bisley.[2] Bronze Age arrow heads have also been found at Stancombe and The Scrubs. On Custom Scrubs there are lines of an earthwork and it has been suggested that there was an ancient camp there but the evidence is slight and the date is unknown.[3] There is however little reason to doubt settlement in the area. Certainly in the Cotswolds as a whole there were hundreds of round barrows built in the second millennium and, in the first millennium, a large number of hill forts and also of oppida, tracts of countryside partly enclosed by banks. There is an example of these on Minchinhampton Common.

Some cultivation took place in the Cotswolds in both the first and second millennia BC. Towards the end of the Bronze Age barley was used for making unleavened bread and, by 300BC, for brewing ale. Large areas of the ancient forests were cleared by the end of the Iron Age. There were domesticated cattle, goats, pigs and sheep. Tame chicken and duck are thought to have appeared by 100 BC. There was a choice of vegetables and of fruit, gathered in the countryside. Slaughter of a large animal would have taken place for a special occasion or perhaps

MAP 2

SIGNS OF THE ROMANS

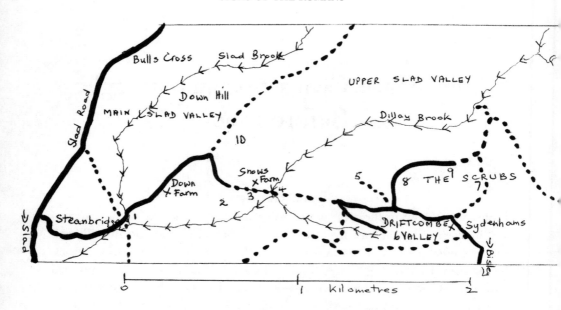

X   EXISTING HOUSES

▬▬   EXISTING ROADS

●●●●   SELECTED EXISTING TRACKS

➔➔   STREAMS

KEY

1   Possible Roman cistern found during excavations for an extension to the present Steanbridge Cottage

2   Site of Roman building south of and between the present Snows Farm and Down Farm[4]

3   A possible Romano-British terrace-way with a turf-covered metalled surface, from Snows Farm to the Slad Brook. It may have continued to 5 below[5]

4   Bridge, known locally as 'the Roman Bridge', linking to the road in 3 above[6]

5   Roman altars, indicating a possible temple site, found in a quarry on the site of the present cottage, Journeys End[7]

6   Bricks, believed to be Roman found in digging a septic tank at the present Driftcombe Farm

7   Crop marks of possible Romano-British enclosures[8]

8   Crop marks of possible Romano-British enclosures[9]

9   A Scatter of Romano-British material found in 1989—pottery, iron slag and gritstone[10]

10 Crop marks NE of the present Down Court, of linear features, possibly forming enclosures, and perhaps related to 2 above, probably 5 cottages but 7 households)

because there was not enough food to carry the livestock through the winter. The normal diet would have been eggs, milk, grains, vegetables and some white meat. Honey was important for sweetening and for making mead which was the drink of nobles and warriors. It is said that a chieftain's bodyguard would fight his battles in return for drinking his mead.[11]

When the Romans came to the area they would have found the Dobunni peoples in occupation. The Dobunni were originally of Belgic origin and had come through Wessex to the rich ill-defended Cotswolds.[12] They inhabited most of the Cotswolds and probably extended their control north-east, perhaps as far as the east coast of England. Their capital was at Bagendon, north east of Minchinhampton. They were skilled smiths and some of their ornaments are amongst the most prized treasures of Celtic art in Britain. Coins were minted in Bagendon in the second century BC. There is evidence that they traded with the Roman Empire before the Romans invaded.

Roman Civilisation Arrives

Before the Romans came the Dobunni had become tributaries of the Catuvellauni. In spite of the fierce fighting between the Romans and the Britons, particularly the Iceni elsewhere in Briton, there is little evidence of military activity in this area after the Romans arrived. It seems that the Dobunni accepted the Romans and were, perhaps, even glad of their protection. Cirencester became the capital of the Dobunni civitas or centre of government. The Dobunni lived in Iron-Age settlements of round houses of wood and turf and these continued to be built in Roman times. In the first and second centuries AD they were also building rectangular wooden frame buildings. The Romans built some forts at strategic positions to keep the borders of the area safe, for example, the border to Wales. They do not seem to have been intended to control the Dobunni, as it seemed that was not necessary. The Romans built villas in stone especially in the third and fourth centuries AD. Some were for the nobles but others were for large farmers who may have been of Roman origin, but intermarriage had blurred the distinction between Romans and Britons.

Map 2 shows the location of known Roman remains found in the two valleys. The extent of the dwellings and other buildings would have been much greater than indicated because many of the buildings would have been made of wood and would have decayed. Other ruins may yet be located.

Two Roman votive tablets were discovered in 1799 and 1801 during quarrying at The Scrubs. Baddeley[13] described the place as 'one of the most beautiful scenes in Gloucestershire on a grassy platform still called Roman Tump.' That name seems to have died out and the grass is replaced by woods. It is believed the tablets were found near to the present cottage known as Journeys End. The find suggests that a significant group was living in the valleys. One tablet bears a figure of Romulus in the guise of Mars. It is about eighteen inches high and twelve inches across. It is said to confirm the theory that, in Gloucestershire, the war god Mars or Romulus was regarded as a fertility god fighting to protect the crops. The other one is slightly larger and is thought to represent a *genius,* a local deity who was worshipped as the personification of some particular society, town or tribe. These two are in the Gloucester City Museum (see Plates 1 and 2). Another was found in 1851 on the same site and is now in the Corinium Museum in Cirencester. The prominent position of the site with a commanding view over the Slad valley suggests a suitable place for a shrine.[14] If the area was in woodland there was probably a clearing there and perhaps a view through to the main Slad valley so that the shrine would have been visible from the villa below. Recently a fourth century Roman coin was found there. Small votive statues have also been found at Bisley Church and at Eastcombe.

The Romans were also settled up the top of The Scrubs at Stancombe and east of Stancombe Plantation. In this area Ashley Dickenson has found eight Roman coins. One of these is of the time of the Emperor Postumus AD 258–268 and another of Constantius AD 337–361. Neptune is on the reverse with a trident and a dolphin. He has also found pottery from the second and third centuries AD, several beads, one of them probably made in Syria, and four brooches.

There was a Roman building, possibly a villa, on the slope down to the stream between Down Farm and Snows Farm. 4th century coins have been found there as well as some flue tiles, now in the Stroud Museum.[15] In a very hot summer, a view from the rooftop of a cottage in the Scrubs showed variations in the vegetation known as crop marks which are often signs of old foundations. There are vestiges of enclosures, possibly related to the villa, north east of Down Court. From this area, and more specifically from Snows Farm, there is what is believed to be a Romano-British track which has a turf-covered metalled surface which descends in a single steep and direct line to the Slad valley. A single span stone bridge with a semicircular arch carries the roadway across the stream.[16] This may have continued to the shrine on the Scrubs. This bridge has always been known locally as the Roman Bridge. It was at one time wide enough to take a horse and cart but was damaged when a load of timber drawn by horses was crossing in the Second World War. It was renovated at its present width in 1994.

The Romans were probably well settled in the whole valley. At the Scrubs, north of Sydenhams on the spur, a considerable amount of Romano-British material was found in 1989. It included pottery, iron slag and gritstone scattered over about one hectare. Aerial photographs have shown two cropmark features at the Scrubs. Their date is not known but they may well have been Romano-British enclosures.[17]

Lower down the main valley at Steanbridge, it is reported that an old Roman cistern was found at Steanbridge Cottage during the construction of an extension.

In the side valley at the site of the present Driftcombe Farm, some remains, thought to have been Roman because of the shape of the bricks, were discovered while a septic tank was being dug. Indeed the latter site is exactly the sort of location favoured by the Romans because it has springs, it is sheltered and is not too far from the place of worship and other Roman villas.

The Romans had introduced new foods, notably pheasants, rabbits and guinea fowl. The last two are said to have died out after the Romans left, the rabbits being reintroduced by the Normans. Cooking at this time was generally by means of an iron or bronze cauldron suspended over the fire. Ovens were less usual and often communal for a whole village. The practice of taking the Sunday joint to the baker, even if the household had an oven, continued into the twentieth century.[18]

The Romans left Britain at the beginning of the fifth century. Troops were withdrawn so that they could defend Italy against the Goths. Slowly British links with Rome diminished. Coins, for example, were no longer being supplied to Britain. The withdrawal was complete by the middle of the fifth century.[19] There followed a general decline in Britain about which little is known. It may have happened gradually rather than as a catastrophic event. The economic framework disintegrated, the standard of living fell and villas became too expensive to maintain and fell into disuse. There is some evidence that the old Iron Age forts were used as markets during this period. This was the beginning of the so-called Dark Ages and conditions similarly deteriorated in most of Europe, as the influence of a Roman civilization waned. However the standard of the workmanship of some of the artefacts found in archaeological digs shows that civilization survived, at least for the upper classes.

ATTACK FROM ALL SIDES

After the departure of the Romans there were raids from the Saxons in the South and Picts in the North. King Vortigen invited the Angle leaders (from the south of Denmark) to help to defend him against the Picts but instead they became the invaders, resisted, according to legend, by King Arthur.[20] The Angles took over much of Eastern Britain and also Mercia, which included the Cotswolds, and much land to the north and east. 'In 577 the Saxons came over from Wiltshire across the Cotswolds to the Severn Valley. There was a great battle at Deorham, near Bath, and Gloucester, Cirencester and Bath were captured.'[21] Bisley and probably the Slad and Scrubs valleys would have been substantially affected. In the ninth century a Wessex king, Egbert, conquered Mercia and briefly came to rule all England south of the Thames. Meanwhile the Vikings were increasing the strength of their raids and gained success in much of the more northerly kingdoms of Britain but left Wessex largely intact.

Over a period of about six centuries many factions were warring in major battles or small skirmishes. So little is known about the whole period that it is difficult to judge the effect on the ordinary inhabitant of this countryside. There is little known about cultivation but wool was very important even in that period. Anglo Saxon wills discuss the disposition of sheep and excavations reveal sheep bones, sheep shears, wool spindles, weaving batons and all the paraphernalia of cloth production.[22] For many generations in this long period life would have continued as usual in the production of food and clothing and in the construction of shelter.

The land was covered with trees nearly to the same extent as in Roman times.[23] It may have been at this time that cultivation in open fields, with each person having strips of land to till, began. Grazing on common land may also go back to this time. Sheep were valued for their milk, meat and wool. Pigs were commonplace. Cattle were, however, the most prized and, presumably, most scarce. Goats were few. Wheat and barley were the main arable crops.[24]

THE UNWELCOME NORMANS

By the time of the Norman invasion in 1066, the manorial system was well established in most of England. The manor was a territorial unit that was originally held by feudal tenure under which the lord occupied the land on condition of homage to a superior lord. Those living in the area of the manor were freemen or villeins. The former paid a rent, often nominal, but the villeins had to work a set number of days on the fields of their lord or give him a share of their own produce. They also had to give a tenth of their produce to the church, the tithe. The villeins did not have the opportunity to earn money. They lived on what they could produce on their strips in the open fields and by grazing on the common pastures, on fallow land and on the open fields after the harvest. There were also an exceptional number of slaves in Gloucestershire. The Domesday Book of 1086 recorded that 26% of the population were slaves, though it is not known whether slavery was prevalent in these valleys. It was this system which the Normans found and used to impose their governance on an unwilling and hostile population.

1. Morton, Richard (1997) Sydenhams Farm, Bisley, Gloucestershire: Archaeological Assessment for Mr Charles Howard, Cotswold Archaeological Trust, Kemble Business Park, Cirencester, Gloucestershire

2. Morton, *op. cit.*

3. NMR Monument Report 114864 Possible earthworks at Custom Scrubs, NMR:SO 80 NE 3, Grid Ref SO 895 080

4. NMR Monument Report 114887 Possible Site of Roman Building NMR SO 80 NE 16, Grid Ref SO 882 081

5. NMR Monument Report 114863 Possible Romano-British Terraced Way and stone bridge, NMR SO 80 NE 2, grid Ref SO 8872 0803

6. NMR Monument Report 114863 *op. cit.*

7. NMR Monument Report 114865 Three Roman altars found at Custom Scrubs indicating a possible temple site, NMR SO80 NE4, Grid Ref SO 8907 0802

8. NMR Monument Report 1074610 Cropmarks north east of Sydenhams, NMR SO 90 NW 69, Grid Ref SO 9005 0804

9. NMR Monument Report 1074621 Cropmark of L shape west of Scrubs Common, NMR: SO 80 NE 85, Grid Ref SO 8948 0799

10. Marshall, A (1991) 'Bisley with Lypiatt, The Scrubs', *Transactions of the Bristol and Gloucestershire Archaeological Society*, Vol 109

11. Summers, Averil (1997) *Pass the Pork Scratchings*, Dean Archaeological Group

12. Finberg, Josceline (1977) *The Cotswolds*, London: Eyre Methuen

13. Baddeley, Welbore St Claire (1907) *A Cotswold Manor being the History of Painswick*, Gloucester: John Bellows, London: Kegan Paul, Trench, Trubner & Co Ltd

14. Rhodes, John (1964) *Catalogue of Romano-British Sculptures*, Gloucester City Museum; Henig, Martin (1993) *Roman Sculpture from the Cotswold Region with Devon and Cornwall*, Oxford: OUP

15. NMR Monument Report 114887 *op. cit.* and 917525 Possible part of enclosures north east of Down Court, NMR SO 80 NE 72, Grid Ref SO 885 081

16. NMR Monument Report 114863 *op. cit.*

17. Marshall, A. *op. cit.*

18. Dean Archaeological Group (2000) *Garlic in my Cauldron: Life in the Early Medieval, Food and cookery following the Romans*, Lydney Glos: Dean Archaeological Group

19. Briggs, Asa (1983) *A Social History of England*, London: Book Club Associates p.50

20. Briggs, *op. cit.* p.51

21. Rudd, Mary A. (1937) *Historical Records of Bisley*, Published privately, Edn 1977, Alan Sutton p.7

22. Lacey, Robert and Danziger, Danny (1999) *The Year 1000*, Abacus: 2000 p.73

23. Grundy, G.B., (1936) 'The Ancient Woodlands of Gloucestershire', *Transactions of the Bristol and Gloucestershire Archaeological Society*, Vol. 58, See map opposite p.65

24. Briggs, *op. cit.* pp.52–3

3

The Rule of the Manor:
The Middle Ages, 1066–1603

INTRODUCTION

There are various interpretations of the term Middle Ages. Here it is used to start at the Norman conquest and continue until the end of the Tudor dynasty at the death of Queen Elizabeth in 1603. There is remarkable continuity over the whole period in the way society was organized and the way the ordinary person lived. The pace of change was slow compared to that of the following centuries. This is evident in the persistence of the manorial system, in spite of gradual developments in the ties of the inhabitants of a manor to their lord. Continuity is demonstrated by the methods of cultivation which altered little over the period, though enclosure and the increase in tenancies were having their effects. Change was however taking place in the making of cloth which developed from a task for each household for its own consumption to a capitalist industry, organized from London and with ramifications abroad. Yet the process had still not greatly altered, only the organization and the scale.

At the time of the Domesday Book (1086) woodland swine pastures were a feature of the South Cotswolds. Bisley Parish was probably then a series of clearings and some of the tenants would have paid part of their dues in honey gathered in the woods.[1] Honey was in great demand and was used for sweetening and for making mead. At the beginning of the period the population lived in small cramped dwellings built of wood and other materials which were not very durable. In the Cotswolds and certainly in these valleys, with the availability of stone, by the end of the period most dwellings were constructed using at least some stone. Lords of the manor and rich clothiers lived in relative luxury in stone houses. The lives of the ordinary cottagers continued to revolve round provision of food, clothing, and shelter. Throughout the Middle Ages the peasants lived in fear of crop failures which could bring hardship and even starvation.

The area was of some importance from at least mediæval times. It is known that the bridge over the stream just above Steanbridge was in existence in 1353 and is thought to be older. There were a number of routes along and across the valley.

MAP 3

SIGNS OF MEDIÆVAL TIMES

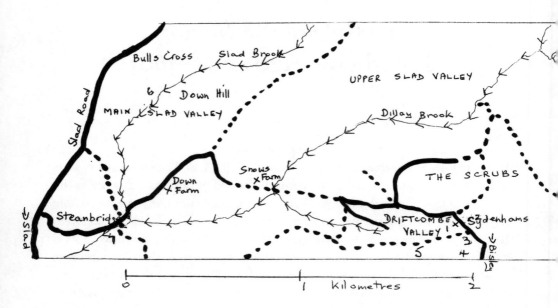

X	EXISTING HOUSES
▬	EXISTING ROADS
●●●●	SELECTED EXISTING TRACKS
→→	STREAMS

KEY

1 Sydenhams
2 Deserted mediæval village at Sydenhams[3]
3 Earthworks south of Sydenhams, date uncertain[4]
4 Lynchets[5]
5 Lynchets[6]
6 The Nap, now Triligate Cottage
7 Bridge over Slad Brook and linking to track

The route now known as King Charles Lane, crossing the valley by the bridge over the Slad Brook, was important as part of the route linking Painswick, Gloucester, Bisley and Cirencester[2] (see Map 3).

THE MANORIAL SYSTEM AND SYDENHAMS

The Norman invasion in 1066 was a turning point in the history of England. Because there was substantial opposition to the Normans, the King had no option but to bring in French noblemen to run the country and ensure compliance with his orders. Twenty years after the invasion nearly all tenants-in-chief were foreign-born. In Bisley Earl Hugh was Lord of Bisley. He was Hugh d'Avranches (commonly called 'le Gros' from his gluttonous habits), a cousin of King William. He would not have spent much time in Bisley for he had other duties to perform. Robert Tilleul, his cousin, was probably his tenant[7] and acted as Lord of the Manor. He would have had some jurisdiction over the area of these valleys. Sydenhams, a lesser manor, was in the parish of Bisley. The land in the valley in Painswick parish was under the Painswick manor. Most of the east side of the Slad valley was then in the parish of Miserden.

The population in the manors consisted mainly of villeins or serfs (also called bordars or cottars) who were assigned pieces of land but they had no legal title to their holdings. They were not allowed to leave the manor. As the slave population in Gloucestershire was high, there were probably slaves in the valleys at the time of the Norman invasion. However, by the twelfth century slaves seem to have been settled on holdings either as bovari, so called because they theoretically had access to the amount of land a man could plough in a year, a bovate, or as demesne ploughmen, working on the land the Lord of the Manor had reserved for himself.[8] There might also have been some freemen within the jurisdiction of the manor.

The mediæval system was very wasteful. The baulks dividing the strips were wide and totally uncultivated. Moreover the cultivation of little plots was fiddly in spite of common use of oxen and horses. Improvement of the land was not practicable. The cattle and other animals grazed on the common land and control over their breeding and over diseases was impossible. Slowly the manorial system altered. One aspect which changed was the relationship of the villein to the lord. Agreements were made to commute the labour and dues of the villein to money payments. These, however, were not linked to inflation, so that the real value of the commutation payments eventually reduced. This commutation was halted temporarily by the Black Death which caused an acute shortage of labour but, by the end of the sixteenth century villeinage was extinct. The former villeins were known as customary tenants or copyholders, because they had a copy of the manorial records giving them the right to occupy their land.

In theory, the lord of the manor had control over his villeins but it was not in his interests to treat them badly as he depended on them for the running of the estate. The treatment of villeins was dictated by custom and this included provision for a villein to pass on his holding to his family. At Bisley in 1354 a villein was able, even during his lifetime, to arrange that:

> Walter Tymbercombe, tenant of a messuage and half a yardland for his own and his wife's lifetime, gives to the lord a fine of 13s 4d in that John, his younger son, may, after their deaths hold the same for the same services.[9]

It seems likely that the messuage and land in question was Timbercombe in the Slad valley from which he took his name.

There are remains in the present manor house of Sydenhams of thirteenth or fourteenth century construction and there was probably a house there even before that time. In mediæval times it was the focal point of wealth and activity in the valley which it so majestically commands. It was one of six independent manors in the parish of Bisley. Sydenhams was a small manor and it seems that its lord had no other manors. Its lands were all in Bisley parish, mainly on the higher ground on the Scrubs and in the Driftcombe valley. The owner of Sydenhams attended the Manorial Court in Bisley.

Map 3 of the mediæval period shows that there was at this time quite a community near to Sydenhams, as evidenced by the remains of a mediæval village in the fields to the east, opposite the house, beyond the buildings of the farm.[10] Houses would have been made of wood or wattle with a thatched roof and there is now nothing left for the amateur archaeologist to see there. The ground was cultivated in the usual feudal strip system. To the south of Sydenhams, on rising ground, are the remains of lynchets, banks of earth between the ploughed strips of mediæval times. The various unidentified linear crop marks showing different levels of cultivation, and therefore the likely position of fields and boundaries, north east and north west of Sydenhams in the fields known as the Common,[11] may have been Roman but they were possibly much later.

Unfortunately the old deeds of Sydenhams are lost and the date and origin of Sydenhams is not known. It is however referred to in mediæval documents, the earliest in 1302.

Manors aimed at being self-sufficient. Although Sydenhams was small, the community would have grown or otherwise produced nearly all its needs. The mill, which was at one time a corn mill, near the Roman Bridge in Miserden parish may have been used in the middle ages or there might have been other corn mills or windmills on the higher land. It seems that Sydenhams Manor conformed to the normal pattern of having the villagers near the manor house and the common fields also close by. The word 'tyning', as part of a field name, indicates that the field was part of the open field system. Almost due east of Sydenhams is The Tyning and, south of that, Great Tyning. The village itself was behind the existing

Dutch barn and therefore between the manor house and the open fields. It is not known where the lord's demesne was but it is possible it was in the field known as Home Ground just north of Sydenhams where there is a linear crop mark. Alternatively Home Ground may simply have meant 'near the Manor House'.

In 1546 Bisley was a Royal manor of Henry VIII. The manorial records tell something of the lord of the manor of Sydenhams. It was reported that:

> The Homage presents that John Smallbrugo who held a close called Rydinge for rent of 2d is dead and the said John held a virgate, Sydhams for 20 shillings and 1 penny a year, whence a relief of 20 shillings and a penny, and that William Smallbridge is his heir and of full age. Thereupon comes the wife of John and seeks to be admitted tenant of the said close—granted.[12]

The homage consisted of twelve homagers or jurors who sat in the manorial court. A virgate was a substantial piece of land up to thirty acres, usually spread about among the common fields and often included rights to use of the commons. It was not unusual for a widow to be given the right to live in her deceased husband's property, or part of it, without paying heriot, a sort of tax imposed on the transfer of property, sometimes in the form of money but often in kind, such as the best cow. The widow was said to be given 'freebench'.

One of the factors which changed the manorial system was the Black Death. The large loss of life in England is variously assessed but Ziegler[13] concludes that it could conceivably be as high as 45% or as low as 23%. A third is not too far out as a rough and ready rule of thumb. It caused a shortage of labour and a rise in wages and enabled some movement of population. It seems likely that it at least hastened the end of villeinage and of the manorial system. There is no information specific to these valleys on the Black Death. Even if there were no deaths in the valleys, the inhabitants would still have been affected by the changes in the economic situation and particularly by the labour shortage. The first major city in England to be affected was Bristol in 1349 and there the plague raged according to an old calendar, 'to such an extent that the living were scarce able to bury the dead.' In Gloucester the Town Council tried to isolate themselves from outsiders, especially those from Bristol, but the rats observed no barriers and the city was badly affected as were villages nearby.[14] One of the indications of the deaths from the Black Death or other plagues is the frequent deaths and replacements of vicars. In Rudd's History of Bisley there are no rapid change-overs at this period, though a vicar did die in 1348 when the Black Death was raging. Rudd comments that there is no record or indication that the plague affected Bisley. There is equally no indication that the area was not affected. The historian Ian Mackintosh has noted that the number of those paying Poll Tax in Bisley dropped from forty-seven in 1327 to thirty-four in 1381. This might not be a result of fatalities from the Black Death but it could be connected through the economic consequences. It might be that it was the plague, or the opportunities it gave for the inhabitants to better themselves elsewhere, which caused the disappearance of the mediæval village at Sydenhams. It seems that St Clair Baddeley did not find any information for Painswick. He says 'whether the Black Death scourged Painswick does not appear'.[15]

FARMING AND FOOD

The arable land was in large fields divided into strips separated by stones, baulks or lynchetts of unploughed land. It is the surviving evidence of these dividing baulks which gives some indication of where the large open fields were. The strips were cultivated either for the lord or allocated to peasants. Each person had strips in all fields. There was an amount of common pasture, sometimes called waste, though it was not useless.

The land would have been used alternately for grain and fallow, although on better land it was possible to have a three field system of two grain crops to one of fallow. After the harvest the land would have been thrown open for grazing. The only winter feed for animals was hay, gathered from strips of pasture, and many animals had to be killed during the winter. The method of cultivation was ploughing by oxen on the flatter land, but on hilly land much cultivation would have been done by hand. Wheat was cut with the sickle or a tool known as a fagging hook, and barley and oats mown with the scythe. Hay was mown, turned and raked up by hand. Threshing was carried out in the winter in the large barns. Yields were low and much of the crop would have been in poor condition.

In the three field system, one field lay fallow while the others were cultivated. The same crop was grown on each strip of land in the field. On one field rye or wheat was grown and on the second barley or oats or beans. In this way the setting and harvesting processes were staggered. Barley was sown in the spring and gathered in the autumn. Wheat and rye were sown in autumn and harvested in late summer of the following year. The yield was six to eight bushels an acre, equivalent to about three to four cwt an acre, though on the Cotswolds it may have been less. In the period to 1500 oats were widely grown on the Cotswolds and especially in the general area of Stroud. There it could be as much as 40% of the sown area. Barley was also important and sometimes barley and oats were sown together and yielded mixed grain, known as dredge. Very few legumes were grown. After harvest the land was opened for the villagers' cattle to graze and the villagers also grazed their animals on the uncultivated common land. This assisted with the manuring of future crops. The villagers appreciated the value of manure which was 'bought, sold, borrowed and stolen', leading to disputes between villagers before manorial courts.[16]

The ordinary peasant's first preoccupation was to survive. Whereas in most years he probably had enough food, there were almost certainly long periods when he was starving or at least malnourished. The climate was not conducive to good crops in some of this period. There was a bout of unstable weather around 1300 with the year 1315 being known as the Great Famine throughout Europe. Torrential rain destroyed crops. The next 150 years saw a period of cool wet summers. In 1371 there had been a year of terrible famine throughout the country and the memory of the conditions at that time stayed in the minds of the peasants for generations to come. There was an improvement in the weather around 1500 but from the second half of the century it was cold again. July was the month when the greatest deprivation was likely to occur because by then the food stored from the previous harvest had often been used up but the current year's harvest had not yet begun. It was also the time which showed the greatest divisions between the rich and poor, because the rich would have had enough grain to store, and could, if need be, afford the soaring market prices.[17] One of the factors which enabled the villeins to survive, even in times of bad harvest, is that in the winter they were usually weaving the wool which their wives and daughters had spun. A surplus could be sold to supplement their income.

There are some data on agricultural wages from the thirteenth century[18] and there are also indices of prices from the same period.[19] The wages of an agricultural labourer were around a third to a half a carpenter's wages. The figures show that the purchasing power of agricultural labourers was as high in the fifteenth and sixteenth centuries as at any time until the end of the nineteenth century.

Sheep have been of great importance to the farms on the Cotswolds for many hundreds of years. By the twelfth and thirteenth centuries England was the principal supplier of high quality wool to Northern Europe. The size of flocks in the Bisley area after the middle of the fourteenth century increased to two or three hundred. Cattle and pigs were also important. Among the pig owners in Bisley in 1431, one had forty animals and another seventeen, three owned ten pigs and two owned eight.[20]

The Development of the Cloth Industry

There is a long tradition in rural England, including the Cotswolds, of the making of cloth in the cottages for use by the household. During the Middle Ages the inhabitants of the area were becoming involved in cloth production as a business. This was particularly appropriate because of the large number of sheep and the excellent quality of the wool. The industry had been important in England as a whole since the eleventh and twelfth centuries but in the thirteenth century the industry was in decline. Edward III (1312–1377) invited Flemish weavers to settle in England to raise the quality of English cloth. Their presence was resented but they were men of substance and developed the industry into a capitalist business with an important export market. In the Stroud valleys the main product was broadcloth, using short staple wool, rather than worsted, though other cloths were produced. There is a tradition, recorded in the eighteenth century, that some of the Flemish weavers brought over by Edward III settled in Stroud, but the development of the industry there postdates their coming to England.[21] Nevertheless at a later date clothiers of Flemish origin may well have settled there.

In the Cotswolds by the mid-fifteenth century cloth production had become a serious business. The processes of the industry were many, with different people engaged at each stage. First the wool had to be sorted, cleaned and, for the production of worsted, combed. Then it had to be spun and woven. In the Middle Ages weaving was solely a home industry. After weaving, the cloth was cleaned of the oil and size used during earlier processes and it was then felted by a process known as fulling. At one time this was done by stamping on the cloth with feet but early in mediæval times it was done in fulling mills by machinery using fulling stocks. The stocks consisted of two wooden feet which were alternately raised and lowered onto the cloth as it lay in a trough with a little water and fuller's earth in it. The power came from a water wheel. The process took up to twelve hours or, for some special cloth, much longer. Fulling was a skilled business. The cloth had to be folded and turned so that the shrinking process was even. Largely because of the suitability of its streams for fulling and the supply of water power, the Frome and its tributaries was by far the most important area for the industry in Gloucestershire. The Slad valley is part of this river system. Fulling was the earliest process to go into mills. A fulling mill was first recorded in Rodborough around 1270 and by the 1400s there were many. As the fulling mills developed, water in the streams of the valleys became overused and numerous arguments between neighbours ensued, leading to the supply of water being a matter for a number of legal agreements and, of course, disagreements.

After fulling the nap was raised by hand with teasles and then finished by removing the uneven knap using shears. The cloth was usually dyed when it was finished but sometimes the wool was dyed before spinning. Much of the cloth was exported undyed, after fulling, leaving the cloth to be finished abroad.

There were constant fluctuations in the state of the industry. There were several reasons for these fluctuations. The price of wool was both a cause and an effect, often being affected by factors external to the industry such as the Black Death. In 1380, the price of a todd (28 lbs) of wool was nine shillings and four pence, by 1421 it was thirteen shillings and a penny and by 1452 down to seven shillings.[22] In the 1570s the price of wool was very high and wool was in short supply. In some cases fluctuations in the wool trade were due to difficulties in export markets, for example, in the 1550s the market for broadcloth in central Europe had declined and the Merchant Adventurers' mart in Antwerp collapsed.

The industry in Gloucestershire was increasingly organised on capitalist lines during the mediæval period, with the clothiers buying the raw wool, or sometimes the spun yarn, and paying others to carry out each subsequent process. In this way they owned the cloth at all or most stages of its manufacture. If they made a profit they were able to treat their subcontractors reasonably well, but in bad times they squeezed the incomes of the persons working for them and reduced them often to starvation levels. The welfare of the weavers in the valleys depended to a large extent, therefore, on the prosperity or otherwise of the woollen industry as a whole.

In these valleys the clothiers would have made some sort of an agreement with the cottagers to produce cloth, paying on a piece-work basis. In the early days of the development of the industry the cottagers of the two valleys undertook most of the processes themselves. The wool for weaving came to the cottages on pack-horses. One of the routes was, at one time, recorded in the inn sign of the Woolpack in Slad. It used to show the well-laden pack-horse and beside it a mile-stone saying 'Bisley 4 miles'. This would have been across the valley by the 'Roman bridge' and up to Piedmont and Driftcombe or, with a different destination, up King Charles Lane to Stancombe. Sadly, the new inn sign has lost the particular reference to these valleys.

The hand weavers working in their own homes were their own masters, not bound by hours of work, and they often combined cloth production with agriculture. This gave them a buffer against bad times in one or the other occupation. At times of urgent demand for agricultural labour, such as the harvest, all would have worked on the land. The coming of the mills during the mediæval period, with the different sort of discipline that they imposed, began to make this flexibility more difficult to maintain.

HOUSES AND COTTAGES

Sydenhams, a lesser manor house with its adjacent mediæval village, has a long history, but there are other houses in the main valley which may have had a similar status. Trillgate Cottage (see photo 21) was well located for the bridge over the Slad Brook. Lionel Walrond, formerly curator of the Stroud Museum, has dated Trillgate Cottage as fourteenth or fifteenth century, which makes it the oldest cottage in the valley. It has very old beams and a large stone fireplace with chamfered sides—features not normally found in cottages. The ends of beams sticking out are burnt, suggesting that a former wing of the house was burnt down (though exposed ends of beams were sometimes charred in order to prevent decay). It is supposed that it was once a big house and possibly a manor house.[23] If it was a manor house it would have had several other dwellings round about. There may also have been other farms with their accommodation for the workers.

Records already referred to show that there was a house at Timbercombe whose tenant was able to arrange for the continued family occupation of this land after his death. Timbercombe as a person or as a place is mentioned in documents in the fourteenth, fifteenth and sixteenth centuries.[24] Although there are buildings and ruins at Timbercombe, it seems that there may have been another more important dwelling at this time. There is no other evidence of the whereabouts of houses in this area before the sixteenth century but there would have been a number in the valleys, some of them probably on the site of dwellings erected at a later date. As with those in the mediæval village at Sydenhams some would have been made of materials not designed to withstand the elements over many years.

Later on in the Middle Ages, and especially in the time of Queen Elizabeth, the clothiers and other persons of influence and wealth built stone houses some of which have survived to this day. One of these is Steanbridge House. The back of the present house is Elizabethan. The present Down Farm was built on the site of an earlier house constructed at the latest in the seventeenth century but possibly in the sixteenth century or even earlier. For most of the population the valleys were a series of communities centred on a small manor or perhaps a subsidiary farm. Each would have had a number of cottages nearby built of wood, mud and straw which unfortunately leave few clues for later generations as to their whereabouts. By the time of Queen Elizabeth prosperity, especially in the woollen industry, was heralding a new era of expansion for the seventeenth and early eighteenth centuries.

This part of Gloucestershire may have been less well served for housing than other parts of the south of the county. An analysis of 413 inventories for South Gloucestershire from 1539–79 shows yeomen's houses as having six to ten rooms, husbandmen's five rooms, labourers' three rooms. Rural craftsmen had rather more than the labourers.[25] By the end of the sixteenth century there were probably no houses of six to ten rooms and perhaps just Steanbridge House and Sydenhams having five rooms. Labourers often had just two.

1.   Finberg, Josceline (1977) *The Cotswolds*, London: Eyre Methuen

2.   Pugh, R.B. (ed.) (1976) *The Victoria History of the County of Gloucestershire*, Vol. XI, published for the University of London, Institute of Historical Research by OUP (The part on the study area was researched by Mr Nicholas Herbert, now working on other volumes) p.57

3.   NMR Monument Report 114916 Deserted Mediaeval Village at Sydenhams, NMR SO 80 NE 39, Grid Ref SO 898 078

4.   Morton, Richard (1997) Sydenhams Farm, Bisley, Gloucestershire: Archaeological Assessment for Mr Charles Howard, Cotswold Archaeological Trust, Kemble Business Park, Cirencester, Gloucestershire

5. Morton *op. cit.*
6. Morton *op. cit.*
7. Rudd, Mary A. (1937) *Historical Records of Bisley*, Published privately, Edn 1977, Alan Sutton p.9
8. Dyer, C.C. (1988) Section 4E, Chapters 6 and 7 in Hallam, H.E. (ed.) (1988) *Agrarian History of England and Wales,* (General editor Joan Thirsk, former editor H. P. R. Finberg) Vol. II 1042–1350, Cambridge: CUP pp.663
9. Page, William (ed.) (1907) *The Victoria History of the County of Gloucester,* Vol. II published for the University of London, Institute of Historical Research, reprinted Dawsons of Pall Mall 1972 p.130
10. NMR Monument Report 114916 *op. cit.*
11. NMR Monument Report 1074610 Cropmarks north east of Sydenhams, NMR SO 90 NW 69, Grid Ref SO 9005 0804 and 1074621 Cropmark of L shape west of Scrubs Common, NMR: SO 80 NE 85, Grid Ref SO 8948 0799
12. Gloucestershire Records Office (GRO) D 1209/1 Bisley Manor Court Records
13. Ziegler, Philip (1969) *The Black Death,* London: Collins p.230
14. Ziegler, *op. cit.* p1.38
15. Baddeley, Welbore St Claire (1907) *A Cotswold Manor being the History of Painswick,* Gloucester: John Bellows, London: Kegan Paul, Trench, Trubner & Co Ltd p.94
16. Dyer, C.C. (1991) Chapters 2, 3 and 7 on the West Midlands in Miller, Edward (ed.) (1991) *The Agrarian History of England and Wales,* (General Editor Joan Thirsk, former editor H P R Finberg) Vol. III 1340–1500, Cambridge: CUP, pp.227, 232
17. Lacey, Robert and Danziger, Danny (1999) *The Year 1000*, Abacus: 2000 pp.101–2
18. Page, *op. cit.* p.172
19. Phelps Brown, E.H. and Hopkins, Sheila V. (1956) 'Seven Centuries of the Prices of Consumables compared with Builders' Wage Rates,' *Economica,* November 1956
20. Dyer, *op. cit.* pp.236–7
21. Pugh, *op. cit.* p.120
22. Page, *op. cit.* p.173
23. *The Slad Valley News* (1986) September
24. Kimball, Elisabeth Guernsey (ed.) (1940) 'Gloucestershire Peace Rolls 1361–98', *Transactions of the Bristol and Gloucestershire Archaeological Society,* Vol. 62 and GRO D2819 Box 16 Victoria County History Notes on the Parish of Bisley
25. Barley, M.W. (1985) Chapter 20 in Thirsk, Joan (ed.) (1985) *The Agrarian History of England and Wales* (General Editor Joan Thirsk, former editor H.P.R. Finberg), Vol. V.2, 1640–1750, Cambridge: CUP p.654

4

Prosperity and Trauma in the Valleys: The Seventeenth Century

TROOPS SHATTER THE PEACE

At the beginning of the seventeenth century there was prosperity in the woollen industry and the general well-being filtered down from the clothiers to the workers in their own homes. Several of the most beautiful houses in the valleys were built at this time. The weavers presumably felt they could afford a better house and workroom and were confident for the future. Unfortunately, the optimism of the cottagers at the beginning of the century was not justified. The wool trade went through bad periods during the remainder of the century. Above all there was the trauma of the Civil War.

The clothiers would have been well informed of the political and religious upheavals of the time. The cloth workers would have had a lesser understanding but undoubtedly they would have been aware of the dissent around them. The church, which almost everyone attended, was a great source of information both from the pulpit and as a meeting place for exchange of gossip. It is unlikely that the cottagers were surprised by the start of the Civil War but they would not have expected to be involved at such close quarters.

This part of the country was a major area of conflict between the forces of Charles I and the Parliamentarians. King Charles crossed the Slad valley on 9 August 1643 on his way from Bristol to the siege of Gloucester. The previous night he had dined at Tetbury and spent the night at Cirencester. He then took the route through Minchinhampton, Brimscombe, Quarhouse and Nether Lypiatt. At Stancombe his route went down what has since been called King Charles Lane. His army crossed the Slad Brook, climbed up Wickeridge Hill, passed over the ridge at Bulls Cross, and dropped down to Painswick. The following 5 September the army was back again in Painswick, but this time in retreat.[1] King Charles Lane was the normal route from Stancombe to Painswick. It crossed the old bridge over the Slad Brook (which was in existence by 1353 and may have been earlier). The soldiers and the camp-followers did damage everywhere they went and caused much distress in these valleys.

DOMINANCE OF HOME WEAVING

The main occupation in the valleys at this time, apart from agriculture, was weaving carried out exclusively in the workers' own homes. At the beginning of the century the initial processes of preparing the wool for weaving—carding and spinning—were carried out by large numbers of women and children but there is little evidence that it was done in these valleys. By the end of the century these processes were largely concentrated round Cirencester and Tetbury. The weaving of broadcloth on a wide loom was a two-person task mainly done by men. According to a survey of males able to bear arms undertaken in 1608.[2] There were as many male cloth workers as agricultural workers in these valleys. In addition, there was a large female workforce involved in the woollen industry. A rough calculation of the number of woollen industry workers in Gloucestershire in 1622 puts it at 24,000 but some of these may have had other occupations too.

The term weaver covers a whole range of social status, wealth and expertise. From the mid-sixteenth century a master weaver had not been allowed to have more than two looms but, as time went on, some of them exceeded that limit, employed a number of men and were in charge of several apprentices. A journeyman was a weaver who did not have his own loom and was employed by a master weaver.

The clothiers managed the overall process of production. They did not need a large amount of capital and small clothiers and independent weavers were able to exist side by side with the large capitalists. Some of the fulling mills were owned by clothiers but in Gloucestershire, there were a large number of independent fullers; in fact, according to the 1608 survey, two and a half to every clothier.[3]

Some of the cloth workers in these valleys would have worked in the fulling mills. They would have walked down the main Slad valley to the Lower Steanbridge Mill in the Parish of Painswick or to the Upper Steanbridge Mill, very close-by, but in the Parish of Bisley. The illustrations of these two mills from the nineteenth century murals at Bishops Cleeve shows Upper Steanbridge Mill as a substantial building, built to fulfil a major industrial task. By contrast The Lower Steanbridge Mill looks like a well-built, very desirable cottage and the architecture, particularly the windows, suggests that it was older than the mill higher up the valley. However, the artist may have been less than accurate in his representation, so the appearance of the two mills on the murals cannot be conclusive evidence. In fact the Lower Steanbridge Mill was not so small by standards of the time. Some of the very early mills were little larger than a garage.[4] Further down the valley there were several other mills of which the most important for the valleys were at the Vatch. There were two mills there, usually run in tandem. They had probably become fulling mills by the early seventeenth century.

During the seventeenth century the Cotswold fleeces, which had been the foundation of the local woollen industry, gradually ceased to be used for the traditional broadcloth. In part, this was due to a deterioration in the quality of the wool, as the sheep became more bulky and better for meat.

Broadcloth, for which Gloucestershire was famous, was different from a number of other woollen cloths, such as worsted, because the special methods of finishing made the cloth smooth and thick so that no individual threads were visible. The process of perfecting this cloth continued over several centuries. Even when the English wool producers elsewhere were producing a variety of woollen cloths, Gloucestershire continued to specialise in broadcloth, though other types were also produced.

In the sixteenth century a machine, called a gig, was invented to raise the nap of the cloth after fulling, using teasles attached to rollers. A large number of gig machines were in operation in Gloucestershire by the seventeenth century. More importantly, the hand process was very labour intensive and there was much opposition by workers in the country as a whole to the adoption of gig machines, fearing that the change would cause unemployment and hardship. Gigs were forbidden by law. The exception was Gloucestershire because gigs had been long used in that county and they were allowed to continue in operation. Some said that their use disguised imperfections in the cloth but, nevertheless, clothiers in other counties sent their cloth to have its nap raised by machine in Gloucestershire.

Much of the cloth produced in the area was exported undyed to be finished elsewhere. Gloucestershire was, however, becoming famous for its spectacular red cloth and also for blue and other colours. Gloucestershire dyed cloth was accepted by merchants, even though it was usual for cloth to be dyed in London. Dying was difficult and there were only a few dyers in the whole county. Generally dyeing of the broadccloth took place after it had been woven and the nap had been raised by the teasles. It was then stretched out on tenterhooks to dry on racks. These racks were part of the landscape and the fields where the racks were erected still include 'rack' as part of their name. The exceptional quality was in part due to the nature of the water but the skill and experience of the dyers may have been even more important.[5]

The century began well with prosperity in the valleys but it did not last. A major factor in the decline stemmed from the ever-increasing dominance of events in London which determined the standard of living amongst the clothiers and their workers. In 1614 the monopoly of the Merchant Adventurers ceased and a new company was formed under Alderman Cockayne. He thought that English broadcloths should be dyed and finished in England rather than being sent abroad to be finished. He had the export of unfinished cloth banned. The Dutch, who were one of the main purchasers of English cloth, refused to buy cloth finished in England and sales fell, and with them, the livelihood of many cloth workers in these valleys.

Map 4

HOUSES AND OTHER BUILDINGS IN THE SEVENTEENTH CENTURY

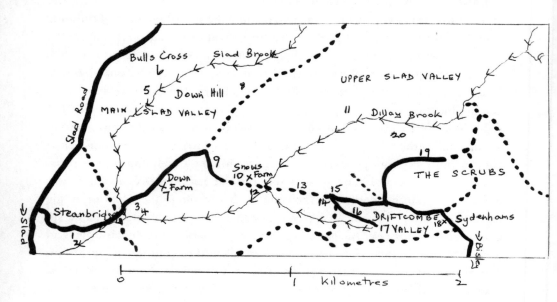

X	EXISTING HOUSES
—	EXISTING ROADS
●●●●	SELECTED EXISTING TRACKS
→→	STREAMS

KEY

1	Steanbridge House	14	August Cottage and Mullions
2	Lower Steanbridge Mill	15	St Benedicts
3	Upper Steanbridge Mill	16	Driftcombe Cottage
4	Steanbridge Cottage	17	Driftcombe Farm
5	Trillgate Cottage	18	Sydenhams
6	Trillgate Farm	19	Woodedge
7	Down Farm (an earlier house than the present)	20	Stonedge House
8	Shepherds Cottage		
9	Down Court (not necessarily all of 1840s building)		
10	Snows Farm		
11	The Old Shop		
12	Snows Mill		
13	Piedmont		

Havoc was caused by the Civil War. Gloucestershire was one of the most fought-over areas. There was plundering of the product of the cloth industry both by troops on their way through and by authority of the king, and this took a heavy toll on the clothiers. The Civil War not only disrupted trade but, because of the fighting in Gloucestershire and even troops going through these valleys, the population suffered from looting and other forms of lawless behaviour. Many people were obliged to pay taxes and make 'contributions' to both sides.[6] In February 1642 the King authorised Prince Rupert to commandeer all the cloth in the chief manufacturing centres of Gloucestershire. The Parliamentary side reported that the royalists 'took away cloth, wool and yarn besides other goods to the utter undoing of them and theirs'.[7]

Yet after the war there was improvement once again. Inventories from about the 1660s to the 1720s show weavers to be well off compared to some other artisans.

ENCLOSURE AND AGRICULTURE

In the country as a whole, enclosure of the open fields cultivated on the strip system took place over a long period of time and often on a piecemeal basis. Some lords enclosed their demesne and also enclosed some of the common land in order to use it for sheep farming. Some even seized the arable fields. Private arrangements were frequently made between the strip-holders to consolidate their holdings by exchanging scattered strips for bigger parcels of land which could be fenced. Rents of arable land increased. Where there was an increase in pasture, the need for labour decreased. The unemployed left the countryside to try to find employment elsewhere, causing acute social problems. Another change which took place was that the lord's demesne was leased to tenants, often with the equipment to work it, instead of being worked by the villeins. Change was well on the way by the end of the sixteenth century. In the seventeenth century the pace of change slowed a little and even as late as 1750 the open field system still existed in many (about half) of the manors in the whole country.

In these valleys it is likely that consolidation and enclosure of the open fields was done by agreement or imposed by the Lord of the Manor fairly early in the seventeenth century or even in the sixteenth century. In July 1641 it had, to some extent at least, already happened at Sydenhams. There was an indenture of 'bargain and sale' which included '30 acres called at that time New Tyning', a name that indicates that it was formerly part of the manor.[8] In Painswick the consolidation of holdings and enclosure was taking place in the late sixteenth and early seventeenth centuries and much of the parish was said to be enclosed about 1703.[9] The process continued, however, well into the first half of the nineteenth century. In Miserden, though not, it seems, in these valleys, there were still at least three open fields in the parish in the seventeenth century.[10]

Agriculture was throwing off the limitations of the strip system and both the open fields and the lord's demesne were by this time often farmed by tenants, rather than the villeins. There was greater freedom to experiment with methods of cultivation and even with new crops. Slowly yields of crops increased. This was achieved in spite of a period of cold winters and cool summers throughout Europe, when even the Thames froze over.[11] Throughout the period there were often disputes. The records of the Bisley Manor Courts provide examples of cases concerned with such matters as the grazing of sheep and cattle on the common land and on the harvested fields, the maintenance of the mounds in between the fields, as well as theft of property.[12]

BUILDING BOOM

Map 4 shows the houses and mills known to be in existence during the seventeenth century. Many of them are thought to have been built during the seventeenth century or at the very end of the sixteenth century so that the number of houses built during the century was more than those known to have been already in existence. This is largely because so little is known of the smaller, less durable properties from an earlier period. Nevertheless, there was certainly something of a building boom especially 1580 to about 1630 but going on, to a lesser extent, to the end of the seventeenth century. It is probable that houses still in existence which were constructed in this period include the following: Beech Cottage, Driftcombe Cottage, August Cottage with Mullions, Driftcombe Farm, St Benedicts, Snows Farm, Steanbridge Cottage, Upper Steanbridge Mill, and Woodedge, The houses built at that time were well constructed of stone. In addition some of those ruins of which there is some record may also have been built at that time, notably Shepherds Cottage. This was the period of the essentially Cotswold style of cottage building.[13] Moreover, it is consistent with the state of the cloth industry when its prosperity was creating a mood of optimism. When they were built these houses were both workplace and home. If they were for weavers, they had a large space on the ground floor, or on the first floor, to hold the loom and materials. In some houses brackets have been found, possibly to keep the machines in place. The large room downstairs would normally have been the living room for the whole family where they cooked and spent all the hours of the day. There might have been one or two bedrooms.

Driftcombe Cottage is thought to be the oldest house in the Driftcombe valley. The artefacts found in work on rehabilitating and extending the cottage include a coin dated 1661, issued by John Hopton of Stroud, found in digging out the cellar. There is no value on the coin. It was probably a trade token minted to overcome the shortage of small coins in circulation. It seems that when Charles I became bankrupt, merchants and others minted their own money.

There were houses in existence in the seventeenth century which are no longer there, on which some information is available. It is possible that the house known as Piedmont was built before or during the seventeenth century. It lay north of the hedge that goes down to the Roman bridge from St Benedicts, just a few yards below the five barred gate.

Stonedge House is mentioned in a will of 1708 in connection with Timbercombe.[14] It seems almost certain to have been in existence in the seventeenth century. It is not known precisely where it was but there is a flat piece of ground below Stonedge Wood which seems a likely site and, at one time, there was some dressed stone in a field wall there.

In addition to the buildings of which something is known, there would have been other cottages of which there is no trace. Moreover, some of the cottages in existence in 1840 and no longer there, may have been constructed before 1700 or they may have been replacements for those which were there in 1700 but later demolished. As the location of cottages is partly dependent on the unchanging shape of the terrain, cottages were often rebuilt where there had already been a dwelling. Thus, the best indication of where cottages might once have been, may well be the location of cottages on the 1840 tithe map. Another clue is the small irregular shaped plots of land, known as assarts, still marked on the ordnance survey map. They often indicate where there was once a dwelling, even if there is no longer one or was not one at the tithe survey. It was not difficult to build and claim a cottage to live in. A plot of land was fenced, the walls of the cottage defined and the chimney built, theoretically all in one day. Once the chimney was in place there was a claim to the dwelling, legalized by the payment of a fine to the lord of the manor.

Sydenhams was extended in the seventeenth century. Families associated with Sydenhams in the seventeenth century include the Burrowes and the Sevills. Samuel Sevill, a clothier, bought it in 1641 when it was a farm of seventy-three acres. The Sevill family continued to own it well into the next century, buying or selling a few acres from time to time. The cross interests of clothiers in agriculture, as well as the woollen industry, was common. Wealth was invested partly in land and the clothiers aspired to be recognized as men of social status. Some of the best houses were old manor houses and suitable for a gracious style of living. In this respect the differences between the seventeenth century and the twentieth century are small.

1. Rudd, Mary A. (1937) *Historical Records of Bisley*, Published privately, Edn 1977, Alan Sutton p.367
2. Smith, John (1902, new edition 1980), *Men and Armour in Gloucestershire in 1608*, Gloucester: Alan Sutton
3. Mann, Julia de Lacey (1971) *The Cloth Industry in the West of England, 1640–1880*, Oxford: Clarendon, pp.92–3

4. Walrond, Lionel F.J. (1973) 'Wool, Woolmen and Weavers' in Charles and Mary Hadfield (eds), *The Cotswolds: A New Study,* Newton Abbot: David & Charles p.187

5. Mann, *op. cit.* pp.8–11

6. Thirsk, Joan (1984) Chapter 6 in Thirsk, Joan (ed.) (1984) *The Agrarian History of England and Wales* (General Editor Joan Thirsk, former editor H.P.R. Finberg), Vol. V.i, 1640–1750, Cambridge: CUP, p.160

7. Tann, Jennifer (1967) *Gloucestershire Woollen Mills*, Newton Abbott: David and Charles, p.36

8. Gloucestershire Records Office (GRO) D1388/III/10 Schedule of deeds relating to Sydenhams 1641–1810

9. Pugh, R.B. (ed.) (1976) *The Victoria History of the County of Gloucestershire,* Vol. XI, published for the University of London, Institute of Historical Research by OUP p.71

10. Pugh, *op. cit.* p.52

11. Luterbacher, Jurg; Dietrich, Daniel; Xoplaki, Elena; Grosjean, Martin; Warner, Heinz (2004) 'European Seasonal and Annual Temperature Variability, Trends, and Extremes since 1500', *Science,* 5th March 2004

12. GRO D745 M6, M7, M8 Bisley Manor Court Records

13. Galsworthy Davie, W. and Dawber, E. Guy (1905) *Old Cottages, Farm Houses and other Stone Buildings in the Cotswold District*, London: Batsford

14. Rudd, *op. cit.* p.111

5

Innovation and Unrest:
The Eighteenth Century

INTRODUCTION

The eighteenth century was a period of technical innovation which affected both the cloth industry and agriculture. Change was also taking place in the pattern of land holding. This century saw the beginning of the important role played by the Townsend family in the valley from Steanbridge to Piedmont. At the beginning of the period they owned Lower Steanbridge Mill and were also, perhaps, established in Steanbridge House but, as the century went on, they acquired land, mills and houses in the whole area. Their dominance as landowners was to continue for about two centuries.

The transport of wool and cloth in the valleys was vital and the tracks developed accordingly. In 1778 the parishes of Painswick and Bisley agreed to share the cost of rebuilding the mediæval bridge across the Slad Brook.[1] This was vital to the use of the road, known as King Charles Lane going from Painswick up to Stancombe. Along the valley there was the packhorse route past Down Farm and up to Driftcombe, Sydenhams and Bisley.

TECHNICAL PROGRESS BUT PROBLEMS FOR THE WOOLLEN INDUSTRY

During the later part of this century great progress was made in the development of machines to increase the productivity of the workers in the woollen industry, many of which involved moving processes, once undertaken in homes, into factories. By the end of the century both a carding and a scribbling machine were introduced to prepare the wool before spinning. This was done in factories, though the prior process of taking the extraneous matter out, known as picking, was still done at home. Spinning itself was also mechanised with the 'Spinning Jenny'. This could be used either in the home or in factories but Steanbridge Mill was also once known as the Jenny Mill, indicating that it was once used for spinning. William Playne, a major local clothier, commented how the spinning jenny, in improving the quality of the thread, had greatly increased the productivity of weavers. Another invention helped to improve weaving.

The flying shuttle, introduced into the Stroud area in the last decade of the eighteenth century, enabled wide looms to be operated by one instead of two persons. It was said it might save a quarter to a third of the time taken to weave a cloth but some denied that it was any quicker.[2] The flying shuttle became important in the next century.

In the early 1700s the weavers were well off compared to other artisans but there was trouble in the middle of the century. Harvests had been bad and food was short and expensive and the wool trade was depressed. There was a great meeting at Selsley and riots ensued. In 1756 the weavers petitioned Parliament about wages and they were on strike for six weeks. Major General Wolfe was sent with six companies of infantry to restore order.[3]

Generally, payment was on a piece-work basis. In 1737 there were about twice as many women as men working on the various processes with women being particularly engaged in carding, spinning and the preparation of the yarn for weaving. Indeed carding and spinning used well over half the total labour employed, while weaving used relatively little. In general, men were paid more than women, sometimes three times as much, but the women finishers of the cloth were well paid. Weavers were paid well compared to other trades, but comparison is difficult because they were paid on a piece-work basis and rates fluctuated with the state of trade.[4]

During the eighteenth century production of a superfine cloth, known as cassimere or kerseymore, became important. It had been patented in 1766. This cloth was much thinner than broadcloth. The yarn was spun differently and it was woven, often with the appearance of a slight rib, on a narrow loom and was then fulled less heavily than broadcloth. This cloth was produced in these valleys before 1815 and probably in the eighteenth century.

In a bad period in 1726–27 Gloucestershire workers petitioned the Privy Council concerning the regulation of their wages. An act was passed providing for the fixing of wage rates by the local magistrates, but the clothiers ignored it and the workers rioted. Another cause of unrest was the 'truck system' by which the workers were paid in tokens to be exchanged in their employers' shops at prices far higher than the market price. This was against the law but redress was on an individual basis at the Quarter Sessions and most workers could not afford the time for this, even if they had the knowledge. Effective truck acts were not introduced until the nineteenth century.[5]

As the capitalist nature of the industry became more intense, to combine work in agriculture with weaving was more and more difficult and, by the eighteenth century, the occupants of these valleys were forced to become either weavers or agricultural labourers. This meant that a prosperous period for one could no longer offset a depression in the other. The weavers in the valleys would still mostly have had their own gardens where they could grow vegetables and keep chickens and possibly a pig. In 1840 all the cottages on the tithe map were described as 'cottage and garden'.

Throughout the history of the industry there were thefts of cloth from the clothiers, the workers perhaps taking what they could not get by legal means. The Gloucester Journal of 31st January 1763 reports the major theft of two pieces of cloth, not scoured, with twenty-one ells in each piece (an ell was about forty-five inches), stolen from John Pegler at Steanbridge. The Courts were constantly dealing with smaller thefts of cloth or wool from the clothiers. The workers almost regarded stealing small quantities of less valuable materials as a perk.

In the eighteenth century the fortunes of the industry went from prosperity to depression and back again, often in as short a period as five years. The dependence on overseas markets for the cloth increased the fluctuations. Rudder[6] estimated in 1779 that more than half the Gloucestershire cloth was sold in foreign markets. This was good in that it created demand, but the overseas market was often erratic. Exports to America, for example, were seriously reduced by the War of Independence in the 1770s.

IMPROVEMENT IN AGRICULTURE AND ANIMAL HUSBANDRY

There were wide fluctuations in climate during the eighteenth century which would have caused some major upsets in agricultural production. The year 1708–9 was the coldest European winter recorded from 1500 to the present. But then there were warmer winters for a few years until around 1730 before temperatures fell again. Summers on the other hand were about average in Europe in the first half of the century but warmed up to near record levels from 1750.[7] The hardship in the very cold winters must have been appalling. It is difficult to know how climate change affected agriculture, especially as there is less information about rainfall than about temperature. In the long run the gradual progress of enclosure was probably more important.

Enclosure of the manorial open fields took many decades and even centuries but it is thought that it was completed fairly early in the area of interest for this book. There is little doubt of its benefits. Rudge in an appendix to his *General View of the Agriculture in the County of Gloucester* of 1807[8] compares yields in the parish of Aldsworth before and after enclosure. He finds that the yield of wheat doubled from six to twelve bushels (about three to six cwts) an acre and that of barley increased from ten to seventeen bushels (four and a half to seven and a half cwts) an acre. In 1796 Marshall[9] quotes the yield of wheat as twelve to twenty bushels (six to ten cwts) an acre or more if it had been sown in the winter. This was two or three times the yields of the Middle Ages.

Another reason for improvement was the introduction of new equipment, such as the drill which increased the quality of crops. The new machinery being developed could all be drawn by horses. Oxen were still used for ploughing but the horse was slowly taking over. In 1796 it was estimated that in the Cotswolds there were two horses for every one ox, in spite of many maintaining that oxen were better for the condition of the soil. Labourers did not like working with oxen.[10]

The cultivation of turnips and other feed crops for sheep and cattle at the beginning of the eighteenth century completely changed the rotation system. The fallow year was being eliminated and replaced by crops of corn in alternate years and turnips and clover in between. Sainfoin, another form of fodder, had become increasingly popular since the latter part of the previous century and in the early part of the eighteenth century was sometimes left down for seven or even ten years.[11] In the Cotwolds by 1796 there was often a seven-year rotation of sainfoin, turnips, barley, grasses, grasses again, wheat and oats or peas. Of these only barley and oats were marketable crops, the remainder being for feeding stock. Specifically in the Cotswolds, the cultivation of turnips was assisted by the old practice of 'paring and burning' old sainfoin layers in preparation for planting of turnips. The Victoria County History describes the process as follows:

> The operation consisted in cutting a thin slice from the surface with the breast-plough, an implement shaped like a spade, and fixed on a shaft with a crossbar at the end, which was held by the labourer in both hands and propelled from his thighs. The slice being cut was turned over by moving the cross handle from right to left. When they were dry the turfs were gathered into heaps and stifle burned, not being allowed to burst into flame. The object of this operation was to destroy weeds, grubs of wireworm, and larvae of other harmful insects as well as provide a fertiliser for the turnip crop.[12]

This process was eventually discontinued because of the rise in the cost of labour and the increase in the use of fertilisers, such as superphosphate of lime and dissolved bones.

The local Cotswold wool, which had once been the mainstay of the woollen industry, had been largely replaced by a Wiltshire breed which cast its fleece. Even when locally produced, wool was not the mainstay of the industry but the number of sheep tended to increase. One of the reasons for enclosure was to enable more sheep to be kept and the selective breeding of animals, which had been impossible before enclosure, greatly improved the quality of sheep and cattle. In previous centuries it had been the practice to send some sheep and cattle down from the Cotswolds to the Vales in the winter. After 1840 the cultivation of turnips allowed them to feed the livestock on their own farms. Roots were fed to the sheep on the field but the grazing was organized in patches and sheep were contained in small areas by hurdles. These were made of ash because, unlike beech, it can be easily split. Improvements in breeding and feed caused the number and weight of sheep and fleeces to increase dramatically. Marshall, writing in 1796 observes that sheep were 'the grand object of Cotswold husbandry'.

Cows were usually fed in their barns, a labour-intensive operation. Nevertheless, as in the case of sheep, the weight of cattle doubled.

Wages were very low. Sir Robert Atkyns, who lived at Pinbury Park near Sapperton and whose memorial is in Sapperton church, wrote *The Ancient and Present State of Gloucestershire* in 1712.[13] He comments in the Preface:

> It is observable that the *Wages of Day-Labourers* were much higher in the times of the *Norman* Conquest than at the present; for then they had a penny a Day when the price of wheat was but a penny a Bushel, whereas now but a Shilling a Day, when wheat is now a Shilling a Peck and consequently the present Wages of a Day-labourer is but the fourth part of what it was anciently.
>
> (Punctuation as original)

The lot of the agricultural labourer was often not a happy one. On the other hand it must be borne in mind that most labourers in the valleys lived in a cottage with a garden and would have grown their own vegetables and perhaps kept chickens or a pig. However, dependence on the local conditions for food as well as income made them specially vulnerable in times of crop failure due to weather or other factors, and starvation was a perennial threat.

Some of the land holdings in the eighteenth and nineteenth centuries were very large, with the farms let out to farmers. The woods were generally kept in the occupation of the landowner, partly for hunting and partly because the investment period for timber is longer than any tenant farmer could manage.

Housing and the Mills

This period was one in which the clothiers became more influential in affairs of the county. In the eighteenth century the Townsend family began to dominate the scene in the valleys, both as clothiers and as landowners. The Townsends were so important in the history of the valleys that their story is told in the next chapter.

It seems that Henry Townsend bought the Lower Steanbridge Mill and Theyer Townsend bought the Upper Mill in 1781.[14] There was another mill below Snows Farm, to the south, known as Snows Mill or sometimes as Down Mill. It was said to have been a flock mill at one time and later a corn mill (see photo 27).

The houses on which there is information in the seventeenth century were still there in the eighteenth century. Sydenhams appeared to be flourishing with the Sevill family who owned it for nearly 200 years. The owners continued to be influential in the neighbourhood. In 1735 Samuel Sevill was a signatory of a document concerning Bisley Commons. It would be normal for the owner of Sydenhams to be a free tenant of the Manor of Bisley and in 1736, for example, he was listed as such in the Court Baron of John Stephens.[15]

Timbercombe seems to have been important in the eighteenth century. In the first ten years of the century it appears in a marriage settlement, in a conveyance and in a will.[16] In the last it mentions some arable and pasture at Gratton Grounds near Stonedge House. It is often difficult to know whether the documents refer to a house or land.

An early reference to Piedmont or Pidemount is contained in a list of children at the Blue Boys School at Bisley in 1756. It seems the boy was disciplined for 'not keeping school'.[17] In 1788 Piedmont was sold by a clothier, Thomas Baghott Delabere of Southam in Gloucestershire to Theyer Townsend together with land up the valley 'called Stonedge and Gratton grounds'.[18] There is a problem in locating all the fields mentioned in the indenture on the 1839 Tithe map. It seems that names had changed in the interim. It does seem fairly certain that the farm lands of Piedmont extended along the south side of the Slad valley and up to the hill towards the Driftcombe Valley. The whole sale of about forty-eight acres was for a sum of £700.

Stonedge House was definitely in existence early in this century. However, in the deed of 1788 there is a reference to where Stonedge House formerly stood. It must have been fairly important to have been mentioned by name. In the same indenture two other dwellings are mentioned as being no longer there (using the term Meeze to denote this). One was described as a tenement called Sidenham and the other was unnamed. All three mentions of properties which were no longer in existence were intended to help locate the area of a transaction. That there were three in one area suggests that the decay and disuse of dwellings was a common occurrence.

The Old Shop was probably thriving in the eighteenth century, if not earlier. It was described as old in the 1840s! There have been various theories as to its function discussed in Chapter 7.

There was very little new building in this century or, if there was, no record of it has survived. A possible exception is the construction of Greencourt Cottage, probably a weaver's cottage, joined on to August Cottage (dated 1676), though Greencourt Cottage may have been built at the end of the seventeenth century. In addition, the rebuilding of Down Farm house took place around this time.

It is notable that, when property changes hands, the indentures refer to the main house and lands and then add 'and messuages', meaning houses and land. These small dwellings were obviously of no consequence to the main landowner, but these are the very cottages where most of the population lived. Some of them were substantial and made of stone and many of those built in the seventeenth century have survived. Others would have been little more than hovels. The problem is that it is not stated how many there were, nor their location, and this makes it difficult until the nineteenth century to get an exact picture of the settlements in the valleys.

1. Gloucestershire Records Office (GRO) P47 VE 2/2 Bisley Vestry Minutes Book 1774–1806

2. Mann, Julia de Lacey (1971) *The Cloth Industry in the West of England, 1640–1880,* Oxford: Clarendon p.229

3. Tann, Jennifer (1967) *Gloucestershire Woollen Mills,* Newton Abbott: David and Charles, p.39

4. Page, William (ed.) (1907) *The Victoria History of the County of Gloucester,* Vol. II published for the University of London, Institute of Historical Research, reprinted Dawsons of Pall Mall 1972 p.160

5. Perry, R. (2003) *The Woollen Industry in Gloucestershire to 1914,* Shrewsbury: Ivy House Books, pp.58–9

6. Rudder, Samuel (1779) *A New History of Gloucestershire,* republished by Alan Sutton in collaboration with Gloucestershire County Library

7. Luterbacher, Jurg; Dietrich, Daniel; Xoplaki, Elena; Grosjean, Martin; Warner, Heinz (2004) 'European Seasonal and Annual Temperature Variability, Trends, and Extremes since 1500', *Science,* 5th March 2004

8. Rudge, Thomas (1807) *General View of Agriculture of the County of Gloucester drawn up for the consideration of the Board of Agriculture and internal improvement,* London: Richard Phillips

9. Marshall, William (1796), reprinted 1979, *The Rural Economy of Glocestershire, Vol. 2, Second District, The Wolds of Glocestershire,* pp.1–84, Alan Sutton

10. Marshall, *op. cit.*

11 Thirsk, Joan (1984) Chapter 6 in Thirsk, Joan (ed.) (1984) *The Agrarian History of England and Wales* (General Editor Joan Thirsk, former editor H.P.R. Finberg), Vol. V.1, 1640–1750, Cambridge: CUP, p.178

12. Page, *op. cit.* p.242.

13. Atkins, Robert (1712) *The Ancient and Present State of Gloucestershire,* London: W. Bowyer. Republished 1974 by E.P. Publishing Ltd. in collaboration with Gloucestershire County Library

14. GRO D2056/7 Sale of Steanbridge Mill to Theyer Townsend in 1781 and arrangement over a mortgage involving Samuel Clutterbuck 1791 and other documents

15. GRO D745/M6 Bisley Manor Court Records

16. GRO D149/T12 and 13 Documents relating to Timbercombe 1701–1707 and Rudd, Mary A. (1937) *Historical Records of Bisley ,* Published privately, 1977 edition, Alan Sutton, pp.110–11

17. GRO D149 R39 Bisley Blue Boy School records 1754–1761 (refers to D. Bucher of Piedmont)
18. GRO D2056/2 Indenture and Bargain and Sale for Piedmount House and Land, 7th September 1788

6

The Townsends and Steanbridge

The Townsends were established at Steanbridge by the late seventeenth or early eighteenth century when Henry Townsend (d.1714) owned Lower Steanbridge Mill in the parish of Painswick. They also owned property at Paradise, including a mill. Their coat of arms, which may be seen in Bishop's Cleeve Church, dates from 1682.[1] In 1691 Henry Townsend was described as a 'Painswick clothier'. The family was clearly of some import as evidenced by references to their witnessing deeds or acting as trustees.

Exactly when the Townsend family acquired Steanbridge House (see photos 3 and 4), some of which is Elizabethan, is not known, but they were probably there in the time of Henry Townsend. In 1721 there was a William Townsend at Steanbridge.[2] In 1736 there were three Townsends mentioned as free tenants in the manor of Bisley of John Stephens.[3] In 1779 another Henry Townsend died. He was one of five boys born to a Mr Townsend, possibly William, described as a reputable clothier at Steanbridge. He owned *inter alia* one fulling mill with two stocks, two grist mills, an adjoining mansion and a dyehouse. His brother, Theyer Townsend, was his heir. Theyer enlarged the family's estate and, in 1781, acquired Upper Steanbridge Mill.[4] In 1788 Theyer Towsend bought a lease of the Cowley estate owned by the Dean and Chapter of Westminster Abbey. In 1788 he also bought Piedmont Farm for £700. Later, probably in 1792, he acquired the corn mill, known as Snows Mill or Down Mill, south of Snows Farm. In the late eighteenth century Steanbridge House was extended to its present grand proportions, almost certainly by Theyer Townsend. When he died in 1801 he left his property, including Steanbridge House and the Cowley Estate to his brother Charles, the third of the five sons to own the estate. He also left £100 to each of the parishes in which he had interests, Painswick, Miserden, Bisley, and Cowley, to establish bread charities for the poor.[5]

When Charles (see photo 9) inherited the Steanbridge Estate he was seventy years of age, a gunpowder merchant living at Homerton in Hackney, London, where he was a prominent member of the Evangelical Church. He does not seem to have had a cosseted early life, as might be expected of one born at Steanbridge House. An obituary in *The Evangelical Magazine* of December 1803[6] describes his life and the development of his faith. It is of interest, not only because for a short time he was the owner of the Steanbridge estate, but also because it throws light on attitudes to religion, to charity and to class at that time. Charles was, it seems a very good man, but it was important to him that the 'lower orders' knew their place. If only one could go back in time and see how his administration of his estates differed from that of his brother! The obituary starts as follows:

> Mr Charles Townsend, the fifth son of Mr Townsend, a reputable clothier at Steanbridge, in Gloucestershire was born there in 1731. Of the earliest part of his life we have no account. His education, like that of others in his condition of life, at a time when a moderate degree of learning was more rare than at present, did not extend beyond the elementary rules of arithmetic. At the usual time he was apprenticed to a fishmonger in London; and such was the severity of his service, that it is believed to have produced the asthma, with which he was afterwards so much afflicted. When his apprenticeship expired, he entered into business; which, after several years, he relinquished, and became a gunpowder merchant. This business he continued until about a year before his death.
>
> There is no reason to believe that he had had the advantage of a religious education; yet he was very regular in his attendance at his parish-church, and correct in his moral conduct. He acknowledged himself, however, at that time, a stranger to the peace which arises from faith in our Lord Jesus Christ. In this state of mind his brother Samuel, who had gained an earlier acquaintance with *the way of salvation,* invited him to hear the late Mr Hart, in Jewin Street. Under his Ministry, by divine grace, he felt the depravity of his nature; and was taught to apply to the great Physician of souls for a remedy. "This," said Mr Townsend, "was just the sort of preaching that I wanted." Our readers will not be surprised to hear that he then went very regularly to hear Mr Hart; and ever afterwards retained a strong affection for him. He was soon missed at church; and did not escape the observation and taunts of his neighbours. "Aye," said one who met him going to hear his favourite minister, "If your father was alive Master Townsend, you durst not go on in this way; he would cut your legs off rather than you should forsake your parish-church." It appeared, as Mr Townsend was one day going to the Rosemary Branch to hear the Revd Ab. Booth, in passing through Devonshire Square, he met the minister of his parish-church: "So, Mr Townsend," said he, and clapped him on the shoulder, "you are going the wrong way." "That is an awful thing indeed, Sir, if it be true," replied

Mr Townsend; "but I hope I am not. I am going, Sir" added he: "where the gospel is preached." "I don't know what you call the Gospel," returned the clergyman; "but I know, if you go to church you will be sure to hear it there." Whatever he might hear from the *reading desk*, Mr Townsend knew he should not hear the gospel from the *pulpit*, and therefore persevered, regardless of the entreaties of his relations and the opinion of the world. The evangelical principles he had embraced, did not lie dormant, but produced such effects, that numbers who hated the truths so precious to his soul, were obliged to confess, that he was a good man, and had no blemish—but his religion. His whole life abounded in acts of extraordinary benevolence. His accounts of expenditure, from the time of his setting out in trade, are filled with items of money applied to the relief of poor people of every description. He paid for the education of some scores of indigent children; and has saved many a needy tradesman from ruin. Poor persons, of honesty and industry, seldom applied to him for the loan or gift of a small sum of money, without success. He had formerly tried his fortune repeatedly in the lottery, in expectation of a large prize; but he made it the constant matter of his prayer, that he might never have one; without the heart to use it to the glory of God. He knew how to relish the happiness of overwhelming a needy person with his kindness. There have been some very affecting instances of this: he could not relate a conversation he had with Mr Winter, of Painswick, last August without tears. Few persons knew more of the motives and principles of the lower order of mankind, or were better acquainted with their manners. It was dangerous to go to him with a false tale of distress, for he could generally detect it. Though he conferred his favours without exacting homage, he took care to let the objects of his bounty know, that he thought they were obliged to him. He had been among the poor as a benefactor, and had encouraged them to consider him under the character of a friend; and their frequent applications to him, in consequence, gave him an opportunity of acquiring an insight into their principles of action. There is a curious story told of his humanity some years ago:—When his eldest brother was in possession of the estate, he sent Charles one day to collect the rents from the poor people; but the good man saw so much misery, that it exercised his compassion; and instead of bringing home the rents, he was money out of pocket.

The principal beneficiaries under Charles's will were his cousins William and Robert Lawrence of Shurdington. The Cowley lease went to William (d.1820) and Steanbridge House and its lands to Robert. The Lawrence family trace their descent to a Robert Lawrence of Ashton Hall in the county of Lancaster. He went to the Holy wars with King Richard in 1190 and was knighted for his services

MAP 5

THE TOWNSEND STEANBRIDGE ESTATE *C.* 1840 AND THE TENANTS OF MAJOR FARMS

THIS MAP HAS BEEN REDRAWN FROM ORIGINAL TITHE MAPS AND APPORTIONMENTS HELD
AT THE GLOUCESTERSHIRE RECORD OFFICE

COURTESY OF THE GLOUCESTERSHIRE RECORD OFFICE

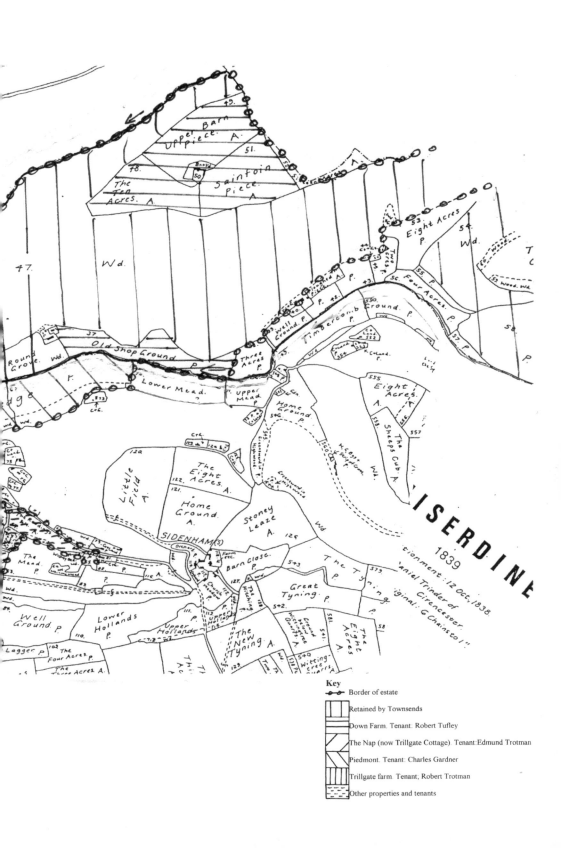

ISERDINE
1839

tionment: 12 Oct, 1838.
'aniel Trinder of
Cirencester.
'ginal. G.Chainsto/"

Key

Border of estate
Retained by Townsends
Down Farm. Tenant: Robert Tufley
The Nap (now Trillgate Cottage). Tenant: Edmund Trotman
Piedmont. Tenant: Charles Gardner
Trillgate farm. Tenant, Robert Trotman
Other properties and tenants

in 1192. They continued to be well connected and remained in Lancashire until 1509 when they sold their estates in the north and bought estates in Somerset, Warwickshire and Gloucestershire. On inheriting the estate at Steanbridge, Robert followed Charles's wish and took the surname Townsend and was thereafter known as Robert Lawrence Townsend.[7]

Robert who had taken Holy Orders by 1794 when he married Anne Walbank, had been from 1795 rector of Alderton, a parish north of Bishop's Cleeve. Nevertheless he took up residence in Steanbridge House and enlarged it, building a south wing in classical style which incorporated an elliptical stairway lighted by a glass dome. In 1815 Robert was appointed Rector of Bishop's Cleeve. For a time he planned to sell Steanbridge House and its lands but he and his wife were fond of it and he changed his mind. They lived much of the time at Bishop's Cleeve. Sometime between 1815 and 1830, Robert had a large upper room in the north wing of the rectory painted with murals depicting scenes from the Slad valley, including one showing a bride arriving at Steanbridge House in a carriage. One explanation is that his wife was homesick for Steanbridge. Another is that it was a way of demonstrating his wealth and position. Photo 3, 5 and 7 show the parts of the mural depicting Steanbridge House and the two Steanbridge Mills. A comparison with the photo of about 1910 shows that the artist allowed himself considerable licence in the portrayal of the house, but it must be remembered that he had to paint from sketches and from memory.

While the Townsend family was living at Bishop's Cleeve, Steanbridge House was let. There was an advertisement in the *Gloucester Journal* in 1815[8] which announced that tenants were sought for:

> A capital MANSION HOUSE called STEANBRIDGE HOUSE (the residence of the Revd Dr Townsend) comprising Dining and Drawing rooms, 25 feet by 18, handsome Vestibule and Staircase, Breakfast and Sitting Rooms, Bedchambers, and convenient Servants' Offices, 2 Four-stall Stables, Saddle Room and Coach-house, Brick-walled Garden covered with Fruit Trees, in full bearing, with 40 acres of Meadow and Orcharding adjoining.
>
> Also, within a short distance, Two FULLING MILLS, in the occupation of Mr. Driver, one employed wholly for Machinery, the other containing 2 Stocks and Gig Mill, with 12 feet diameter over shot water wheels, well supplied with water in the driest season, and never flooded in winter.
>
> Also within a quarter of a mile of the House a very advantageous situation for erecting a building for carrying on business to any extent that requires great power of Water having a fall of 24 feet.

The above premises are within 200 yards of the Turnpike Road leading from Cheltenham to Stroud and Bath, to which there is an easy access and where a coach passes daily to those places, Birmingham etc.

Also an excellent DWELLING-HOUSE, with every convenience for the family residence of a Manufacturer, with 12 Acres of Pasture Land adjoining, within a short distance of the mills. Together with 24 COTTAGES, standing at a short distance from the above Premises, chiefly occupied by persons employed in the Manufacture of Kerseymore[9] and Superfine Cloths.

In 1820 the house was let to a Mrs Smith where the house was called Steevensbridge. The mill was leased to a Mr Benz.[10] It is said that one of the tenants of the house was a couple by the name of Rooker. They were involved with the Cottage Church Sunday School at Slad. After a spell when it was housed at what is now the Old House in Slad, it was moved, about 1828, to the top of Steanbridge Mill (described as the old Elizabethan part of Steanbridge House). The Rookers also formed a day school where the children were taught reading and spelling (but curiously, not writing or arithmetic) and work skills. The latter consisted, for example, of straw plaiting for boys and sewing for girls. The arrangements did not last very long, as the Rookers had to leave Steanbridge House.[11]

Robert Lawrence Townsend died in 1830 at the age of sixty-four and was buried at Bishop's Cleeve. Steanbridge House then passed to his son, also Robert Lawrence Townsend. According to the tithe records the house was let to William Clissold around 1839. In 1839 Robert owned much of the property in the two valleys, as shown in Map 5, including Lower and Upper Steanbridge Mills, Down Farm, Snows Farm and the corn mill below it. Included in his ownership were at least twenty-four cottages. By 1841 Robert Townsend was resident there with his wife and two children. He gave his occupation as army. He was also there in 1861. As would be expected in a house of that quality, they had a number of staff. In 1861 the staff living in at Steanbridge House were a cook, two housemaids, a butler and a coachman. There would have been others living in cottages round about.

The leases for Down Farm, Snows Farm and Trillgate Farm are interesting for the way in which the freeholders kept control of various aspects of the leased farms, including of the way in which they should be cultivated. Hunting and shooting rights were generally reserved to the freeholder. The rent of Snows Farm was to rise from 1860 over its twenty-one year life, whereas those of Down Farm and Trillgate Farm, determined in 1876, were fixed. One could speculate that Snows Farm had not been well farmed for a while and that the owner was determined that it should improve, thus enabling it to support a higher rent.

After Robert Townsend's death in 1877, the estate passed to his son, a third Robert Lawrence Townsend. The latter continued to own the estate until at least 1892 and probably until it was sold in 1901. He may never have lived at Steanbridge House. In 1892 he was living at Terhill House, Pittville Circus, Cheltenham. He was however active in running the estate. In 1886 and 1892 rents were reduced at Down Farm and Trillgate Farm.[12] This was the period sometimes known as the Great Depression. In the mid 1880s prices were falling and after a short pause, fell further to the mid 1890s. There would have been problems in farming profitably and a good landlord would have taken that into account.

In 1891 the house was rented and occupied by John C. Collins, a retired Surgeon Major in the Indian Army, his wife who was born in Calcutta, two children and four living-in servants, a cook, parlour maid, housemaid and kitchen maid. The end of the estate came on 5 July 1901, when it was sold in several lots at auction in the George Hotel, Stroud for a total amount of £9,840.[13] This was a milestone in the history of land ownership and usage in the valleys which brought changes in the social structure of the area, as the farmers ceased to be tenants and became owners.

1.   Were, F. (1905) 'Note on Heraldry in Churches', *Transactions of the Bristol & Gloucestershire Archaeological Society*, Vol. 28, p.92

2.   Gloucestershire Records Office (GRO) D1388/III/10 Schedule of deeds relating to Sydenhams 1641–1810

3.   GRO D745 M6 Bisley Manor Court Records

4.   GRO D2056/7 Sale of Steanbridge Mill to Theyer Townsend in 1781 and arrangement over a mortgage involving Samuel Clutterbuck 1791 and other documents

5.   Jurica, John (1979) *A history of the ancient parish of Miserden and its principal estates*, Typescript presented to Mrs Koechlin-Smythe of Sudgrove House, Miserden, copy in GRO ROL G4

6.   *The Evangelical Magazine* (1803) 'Memoir of Charles Townsend, Esq.', Vol. XI, December, pp.509–13

7.   GRO D1815 Townsend (Location 7.79.3) Documents relating to the Townsend family and estates and leases for Down Farm, Trillgate Farm and Snows Farm, nineteenth century

8.   *Gloucester Journal* 3rd July 1815 Advertisement to let Steanbridge Estate

9.   Kerseymore or cassimere was a superfine woollen cloth (see Appendix 1 and Chapter 5).

10. GRO P244a M1 1/5 Painswick Parish Map of 1820 and references

11. Jones, Brian (1982) 'Slad School and Church in the 19th and early 20th centuries' in *The Slad Valley News*, No.11, Sept 1982

12. GRO D1815 Townsend (Location 7.79.3) Documents relating to the Townsend family and estates and leases for Down Farm, Trillgate Farm and Snows Farm, nineteenth century

13. *Gloucester Journal* 1st June 1901 Advertisement for sale of Steanbridge, p.4 and 6th July 1901 'Important Sale of Property at Stroud'

7

The Demise of the Cloth Industry and Degradation in the Valleys: The Nineteenth Century

PEOPLE AND HOUSES

Suddenly in the nineteenth century there is some detailed information on the land holdings in the valleys and also on the families who lived there. The first reason is that in the late 1830s there was a survey of properties in order to assess the tithe situation.[1] The second reason is that the censuses of 1841 and of 1851 give some excellent data on people and where they lived. Detailed information from the survey and from the censuses is contained in the Gazetteer later in this volume. Map 5 shows the dwellings and mills in existence in the middle of the nineteenth century, with their names, where known.

In the area of the two valleys there were in 1851 about twice the number of dwellings and four times the population of the present time. The number of dwellings was about 50 and the population over 200. The early nineteenth century saw a number of new cottages. It is thought that five dwellings were constructed in the first half of the century around the Scrubs Common. These, it is understood, were not as well built as those of the earlier building boom of the seventeenth century. The fall in the number of occupied dwellings began later in the century, certainly before 1891, and continued to 1901 and probably to the 1950s. The 1890s were a period of recession in the whole country and in Gloucestershire the woollen industry was in decline. It was also a bad period for agriculture. The dwellings which were 'lost' were often left unoccupied for some time and were sometimes pulled down for the stone to be used elsewhere, as in the case of Piedmont.

The reason the population was as great as it was about 1851 was partly that families were large. Some families had six, seven or eight children and in some of these cases the wife was still of child-bearing age. The crowding in the small cottages was, by present standards, desperate, but the families did not know any other situation, except what they saw in the large mansions where some of the people from the valley worked. The 1891 census contains information on the number of rooms. Less than eight of fifty-seven houses had five rooms or more. We know that some of these eight were almost palatial. According to an 1810

Map 6

HOUSES AND OTHER BUILDINGS *C.* 1840 (BASED ON THE TITHE MAPS AND APPORTIONMENTS)

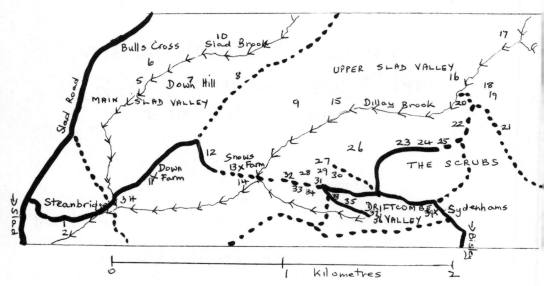

X	EXISTING HOUSES
▬	EXISTING ROADS
••••	SELECTED EXISTING TRACKS
→→	STREAMS

KEY

1 Steanbridge House
2 Lower Steanbridge Mill (now site only)
3 Upper Steanbridge Mill
4 Steanbridge Cottage
5 Trillgate Cottage
6 Trillgate Farm
7 Down Cottage (3 families there)
8 Shepherd's Cottage (now site only)
9 Down Common (now ruin)
10 Detcombe (at least one cottage, 1851 5 families or cottages)
11 Down Farm
12 Down Court (probably 5 cottages but 7 households)
13 Snows Farm
14 Snows Mill (now ruin)
15 The Old Shop (now ruin)
16 Dillay Farm
17 Cottage east of Dillay Farm (now site only)
18 Beech Cottage, Nottingham Scrubs
19 Two cottages near Beech Cottage (now ruins)
20 Timbercombe (not on Tithe map)
21 Highwood Farm (now a shed)

22 Two or three cottages at Timbercombe (now ruins)
23 Woodedge
24 Yew Tree Cottage
25 Cottage east of Yew Tree Cottage (now site only)
26 Cottage far side of Common (now site only)
27 The Scrubs (formerly 2 cottages)
28 Journeys End
29 Colombine Cottage
30 Building up the road from Colombine Cottage (now site only)
31 St Benedicts (probably 2 cottages)
32 Piedmont (now site only)
33 Primitive Methodist Chapel (built 1840, now Scrubs Bottom)
34 Greencourt, August Cottage and Mullions
35 Driftcombe Cottage
36 Driftcombe Farm
37 Two cottages behind Driftcombe Farm (now ruins)
38 Two cottages below St Benedicts (now ruins)
39 Sydenhams

inventory for sale of Down Farm, it consisted of kitchen, parlour, pantry, dairy, cheese room, fourteen bedchambers and two large drink-houses, as well as a stable and barns.[2] Some of the bedchambers may have housed farm workers. Ordinary people were living on average at a density estimated at 2.5 persons per room, but there were often husband and wife and five children in a two-roomed cottage. Sometimes the rooms were divided by wooden partitions.

In the nineteenth century nearly everyone who lived in the valley worked in the valley or at least in the Slad Valley as a whole. The exceptions, at the top of the social scale, were landowners who might be in the army or the church, and, at the bottom of society, those unable to work, retired persons and people who could not get work, some of whom were paupers. These latter categories overlapped. In 1851 several persons were listed as paupers. One man aged seventy was a crippled pauper. There were three women paupers, one on parish relief aged eighty and two of sixty-seven years old. Some families took lodgers. In 1851 there were two lodgers in one house in the Scrubs and one in each of another three houses.

Home weaving was in decline from before 1841 but the ten years from 1841 to 1851 witnessed a major decline in the cloth industry and in the importance of wool in the valleys. In 1841 cloth workers of various types were distributed over the two valleys, with three cottages at Driftcombe with eleven weavers, a weaver at Down Hill and another at Trillgate Cottage (The Knap). At Down Court there were three weavers in two cottages and about four carders. At Detcombe there was a spinner and a cloth worker. They were probably all working with wool. Then by 1851 the whole situation had changed, in that Driftcombe was the only area in these two valleys with cloth workers. According to the census, six of the eleven cottages were occupied mainly by farm labourers and four were inhabited by some sort of weavers or other wool workers. The eleventh had members of the family who were wool workers or cloth workers, although the head of the family was an agricultural labourer. Fortunately, the census of that year was very detailed in its description of the weavers. In five houses there were thirteen handloom weavers and two power-loom weavers. Four of the handloom weavers were under fourteen years old. In addition, some of the younger children of five or six were described as assistants. The power-loom weavers must have worked in a mill, and there were some in walking distance (see Chapter 4). One family, the Harriers, had eight children from twenty-one years to three months. The head of the family, aged forty-nine, was a handloom weaver but his wife and eldest daughter were power-loom weavers. All the others were handloom weavers and the boy, aged six, was an assistant. Another family, the Browns, were all handloom weavers and the girl, aged five, was an assistant. It is possible that the others, or some of them, were still home weavers. That possibility is increased by the age of the children. Since 1833 it had been illegal for children under the age of nine to work in woollen factories. It would have been much easier to employ young children at home where there was no limit at all on the age at which children could work. Moreover, Marling, an influential clothier, told the Factory Inspectors that in 1834 most weavers were working in their own homes, although that practice was dying out.

By the 1861 census Driftcombe was included with The Scrubs and it becomes more difficult to identify individual properties. In The Scrubs there were six cottages with some cloth-workers but it was not the occupation of whole families. There was a total of eight woollen weavers, three silk workers and one unspecified cloth worker. There was also one in 'silk manufacture' in the Down Hill area but the eighteen year old girl was probably working in a factory. By the 1860s silk was being produced in the Slad Valley at Peghouse or Woodlands Mill. The centre was the area round Chalford. In 1871 there were still some weavers in the valley but the census is not sufficiently detailed to inform where. By 1891 none was left.

Other occupations in the 1851 census included stone mason, maltster, nurse, shepherd and gardener. One man of sixty-three gave his occupation as pensioner, Greenwich. In 1891 the range of occupations was wider, including a shoemaker, coach trimmer, pin packer, refreshment-house keeper and engine driver. Robert Townsend of Steanbridge House was listed as army in 1861. In 1891, when Steanbridge House was lived in by John Collins, his occupation was given as Surgeon Major, Indian Army. Apart from those of the gentry, nearly all these occupations would have been carried on locally. The pin packer may have worked at the Painswick pin mill.

In 1851 most of the residents were born in the parish in which they lived or in adjacent ones in the same area. By 1891 several came from other counties, including Oxfordshire and Worcestershire. In 2004 nearly all the population came from other counties and at least five were born abroad. The world of the occupants of the valley in 1851 was bounded by Bisley, Slad and Stroud, though some might have made forays outside these narrow confines. In 2004 it would be unusual to find someone in the valleys who had *not* been abroad at some time.

Among the gentry and the farmers, residences often passed from one member of the family to another. For the agricultural labourers it seems likely that, as the size and age of the families changed, so they would move house, staying in the same area. The surnames of cottagers (sometimes with varied spellings) which occur again and again from the 1841 census to the 1891 census include Davis, Ireland and Woodward. Additionally, many names carry on at least from 1841 to 1861: such as May, Gardiner and Dickenson, often with several cottages occupied by persons with these names. The houses actually connected with the same family would have been even more, perhaps double, because of the women-folk married to another family. Many of these names of the 1840s are still to be found in the wider Bisley area.

The close family relationships in the valley together with the unifying influence of the Primitive Methodist Chapel, with all the values it stood for, must have helped to keep the residents of the valley in good behaviour. Imagine a young lad, out and feeling restless, and everywhere he went there was a house with a relative or a friend of his parents. It must have been very difficult to get up to mischief unobserved, let alone something worse. The saga of the Primitive Methodist Chapel is told in the next chapter.

An Industrial Woollen Industry and its Demise

After a period of great activity and prosperity from the mid eighteenth century to about 1820, the woollen industry entered a period of poor market conditions, especially in exports. The English had to compete in overseas markets with cloth from Germany, Flanders and France. High foreign tariffs reduced woollen exports to the continent and the USA. It was at this period that the change to steam-power was taking place. Initially, water power and steam power were often used in the same mill. In the summer and autumn there was a shortage of water to drive the water wheels and steam power helped to even out the supply. At the same time as the use of power was increasing, there were developments in the means of production which speeded up the processes. These included machines invented in the eighteenth century and introduced in the nineteenth century, including carding machines for use in factories, the spinning jenny and the flying shuttle. Soon after the flying shuttle was introduced, clothiers started to move weaving into factories even though they were still using hand looms. In the Stroud Valleys in 1802 there were no looms in factories and in 1833, as Marling told the factory inspectors, most of the weaving was done at home. By 1840 about three quarters of manufacturers had installed some handlooms or power looms in their mills and many mills, including the Vatch, had both at the same time. By 1851, although there were still some home weavers, including in the Driftcombe Valley, the factory had become the main workplace. It tended to be the women who worked at the power looms. In 1851 the only two power loom weavers in the valleys of this history were women. William Playne in 1838 said:

> 50 years ago broad looms were all worked by two persons but for the past 25 to 30 years the flyshuttle has been generally used and the yarn being much better spun since it had been done by machinery one man can certainly weave more than 2 did 50 years ago.[3]

This optimistic claim of productivity gains was not universally accepted.[4] All these inventions were good for the clothiers but not necessarily good for the workers. Overall fewer workers were needed to produce the same output and the movement to factories meant that the family, all working together and being able to care for and teach children, was undermined. The fulling process remained tediously slow, needed an enormous amount of power and required large numbers of fulling mills. Not until the use of newly developed milling machines after the middle of the century was this situation substantially improved.

From 1823–38 over 60% of the total yardage of cloth produced in Gloucestershire was broadcloth. The advertisement for the renting of Steanbridge House and the mills and surrounding houses and cottages in 1815 states that most of the twenty-four cottages were occupied by persons employed in the manufacture of Kerseymore and superfine cloths (high quality broadcloths). These were the second most important group of types of cloth produced in Gloucestershire. An observation by William Playne giving evidence in 1838 to Mr Miles confirms that at that time there was a high level of demand for cassimeres:

> Fifty years ago there was not a casimere loom in the county of Gloucester but for 30 or 40 years since that time there has been a great demand for caseymeres until within about 5 years.[5]

The installation of the necessary machinery for these new developments, for whatever type of cloth, required much capital beyond the means of the small clothiers. The clothiers who survived were those able to weather the storm with large premises and adequate machinery. Whereas in 1820 there were some 175 cloth mills in Gloucestershire, including ten in the Slad Valley, by 1840 there were about half that number. Soon after 1838 Upper Steanbridge Mill became a saw mill. Many of the small clothiers went out of business. Several of the well-to-do clothiers, such as Nathaniel Samuel Marling, operated more than one mill. The Vatch Mill, owned by Marling, was one of those which survived and prospered. Between 1822 and 1839 the rateable value of The Vatch had more than doubled while that of many smaller mills was static.[6]

Perry lists a number of factors often blamed for the overall decline in the industry, including poor transport, the high price of coal, and competition from the Yorkshire clothiers. Although he acknowledges that these played a part, he maintains that they alone did not deliver the fatal blow. He concludes that the main reasons were, first, a failure to diversify production, for the Gloucestershire clothiers were proud of their high quality cloth and never switched to cheaper but more marketable worsteds, and secondly, an inability or unwillingness to inject more capital into the business.[7]

The hardship of the weavers, and especially of the home weavers, in this period of restructuring of the industry was desperate. In 1839 the Government set up an *Inquiry into the Condition of the Handloom Weavers in the United Kingdom* and Mr. W. A. Miles was asked to report on Gloucestershire.[8] This was all rather late in the day, for the home weavers had been in trouble for some years and, as is reported below, there had been riots in desperation at the condition of weavers. Moreover, emigration, intended as part of a solution, had already been arranged by various parishes, including Bisley.

In the Miles report there are many examples of poverty and hardship, including near starvation. Most of them are not from the parishes in the valleys of this book but there is no reason to doubt that the same conditions applied. Evidence taken included information about Francis Berry of Randwick, a journeyman working for a master weaver, whose average earnings were five to six shillings a week. The family income in 1838 was as follows: himself 5s 6d, wife 'charring' 3s 0d, boy in factory 2s 0d, girl in factory 1s 0d, giving a total of 11s 6d. This was supplemented by a parish allowance of 4s 0d a week. The expenditure of the household was quoted as follows:

	s.	d.
3 pecks of potatoes @ 10d a peck	2	6
24 loaves, 2lbs in a loaf @3½d	7	0
Scraps of meat, flick (fat), etc.	1	6
Vegetables	0	6
Firing 1s 6d, soap and soda 6d	2	0
Rent	1	6
Rates	0	1½
TOTAL	15	1½

His employer, a master weaver, stated that 'the clothes of Francis Berry are all pawned. He is in debt for rent and owes £2 to the baker. He was in the workhouse for ten weeks. He now receives 4s a week from the parish. He thoroughly understands his calling; is an honest, hard-working man. He had tasted neither tea nor sugar for some time and his breakfast was nothing more than some bread, hot water and salt.'[9]

This person's situation was by no means unusual. Similar are reported in all parishes and all commentators were in agreement that the weavers were in dire straits. Indeed many weavers considered that the condition of a prisoner was superior to their own, inasmuch as he is supplied with food and clothing and they could scarcely obtain either the one or the other. Expenditure in Horsley Prison for food and clothing for five persons exceeded the total earnings of a family of five, as did the cost of food alone for five persons in the workhouse.

Another case reported is that of a woman with three children, one of whom was breast-fed, who had had no food all day. Her cottage had no furniture as it had all been sold. Another instance quoted is of a weaver with three children and a wife near her confinement who had no food in the house, not even a piece of bread or a potato. The informant gave him a shilling and obtained another shilling from a friend to buy some food for the family. It is not surprising that there are reports of the men looking 'spent and wan and the females thin and exhausted'.

The master weavers earned more than the journeymen whom they employed. Their average earnings in 1838, according to the Miles report, were 8s 1½d a week compared with the average for journeymen of 5s 7d. However only one person in the family would normally be a master weaver so the earnings of the whole family would still be very low. Indeed the master weavers were faring badly and between 1815 and 1840 their earnings fell by 37%. Their journeymen employees were even worse off.[10]

The average earnings of the factory weaver in 1838 were 11s 9d a week and were fairly steady. This, though low compared with other skilled persons, was considerably higher than the outdoor workers. Moreover, in times of low demand the mill owner gave work to those in the mill and not to the home worker. Yet the Miles report observes that, though the factory weaver was most favoured, he was most dissatisfied with his lot. 'He considers the factory system to be an infringement upon the trade of weaving and a "breaking up" of his domestic comforts.'

One of the main conclusions of the Miles report was that:

> The condition of the outdoor weaver is depressed without any prospect of remedy; for if a demand for labour should arise from any change in the trade, wages will not be allowed to exceed in any great degree the cost at which power can perform the work. The lowness of the outdoor weavers' wages and earnings are fully attested, and show his condition to be below that of any other labouring class, where skill or knowledge of a trade is requisite, women and young persons have been found adapted to the work, and the market is overrun.[11]

One observation gave the weavers a good moral report despite their low condition. Miles said that 'The weavers are not, however, a race of people addicted to daring crime or hardened theft. Their pilferings are confined to vegetables, or to obtain a little wood for firing, and to minor offences emanating from extreme distress.' The exception was embezzlement, known as slinging, or the taking of materials or cloth from a poor-paying master. This practice was commonplace and regarded almost as a right.

It is perhaps surprising, in view of the appalling poverty, that there was not more protest and violence. There had been strikes and riots in the Stroud area on many occasions but it is not known how far the weavers in the Slad valley were involved. However in 1825 there was serious and widespread protest in the area. In the Stroud valleys on the 28 April 1825:

In about forty-eight hours all the shuttles were laid in the silent grave and the membership of the Stroud Valley Weavers' Union increased in a few days from 400 to 5000.[12]

In the Stroud area strikes were followed by riots and The Vatch Mills were seriously affected.

On the 3rd of June a mob of about 200 went to Vatch Mills and some of the men held sticks over the heads of Mr Peter Wyatt and Mr George L. Wyatt, two of the firm, and threatened to knock out their brains and destroy the mill. On the 4th of June Mr Peter Wyatt went to the Magistrates' Office to prefer a complaint and was assaulted by a mob in front of the office.

On the same day a body of about 3000 assembled at Vatch Mill and took back several pieces of cloth in an unfinished state which they had taken from the weavers.[13]

The decline of employment and earnings continued in spite of protests. In 1837–8, 561 persons in Bisley, of whom 233 were outdoor wool workers, were in receipt of parish relief.[14] There were those who blamed the condition of the weavers to some extent on their own improvidence but, even if they had had savings, by 1839 after several years of earnings below subsistence levels, they would have been destitute. Others blamed the expenditure on alcohol in the beer shops but, by this time, even that had decreased to very little and again the comparison of wages and expenditure speaks for itself. Not surprisingly a remedy was sought in emigration and persons from several parishes went to Canada or Australia. 'In 1837, a party of sixty-eight men, women and children left Bisley for South Australia, eight of the thirteen men being weavers. They were taken to Bristol and put on a steam packet that took them out to an emigrant ship lying in the Channel. For this the parish borrowed £200.'[15] Whether or not any of these emigrants came from these valleys, the fall in their standard of living would have followed the general trend, that is, always downward.

Sometimes the outdoor workers tried to get work on the farms when they had no weaving work. One journeyman weaver reported, however, that this was difficult because the farmers did not think a weaver capable of doing *their* work. He had had some work at potato digging, grubbing trees and sawing wood. He could earn 1s to 1s 4d a day, the highest wage being for harvesting.

There was also concern from the beginning of the century for the conditions of those working in the mills. From 1802 Parliament began to regulate the employment of children. The first Factory Act of that year dealt only with apprentices in cotton and woollen factories and limited their hours of work to twelve per day, as well as regulating their living conditions. This Act was not effective until the 1833 Act included the appointment of factory inspectors, after which the law began to be enforced, though with only four inspectors for most of the country their impact could not have been substantial. The 1833 Act prohibited the employment in woollen factories of children under nine. The mill owners claimed that children were essential to carry out certain processes. For example, young children (that is, small in stature) were employed in the gig pits to clean the flock from the revolving roller. The children sometimes became crook-legged doing this job. Later a revolving brush cleaned the rollers automatically.[16] William Marling and Sons, in response to factory inspectors in 1834, said that children were most generally employed at the age of nine. Nevertheless, the factory inspectors questioned very carefully about the employment of children and seemed not to like the situation.[17]

Once the change was made to a larger scale industry, there was a rather short-lived period of prosperity for the mill owner, though this did not halt the decline in the number of outdoor workers in the cottages. Cotswold cloth was still very well regarded. It is said that, in the 1860s at Ebley Mill, buyers from London would come and mark the cloth on the looms before the pieces were finished, and give their orders for what was known as 'West of England blue and black broadcloth'. Other woollen cloths sometimes produced in the wider area, although probably not in these valleys, were serge and worsted.

The old clothiers were proud of the quality of their cloth and the workers must have had some satisfaction in the finished cloth although, with so many processes, the weavers, for example, did not see their cloth in its finished state. There is a nice story told of Samuel Stephens Marling at Ebley Mill. A customer was looking out of the window at some sheep grazing in the field next to the factory. He complained at the late delivery of some cloth and said that things were done much quicker in the old days. Marling replied, 'We can do just as well and better than in the old days. I will make you a coat out of the wool of those sheep in twenty-four hours.' A small bet was made. The sheep were sheared, the cloth made and dyed, a tailor was sent for and the coat was on the customer's back in twenty-three hours ten minutes.[18] No comment is recorded on the quality of the cloth. It cannot have been very good!

In spite of some prosperity after the middle of the century, the period of decline in the woollen industry continued during the second half of the century to the point of its extinction in the Slad and Scrubs Valleys. In the wider Stroud area there were in 1900 still eleven surviving firms of cloth manufacturers.[19] In 1861 the number of woollen industry workers in Gloucestershire is estimated at rather over 6,700 but by 1900 that was down to about 3,000. This compares with about 24,000 in 1622.[20] The mills which had played such a vital part in the life of the valley were demolished or turned to other uses. The Lower Steanbridge Mill was demolished before 1895. The other mill, the Steanbridge Mill or the Jenny Mill, was converted to a saw mill by 1861 and then to a house before 1882[21] and was known as Steanbridge Farm and later again as Steanbridge Mill. The Vatch was closed sometime before the 1890s and it was demolished before 1901. After that time the clothiers were first and foremost businessmen, and only secondarily the gentlemen clothiers who combined a comfortable lifestyle of farming with the production of cloth.

THE MARLING CONNECTION

The Marling family, and particularly Nathaniel Samuel Marling, had a close connection with the valleys. An early reference to the family is the will of Edward Marling, yeoman, in 1544. There were weavers in the family from as early as 1608. By 1776 the family had a mill at Woodchester. William Marling was, to some extent, a spokesman for the industry, giving evidence to the factory inspectors. By the 1830s Nathaniel Samuel Marling was established at the Vatch. He acquired other mills, including the mill at Kings Stanley in 1839 at a price of £27,000. He retired from the business in the 1850s, receiving £700 a year from the profits of the firm.[22]

Nathaniel Samuel's name occurs again and again in the story of these valleys. He owned Lower Steanbridge Mill, and was a tenant of the Upper Steanbridge Mill. Thus, with his ownership of The Vatch, further down the Slad Valley, he must have been the main employer of the cloth workers in the area. Around 1840 in the Driftcombe Valley, he owned the houses in the terrace of three, as well as Driftcombe Cottage and land to the west of all these cottages. This plot of land was sold on 4th May 1840 as the site for the Primitive Methodist Chapel.

INTERMITTENT AGRICULTURAL PROSPERITY BUT NOT FOR ALL

The Napoleonic Wars were periods of prosperity for the landlords and farmers, partly due to the large price increases and rises in rents. The labourers and small holders did not benefit because of the lower quality of their produce and because agricultural wages in this period fell. In order to keep prices high after the wars the Corn Law of 1815 was introduced. It limited imports of wheat if the price fell below a certain level. This was intended to benefit the landed but was detrimental to the population at large. It caused high prices of food but did not, as intended, stabilize the wheat price because exporters from abroad were not interested to export irregularly. Farming became a gamble and rents fell.

The Miles report compares the agricultural wages with those in the woollen industry. The agricultural labourers were not well paid, but they were better off than the weavers in the valleys, though they earned a little less than those woollen industry workers in factories. One respected farmer in Bisley Parish employed a carter hired by the year for 9 shillings a week. In addition, he was given a cottage and garden rent free, as well as other perquisites which all together meant that his earnings were about 11s a week. A herdsman, rick-maker or thatcher would have received about 10s a week.[23]

The agricultural depression continued to the 1840s. The Corn Law was repealed in 1846 and, contrary to expectations, by 1850 a period of prosperity commenced which lasted until about 1875. Then a series of bad summers knocked yields of arable crops and provided the conditions for the spread of disease among sheep and cattle. In theory it was becoming easier to feed sheep. They could be given supplements of corn through the summer and later in the year they could be fed white turnips, corn or oilcake.[24] If the crops were poor, however, this practice would have been limited. At the same time foreign competition became fierce, especially as steamships facilitated the import of meat from Argentina and the USA and also wheat from Canada. Prices tumbled. The farmers wanted to reduce the already low wages but the labourers pressed for more and eventually deserted the land to work in the towns or emigrated. The situation did not improve until early in the twentieth century and even then prosperity was limited.

In Painswick Parish in 1854 the arable and pasture were approximately equal, but by 1901 there were 1892 acres of arable and 3093 of pasture, though the pasture was not necessarily all fully grazed. In the area covered by this book in 1840 about 270 acres were arable, 250 pasture and 260 woods. Unfortunately there are no such detailed data for the end of the century.

LAND OWNERSHIP AND FARMS

The enclosure of the commons took place much later than the enclosure of the open fields. The large piece of land now known as the Common, or Scrubs Common, and formerly as Custom Scrubs, had no owner designated on the tithe maps of 1840 and was still common land. There the villagers would have had rights to graze cattle, take firewood and so on, according to local custom. The name Custom Scrubs derives from the rights of villagers. It was used in the 1841 census but after that seems to have disappeared from official records to be replaced by The Scrubs. In the eighteenth century enclosures were achieved by special acts of Parliament. In Bisley or Nash End there were 845 acres of commons: Oakridge (including Bourns Green), Nottingham Scrubs, Custom Scrubs and Dunkite Hill. Attempts were made in 1733 and again in 1815 to enclose the Bisley Commons. The Act of Parliament authorizing enclosure of Bisley's Commons was passed on 13 July 1863 but it took until 10 December 1869 to implement.[25]

Custom Scrubs and Nottingham Scrubs were the smallest of the Bisley Commons. It was said in 1839 that Custom Scrubs Common 'does not contain about two or three acres that would be worth cultivating. Thorns and brushwood now grow upon it, which the parishioners have a prescriptive right of cutting whenever they like.' Of Nottingham Scrubs it was said 'though perhaps of a somewhat better soil, still it would not be worth cultivating, either with the spade or the plough. Thorns and brushwood is present produce.' The value of these commons if sold was estimated at £5–8 per acre.[26]

The owners of Steanbridge House, the Townsend family, held large areas of land up the valley as well as two cloth mills and around thirty houses and cottages. Map 5, based on the information from the tithe surveys of around 1840 shows the extent of their holdings. They amounted to nearly 750 acres of which about 500 was in the parish of Miserden, 150 in Painswick and 100 in Bisley. Each of the farms was let. It is clear that in the middle of the nineteenth century there were several substantial farms for, although the Townsend family owned the land, they farmed only a tiny proportion of it themselves. They retained most of the woodland to themselves. This was partly because they wanted the woodlands for hunting which was an important pastime. Leases of farms usually retain the hunting rights for the freeholder. Moreover the gestation period of a timber crop is too long to be attractive to the farm tenant. There was a penalty, of ten pounds in some leases, payable for any tree lopped or topped. Forestry was profitable because of the high demand for timber especially in the Napoleonic Wars and, as a result, many forests were decimated.

The leases of Snows Farm, Down Farm and Trillgate Farm for the 1860s and 1870s are preserved.[27] It is interesting that the rotation system was laid down by the landlord for his tenant to observe. In part this was intended to maintain the quality of the land in case the tenancy ceased and, no doubt, to ensure that the income was such that the tenant would be able to pay the rent. In the case of Trillgate Farm, of over 118 acres in 1876, the farmer must:

> not take two successive crops of corn, grain or pulse from any part of the said lands and that every crop of winter corn or pulse shall be taken upon land broken up from seeds or grass of one years lying and that immediately after every such crop of winter corn or pulse they (the tenants) will summer till the land on the fourth earth system and sow good turnip seed thereon and cause the turnips produced there from to be hoed scoured and preserved for a crop and immediately after such crop of turnips they (the tenants) will take one crop of Lent or summer corn lay the land down with sound grass seeds and continue the same so laid down for one year to be computed from the 1st day of August next after sowing such grass seeds and will at the end of the said term leave the said arable lands in four equal divisions or shifts (as near as the pieces will admit) according to the course or mode of husbandry above described and leave all the last years hay and turnips for the benefit of the said Robert Townsend his heirs and assigns on having been paid for the same according to a valuation to be made.

It was also specified that they must make and appropriately spread manure, dung and compost.

Down Farm was the largest of the Townsend rented farms, in succession farmed by Robert Tuffley, Charles Gardner and Robert Trotman, father and then son. At the 1841 and 1851 censuses Down Farm was lived in by Charles Gardner, described as a farmer and maltster, who in 1841 had farmed at Piedmont. By that time Down Farm covered 250 acres and employed 18 labourers, a governess and house servant. It was clearly a prosperous time for the farm and during the century the house was substantially enlarged.

In 1839 Snows Farm was part of Down Farm but, in the 1851 census, it was said to be a farm of 50 acres and it was rented by George Ayers whose family were to farm there for at least 120 years. It seems there was considerable change in the territories of various farmers, as their circumstances and fortunes fluctuated. The mill below Snows Farm, sometimes known as Snows Mill, sometimes as Down Mill, was in 1840 owned by the Townsends and occupied by William Clissold. It was granted on lease to Snows Farm in 1860. The mill was worked as part of a baker's shop in the late nineteenth century but by the 1960s the buildings had disappeared. All that remains now is the depression of the mill-pond and a wall about 3ft high linked presumably to the mill machinery (see photo 26).

Trillgate (also known as Thril Yat) was also owned by Robert Lawrence Townsend. In 1839 it was occupied by Robert Trotman and it was farmed by the Trotman family for over sixty years, latterly farmed by women. Later the Cook family of clothiers lived there and they probably made some alterations to the house, though it is not known whether it was they who added large extensions on each side of the original building (see photo 22).

Another of Townsend's farms was Piedmont, running along the Slad Brook on the south side. It had seventy-nine acres, unusually, almost all pasture. This was farmed by Charles Gardner, who later farmed Down Farm. The land he rented included the place in the field, known as Stonedge, where Piedmont House stood and also Piedmont Orchard. Some thirty years ago it was possible to trace the boundaries of the garden of Piedmont House by standing at Snows Farm and looking across the valley, but the trees and undergrowth have grown so that is no longer possible. The house would once have been on the track going down to the Roman Bridge which is now enclosed between two fences and overgrown. This was the track used by Mrs Timbrell to take furniture from the Driftcombe Valley to Down Hill in the main valley on her marriage.

The need to determine the exact location of Piedmont House and lands has assumed serious proportions in the discussions in the Valley. There were protagonists who wished the name to apply to the whole of Driftcombe Valley. There were also endless hypotheses as to the origin of the name. Some of this is reported in Appendix 2. It seems, however, that Piedmont was more part of the main Slad Valley than the side valley and that the area marked as farmed by Charles Gardner on Map 5 defines the extent of Piedmont Farm. Gardner did not live in Piedmont House which, for a well-to-do farmer, was too modest a dwelling. By the standards of cottagers, however, it was a big house, as remembered by Lizzie Timbrell. In 1841 it was inhabited by a farm labourer, Henry May. This may be the Henry May who was party to the inventory for the land for the Primitive Methodist Chapel (see Chapter 8). He was described as a labourer from Custom Scrubs. He could not sign his name and simply made a mark. Piedmont House was later owned by Snows Farm. Mrs Timbrell helped to knock the house down when she was a schoolgirl, say 1895–1900. She helped load the stone into a cart. It was to be used in construction of a house for one of the Winterbotham family of clothiers.

Higher up the Valley on the north side of the Dillay Brook is Dillay Farm. In 1838 the farm was owned by John Partridge. The Townsend estate did not extend this far. On the other side of the Dillay Brook is Highwood Farm (now a shed used for storage). In 1851 it was a farm of forty acres. Lizzie Timbrell née Mansell was born there around 1887. She described it as a beautiful house but said it was not really a farm, just called one.

Up the side valley was Sydenhams, the largest farm in this valley with a history second to none. All was not well in the nineteenth century. In 1810 William Sevill, a clothier, perhaps feeling the financial drain of all the developments in the cloth industry, mortgaged Sydenhams to Thomas Parker for the very large sum at that time of £4,000. It is thought that Thomas Parker foreclosed on the mortgage and that it passed through him to Thomas Baker of Bakers Mill.[28] At this time it consisted of over ninety-six acres, of which about forty-five were arable and the rest pasture. Then, by 1851, came the Driver family, probably owning it until 1927, though not always occupying it themselves. Later Henry Williams, father of Norman, lived there with his mother who worked the farm, probably renting it from the Driver family. Her husband was butler at one of the large Gloucestershire houses. The Williams moved to Stancombe soon after 1900.

Driftcombe Farm in 1841 was a small farm of thirteen acres of pasture below Sydenhams also owned by Thomas Baker. In 1898 about twenty-six acres of land at Driftcombe was sold for £250 following the deaths of Henry Driver in 1895 and his wife Maria in 1897.

Disappearing Cottages

Although many farms were owned by the Townsend family of Steanbridge House or other landlords, the farmers who rented their land were largely their own masters. There were also about thirty to thirty-five cottages occupied mainly by farm labourers, with the whole family putting that as their designation. Indeed, children as young as four or five years old were recorded as being farm labourers. There were also a few cottages occupied by weavers or others.

Many cottages in the area in the nineteenth century have since fallen down. They were poorly built, in spite of being mainly of stone, and normally one-up and one-down. Rudge comments on the attitude to agricultural cottages in 1807.

> Landlords generally deem building cottages an unprofitable way of spending money; yet a land owner should recollect that he cannot expect tenants for his lands if proper places are not provided for the residence of labourers. A tenant indeed taking a farm seldom, if ever, troubles himself about the number of cottages annexed to it. Overseers are not often aware of the power the law gives them of erecting cottages on the waste; and hence it follows, that more families are crowded together than is either consistent with comfort, health, or decency; or a remedy is applied, worse possibly than the disease, which is to build a workhouse, into which every person wanting relief is crammed, without distinction of age, sex, or cause of distress.[29]

Rudge goes on to discuss the type of cottage and garden a labourer should have. He sets limits however and says that one does not want such beautiful cottages as to make the distinction between the proprietor and the labourer too faint 'as without this distinction, neither agriculture nor commerce can flourish'.[30]

Some of the cottages in the valleys at the tithe survey had appeared in records before that date and are referred to in previous chapters. These include the ancient Trillgate Cottage, which in 1840 was known as the Nap or Knap and was owned by Robert Lawrence Townsend but lived in by two agricultural labourers, a stonemason and a weaver. The terrace of three cottages, now known as Greencourt, August Cottage and Mullions, were all owned by Nathaniel Samuel Marling in 1840. They were lived in by two weaver families. At the end of the century St Benedicts was occupied by the Mansell family. Further along the Valley is Driftcombe Cottage. In the later nineteenth and early twentieth centuries this seventeenth century cottage had strong connections with the Timbrell and Mansell families (see Chapter 9). Bits of clay pipes were found which probably date from this time. Under the floorboards there were clay stands for use in firing pottery. In the foundations of the lean-to a coin of George IV (1820–30) was found with the Roman numbers unusually written as IIII. This coin is thought to be a forgery.

Down Court, built in the seventeenth century, was five cottages in the mid-nineteenth century. Around 1840 it was owned, as was all the land around, by Robert Lawrence Townsend. Two of the occupiers were signatories of the indenture to purchase the land for the Primitive Methodist Chapel. According to the 1841 census the five cottages were at that time inhabited by five families but there was also a boy of twelve seemingly living separately. The head of the household in four of the cottages was an agricultural labourer, the other being a weaver with his wool-worker family. There were also wool workers in some of the other cottages.

There is another category of cottage, inhabited around 1840 and probably built in the nineteenth century. Most of these are situated in The Scrubs and were built on the Common. It seems that there was a small building boom at the beginning of the nineteenth century. Four cottages were built on the promontory overlooking the Slad Valley and one on the edge of the existing arable land. All were on the original common. It is not known who lived in them but most were probably built for agricultural labourers or perhaps for factory cloth workers. If they were used by home weavers the looms were likely to have been on the ground floor, as was more usual after 1800.[31] Yew Tree Cottage, at the end of the road across the old common, was built in 1823–4 by Bisley Parish as an overflow for paupers of the Bisley Workhouse. It is assumed that it fell into disuse as a poor law house after the Poor Law Amendment Act of 1834.[32]

Another cottage built in the nineteenth century is Timbercombe Cottage, now listed as one of the last examples of the traditional two-up, two-down cottage. It is currently in a poor state of repair and is unoccupied. It is hoped that it can be modernised so that its origins are still apparent (see photos 29–32) .

Lastly there are the cottages which were included in the tithe survey of about 1840 and some further cottages which were occupied in 1851 but are now ruins or have completely disappeared. There were a surprising eighteen such cottages. Indeed it seems that two whole but linked communities vanished. One of these lost communities was at the north side of Down Hill and at nearby Detcombe. In 1851 there were ten cottages believed to be in this area of which four were uninhabited. Thereafter there were four or five in the censuses. Now the only one is Down Cottage, believed to be two of the cottages at Down Hill turned into a single house. It was certainly the only inhabitable cottage there in the 1930s, although there was also the nearby Trillgate Cottage.

Something is known of the history of some of these lost cottages. On 6th June 1840 Robert Lawrence Townsend bought two cottages at Down Hill from the Guardians of the Poor of the Stroud Union and the Parish of Miserden for £40. They were then occupied by Thomas Ireland and Richard Thirsk. Robert Townsend assigned them to the use of a Joseph Watts.[33] They had formerly been workhouses. It is difficult to know which cottages these were because, according to the tithe surveys of 1838 and 1839, all the cottages in the area seemed already to have been owned by Robert Townsend. It may be that, as the cottages were partly owned by Miserden Parish, they were not included in the survey and not marked on the map. Cottages lived in by Joseph Watts have not been traced either in 1841 or 1851, but the indenture does not state that he was going to live there, only that they were for his use. He may have let them. If they were additional to those on the tithe map that means there were even more cottages than previously thought.

Even further over from Down Hill is Detcombe. Access is by a track from the Slad Road uphill from Bulls Cross. In 1820 it was owned by Robert Lawrence Townsend and three men and a woman, all with different surnames, were living there. In 1840 it was shown on the tithe map as one cottage and garden. It was owned by Robert Lawrence Townsend. In the census of 1851 there were three inhabited houses and two uninhabited dwellings at what was called Detcombe. The ruined cottage referred to in Laurie Lee's *Cider with Rosie* as Hangmans Cottage where he said that he and his friends used to play when he was a boy was in fact at Detcombe. One can now only guess where the cottages at Detcombe might have been and there have been no habitable dwellings there in living memory.

On the south side of Down Hill there was a cottage known as Shepherd's Cottage. In 1840 it was owned by Robert Lawrence Townsend and it had a tenant. A photo taken in 1974 shows it as a ruined barn but the stairs in the corner of the house were still visible. It had probably been built in the seventeenth century. A small stone mullion window was well crafted and appeared to belong to that period. Another small mullioned window was made from one piece of stone and was very old (see photo 28). The cottage fell into disuse by the early 1900s. As a shed it was used by Mr Mansell of St Benedicts to make hurdles during the winter. Some time after 1974 it was demolished and the stone was used for some building work. The stone windows had already 'disappeared'. Now all that remains is a small heap of rubble stone.

On Down Common, according to the tithe map, there was another cottage owned by Robert Townsend. This is at the north edge of what was then wood but is now pasture. Curiously, on the south of the location of the cottage, on the Old Shop Ground, there is now wood but it was previously pasture, so that the land usage has been reversed. In 1838 the house was occupied by Daniel Davies.

The area round Timbercombe, at the top of the Slad Valley, sometimes known as Dillay Bottom is another area where a community has disappeared. In the nineteenth century Dillay Farm would have been the most important farm in this secluded part of the valley and there was also Highwood Farm (see photos 29 and 30). Much reference has been made to Timbercombe over several centuries but with little hard evidence as to where the dwellings were located. According to the tithe map and apportionments in the woods off the path from Timbercombe there are ruins of two or three cottages. Around 1900 they were still inhabited. Mr Hopkins who lived at Dillay Farm for about 20 years before and during the Second World War, was convinced there had been a shop and a pub there at one time.[34] As in those times both of these amenities could be very simple, that is a possibility. Higher up the valley towards Nottingham Scrubs were three other cottages of which just one, Beech Cottage, survives and east of Dillay Farm there was a further one. Now Dillay Farm, Beech Cottage, the nineteenth century Timbercombe Cottage (see photos 31–34), now in danger of decay, and Highwood

Farm, now a shed, are all that remain of the seemingly important Timbercombe or Dillay Bottom of earlier centuries. The area may indeed be called a lost village. Whereas, in the area as a whole it seems that one in two cottages survived from 1840 to the twenty-first century, in the case of Dillay Bottom the survival rate was about one in five. One puzzle is what all the inhabitants there did for a living. Census information tells that they were nearly all agricultural labourers. No woollen workers have been found in the censuses though this may be because the first useful censuses did not appear until the industry was declining. The area now is largely covered in fairly young woods, but a photo of Timbercombe in about 1910 shows it surrounded mainly by pasture (photo 31), and there, in the original land use, lies at least a part of the answer to the local occupations.

It is possible that a cottage was later built on the site of Stonedge House. Mrs Timbrell used to play as a child in a ruin in that location which they called Suicide Cottage because someone had killed himself there.

There are ruins too in the Driftcombe valley. Behind Driftcombe Farm are the remains of two houses. They were occupied in1840. Mrs Timbrell said she remembered people living in them, say 1895–1900. When they were bought by the Revd Herford, Bishop of Mercia in 1903, they were described as ruined.

In the woods above the garage near to Greencourt and below St Benedicts is a ruin in the woods. Curiously it is not marked on the tithe map of about 1840. Mrs Timbrell said that there were two houses there of which one was lived in by the preacher on the Easter tea party photo about 1900. The house can, with imagination, be seen on photo 35 of the Scrubs of 1910. Some of the stones from this house were used in the renovation of St Benedicts in the early 1960s.

Up on Scrubs Common there was a cottage in existence in the 1840s to the east of Woodedge. It was owned by Thomas Dickerson who lived in a cottage above Timbercombe. It was unusual for a cottage to be owned by another cottager. At the far side of the Old Common was another dwelling of which no sign has been found. It lay on the southern edge of Stonedge Wood. It was owned and occupied in 1840.

Nearby downstream, but on the south side of the valley is the Old Shop, now in ruins but still in use in the nineteenth century (see photo 41). There has been much speculation about what sort of shop this was. The first thing to note is that it was 'old' in 1838 and owned by Robert Lawrence Townsend. In the censuses from 1841 to 1871 it was occupied by farm labourers. After 1871 the Old Shop is not mentioned by name in the censuses. Mrs Timbrell could not remember anyone living there but her husband recalled two people there, say about 1895, and they were in the photo of the Easter tea party at the Chapel. By 1926 it was described in the ordnance survey map (25 inches to the mile) as 'in ruins'.

The speculation about the use of the Old Shop includes gin and prostitution, a bakehouse, a shop to sell to the locals, a cloth workshop and a farrier's.

Wesleyans were active in the eighteenth century and nineteenth century and it is said that they drove out undesirable elements from the towns and villages to the countryside which lends support to the gin and prostitution theory. Moreover it is said that to have visited the Old Shop was, in itself, grounds for divorce. It could have also been a shop selling provisions and this may well have included bread. It is said that there were two buildings of which one might have been the bake-house. One of the Miss Ayers said that her mother remembered buying sugar from there and Jack Timbrell also said that sugar was sold there. Miss Ayers' mother was born in 1849 or 1850 at which time the Old Shop was lived in by a farm labourer. But it is possible that a farm labourer's wife might have had a few goods to sell to neighbours and travellers. As it was on a probable packhorse route from Miserden to Stroud, it is not unlikely that it was a shop stocking supplies. Norman Williams said that before his time, say 1900, it was a farrier's. Lastly, the word shop was used to designate any type of business premises. A rating survey of 1822 found that, of the 'shops' in the Stroud area, the great majority were weaving shops. This could easily be the meaning of the name in this case. None of these solutions to the problem is mutually exclusive. Any place on a route for travellers would have required many different types of services! If Timbercombe was a more important area, then the need for the services offered by the Old Shop would have been even greater. On balance, however, the brothel and a shop with probably a baker's is the most likely. This is supported by memories from Elcombe.[35] There it is said that there is a story that 'there was a brothel in the middle of fields at The Scrubs, a mile or so up the valley.' It goes on: 'According to a reliable source from an old farming family, this house of ill repute shared a small stone building with a shop. Anyway, both businesses must have suffered a recession a long time ago. All that is left, this informant says, are some ruins of a building.' A photo of the Old shop about 1966 before the chimney fell down, indicates that it was a fairly substantial building (photo 41).

There was another amenity in the valley, the Old Ale House, the name and location of which has been passed down by word of mouth. It was nearly opposite Driftcombe Cottage and is now a ruin, still visible in photo 49. In 1974 it was possible to see where the rooms had been, but now all that remains are a few stones. Although there has not been any doubt about its description, it is very difficult to know when the last glass of beer was sold or, indeed, when the first one was sold. The census throws a little light on the matter. Around 1840, the cottage and the field in which it is are referred to as 'Reddings and houses' and they were occupied by Robert May. He was 80 years old and retired. In 1851 there was another Robert May living there with his wife and eight children and in 1861 he was still there. In 1851 he was described as an agricultural labourer but in 1861, by which time he was 63, he was described as innkeeper. Mrs Timbrell's husband, Jack, remembered the Old Ale House and said that around 1890 it was open only on Sundays. The ale or beer was delivered by donkey. They would also have brewed their own beer. There are still hop plants growing on the site by the building. In 1891 Edwin Partridge lived at Driftcombe Farm and described himself as a refreshment-house keeper. He may have been linked to the Old Ale House. When Driftcombe Cottage opposite was sold in 1938 it was described as having a brewhouse which may have had a connection at one time to the Old Ale House. In spite of the uncertainty about dates, the local stories still get handed down the generations. It is said that the Old Ale House had wallpaper, but it was no longer beautiful because the pigs had eaten it, tempted by the flour and water paste, as far up as they could reach.

The report on the condition of the handloom weavers refers at length to the injurious effects of the Beer Shops, known as 'kidley winks'. Miles observes that 'there is scarcely a factory which has not a beer shop, or many beer shops in its immediate vicinity. If there is a spot more secluded than another in the parish, I generally expect to see a beer shop in the midst of that seclusion.' There were 35 Beer Shops in Bisley Parish in 1838 of which seven had a chandler's shop attached. This was in addition to 15 public houses. It is not known how many others there were which were not licensed. The Old Ale House was probably one of these Beer Shops and in its earlier life may well have done good business. Indeed, the Old Ale House may well have been in existence from quite early times—long before there is written or anecdotal evidence of its existence. It may be that it was open only on Sundays in the period of its decline and/or because the landlord was working as an agricultural labourer on all the other days of the week. It was very usual for ale-houses to provide an extra source of income for people working at other jobs, the wife often doing the brewing and serving customers.[36] There is also a possibility that it was used for nonconformist worship in the mid 1820s (see Chapter 8).

George Turner of Dowdeswell, writing in 1794, was very critical both of ale-houses and of chandlers' shops. The former, he says, 'hold out too great a temptation to the labourer to waste that money in debauchery, which ought to find bread for his family …' and 'Chandlers' shops—retail in small quantities and at extravagant rates the worst of commodities'. He was worried about the drain on the income of the poor and also, in the case of alcohol, the effect on their work.[37]

Nothing illustrates the decline in the valleys in the nineteenth century better than the decay and disappearance of all these cottages and related amenities. The valley at the turn of the century must have been a dejected place with a down-hearted and down-trodden population. Some of the people who had lived there had simply tried to find work in the towns; others had taken more drastic action and emigrated even further afield.

1.   Tithe Survey maps and apportionments for Bisley, Miserden and Painswick

2.   Gloucestershire Record Office (GRO) D2080/77 Inventory and Sale of property at Down Farm, 1810

3.   Mackintosh, Ian D (1993) 'The Playnes and Industrial Change', Typescript, Jan 1993

4.   Mann, Julia de Lacey (1971) *The Cloth Industry in the West of England, 1640–1880*, Oxford: Clarendon p.229

5.   Loosley, John (1993) *The Stroudwater Riots of 1825*, Stroud, Glos: The Stroud Museum Association, p.62

6.   Loosley, *op. cit.* p.5

7.   Perry, R. (2003) *The Woollen Industry in Gloucestershire to 1914*, Shrewsbury: Ivy House Books, pp.103–7

8.   Miles, W.A. (1839) *Report on the Condition of the Handloom Weavers of Gloucestershire for Her Majesty's Commission of Inquiry into the Condition of Handloom Weavers in the United Kingdom*

9.   Miles, *op. cit.* p.419

10. Perry, *op. cit.* p.119

11. Miles, *op. cit.* p.359

12. Loosley, *op. cit.* p.7

13. Loosley, *op. cit.* pp.15–16

14. Miles, *op. cit.* p.417

15. Perry, *op. cit.* p.124

16. Mackintosh (1993) *op. cit.*

17. Mackintosh, Ian D (1993) 'Responses by William Marling & Sons to the Factory Inspectors, 1834' Typescript, Feb 1993

18. Marling, Percival (1931) *Rifleman and Hussar*, London: John Murray, p.3

19. Page, William (ed) (1907) *The Victoria History of the County of Gloucester*, Vol. II published for the University of London, Institute of Historical Research, reprinted Dawsons of Pall Mall 1972, p.196

20. Tann, Jennifer (1967) *Gloucestershire Woollen Mills*, Newton Abbot: David and Charles, Chapters 2–4

21. Pugh, R.B. (ed.) (1976) *The Victoria History of the County of Gloucestershire*, Vol. XI, published for the University of London, Institute of Historical Research by OUP, p.53

22. Moir, Esther A.L. (1955) 'History of Marling and Evans Ltd., Woollen and Worsted Manufacturing, Kings Stanley and Ebley, Glos' Typescript

23. Miles, *op. cit.* pp.416–7

24. Moore-Colyer, R.J. (1989) Livestock Section in Chapter 4, Farming Techniques, in Mingay, G.E. and Higgs J.W.Y. (eds) (1989) *The Agrarian History of England and Wales* (General Editor Joan Thirsk, former editor H.P.R. Finberg), Vol. VI, 1750–1850, Cambridge: CUP, p.332

25. Board of Agriculture (1893) *Return for all Inclosure Awards Deposited with the Board of Agriculture*

26. Letter from Mr Sevill of Burleigh House to Mr Miles in Miles, *op. cit.* p.520

27. GRO D1815 Townsend (Location 7.79.3) Documents relating to the Townsend family and estates and leases for Down Farm, Trillgate Farm and Snows Farm, 19th century

28. GRO D1388/III/10 Schedule of deeds relating to Sydenhams 1641–1810

29. Rudge, Thomas (1807) *General View of Agriculture of the County of Gloucester drawn up for the consideration of the Board of Agriculture and internal improvement*, London: Richard Phillips, pp.47–9

30. Rudge, *op. cit.* p.50

31. Walrond, Lionel F.J. (1973) 'Wool, Woolmen and Weavers' in Charles and Mary Hadfield (eds), *The Cotswolds: A New Study*, Newton Abbot: David & Charles p.87

32. Pugh, *op. cit.* p.31 and a letter from the County Archivist to J Duce Esq 25.8.87

33. GRO D2056/6 Purchase by Robert Lawrence Townsend from the Overseers of the Poor of Miserdine of two cottages on Downhill 1840

34. *Stroud News and Gloucester County Advertiser*, Spring 1947 'In search of a lost village: a visit to Dillay Bottom'

35. Sharp, Robin (2003) *All About Elcombe: The intimate history of a Cotswold hamlet*, London: Wygesty Publishing

36. Hey, David (1996) *The Oxford Companion to Local and Family History*, Oxford: OUP

37. Turner, George of Dowdeswell (1794) *General view of the Agriculture of the County of Gloucester with observations on the means of its improvement*, London: J Smeeton, pp.25–6

8

The Primitive Methodist Chapel

Worship on Sundays in the eighteenth and early nineteenth centuries was *de rigeur* in the Church of England churches in Bisley and Slad. The large farmers would have attended and they would have expected to see some of their employees there too. Some, however, would have gone to nonconformist establishments including the Methodist church. The west of England had been a stronghold of Methodism established by John and Charles Wesley in the eighteenth century. The practice was to have itinerant lay preachers. The Primitive Methodists broke away from the main stream of Methodism in 1812 and soon became the second strongest of the Methodist sects. Across the country it was the humbler people in every walk of life who became part of the Primitive Methodists. Feeling for this form of worship was clearly very strong in these valleys amongst the agricultural and cloth workers.

In 1825 permission had been obtained by Robert May from the Bishop of Gloucester for Primitive Methodist worship to be held in 'that certain building or kitchen now in his occupation in the parish of Bisley'. In 1841, according to the tithe maps, there was a Robert May, occupying the Old Ale House, and, according to the census there was a Robert May, aged eighty, living at Driftcombe. These are presumed to be the same person. There was another Robert May, aged forty, living at Custom Scrubs. In 1828 a William May was given permission to use his own cottage at Custom Scrubs as a place of religious worship.[1] In the census of 1841 there was a William May, aged thirty-five, living at Driftcombe, but it is not known in which cottage.

A more ambitious scheme was afoot. It was decided to build a chapel for the valleys and the surrounding area. A farthing fund was set up to buy the land for a chapel and the materials for its construction. The site which they were able to buy was in the Driftcombe Valley between Piedmont House and the three cottages in a terrace, later known as Greencourt. According to an indenture of 4 May 1840,[2] the land for the chapel and for a school and burial ground, previously wood or woodland, was bought from Nathaniel Samuel Marling for £5 by eleven persons living no further away than Stroud. The only cottages mentioned in the indenture for identification purposes, are to the east, presumably the three cottages at Greencourt. Prior to 1840, the land had been in the possession of James Woodfield or his under-tenants.

The eleven signatories of the purchasers of the land were:

Thomas Russell	Primitive Methodist Preacher of Stroud
James Pegler	furrier of Stroud
James Woodfield	clothworker of Stroud
James Collett	clothworker of Rodborough
Richard Davis	labourer of Downcourt
William Davis	miller of Downcourt
John May	labourer of Custom Scrubs (could not sign his name)
William May	labourer of Custom Scrubs
Robert May	labourer of Custom Scrubs
Henry May	labourer of Custom Scrubs (could not sign his name)
Thomas Claridge	

The Chapel was built in 1840. It was the original part of the building which is now known as Scrubs Bottom, although the Chapel consisted only of the one room on the west of the present house. It was very important in the Valley not only as a religious centre but also for its unifying influence on the whole area. The congregation came from the main Slad Valley, from Driftcombe and The Scrubs and also from as far away as Leonard Stanley. The Chapel claimed a congregation of about forty in 1851, thirty-six attended in the afternoon and thirty-eight in the evening.[3]

A register of baptisms in the Primitive Methodist religion was kept for an area in Gloucestershire from 1829.[4] It gives the name of the child baptised; the names of the parents, including sometimes the maiden name of the mother; where they lived; where they were born or lived formerly; the occupation of the father and the name of the Minister. With one exception there is no statement as to where the ceremony took place and the place of abode is often described broadly, such as Painswick, which may refer to the parish rather than the village. From 1840 to 1918 there were only twenty-two baptisms where the child or its parents lived in the area of this study—at Scrubs (spelt Scrubbs) (14), Downcourt (4), Downhill (2), Sydenhams (1) and Detcombe (spelt Dedcombe)(1). Richard Davis, one of the signatories, had three children baptised from Downcourt in the early 1850s. It seems curious that there were not more baptisms from the area of study, particularly that there were no Mays.

As far as is known, there were no burials on the Chapel land. Similarly no reports of it being used as a school, except for Sunday School, have been heard.

The preachers for the Chapel were, as was normal for the Primitive Methodists, lay people. Sometimes they walked great distances. One such was John Autumn who frequently walked from Sheepscombe to preach at The Scrubs. He died around the mid-1930s aged eighty-six.[5]

Photos 45 and 46, from around 1890, of an Easter Sunday tea party outside the chapel are still in existence and two of them are reproduced in this book. Information on the people in the larger group and where they lived comes from the late Mrs Timbrell and Mr Wilf Merrett.

The Ansloes lived at St Benedicts.

Mr and Mrs Mansell (possibly far left) and their daughter, Lizzie (later Mrs Timbrell) lived at Yew Tree Cottage. Lizzie Mansell, (in the front row) was then about ten years old. Mr Mansell was a hurdle maker. Edith Mansell was later caretaker at the Chapel. Further information on the Mansell family is included in Chapter 9.

Mr Timbrell and his father and mother (possibly far right back) lived at Driftcombe Cottage and there are photos of them outside that cottage. Mr Timbrell worked on the farm of Sir John Dorrington at Lypiatt.

Mr and Mrs Holloway (possibly left of doorway) lived at Colombine Cottage. The preacher lived in the cottage (now a ruin) below St Benedicts in the woods.

In addition in the photo are two families from Down Court, a family from Slad, walking preachers and Nurses of Mercy from Bisley. The names Ansloe, Mansell, and Timbrell and also Gardiner (see St Benedicts) all appear in the record of baptisms from 1874.

On 1 April 1921 a note in the *Stroud Journal* described Good Friday at the Chapel:

> Fortunately for those who prepared the open-air tea at picturesque Scrubbs on Good Friday the warmth of the sunshine enabled the large muster of visitors to take their meal in comfort. So many attended from Stroud, Painswick, Bisley and elsewhere that rugs and wraps had to be spread on the grassy slopes in front of the little chapel, but although Catswood opposite was in shadow, the chapel side of the valley was bathed in sunshine, and picknicking in March was voted a great joy. The chapel would not have contained all those who attended the tea, and for that reason it was just as well that those living at a distance did not remain for the evening meeting. This took the usual form, there being present the Revs. J. Burton and C. Durham and Messrs Jesse Wall, S. Fern, Mr. and Mrs. Mansell and others who have worked devotedly in connection with the Primitive Methodist cause at Scrubbs.[6]

There was a Whitsun tea party, too. Some of the congregation of the Chapel in Parliament Street, Stroud used to walk to The Scrubs, via The Vatch and Swift's Hill for the Whitsun tea party at the Chapel. Bread for the tea parties was baked in the bread oven of St Benedicts. Miss Stevenson organized the services at the Chapel and the Gardiners looked after the building.

The later history of the Chapel is patchy. The changes which took place in the First World War and the depression of the 1930s would have diminished its congregations, though in the 1930s Jim Dickenson sometimes used to go with his friends to a service in the Chapel instead of going with his family to church in Slad. In 1932 the Primitive Methodists had united with other groups to form the Methodist Church of Great Britain. This would probably have had only a small effect on the Chapel at The Scrubs. The reason for the fall in Primitive Methodist worship at the Scrubs was the serious economic situation of the inhabitants in the 1930s, leading to many of the supporters of the Chapel leaving the valley. It is known that in the period 1937–9 Easter services were never missed. In these years Austin Magor, well into his eighties in 2005, played the organ at the Chapel for services held once a month. Attendance for the latter was only ten to twelve persons. The date at which all worship ceased is not known but probably coincides with the beginning of the Second World War.[7] By 1940 people were living in the old Chapel. It had become a house. This was the end of an era. The influence the Chapel had had on the lives of the woollen and agricultural workers and on their substantial families in the Valley in the difficult nineteenth century is immeasurable. The mutual support of the members of the congregation would sometimes have helped to make their lives a little more bearable then and in the first part of the twentieth century.

1.   Gloucestershire Records Office (GRO) Hockaday Abstracts, GDR 350 p.42 Certificate to the Bishop of Gloucester by Robert May, labourer, 16th July 1825, and p.92 Certificate to the Bishop of Gloucester by William May of Bisley, Labourer, 2nd August 1828

2.   Indenture for the purchase of land for the Primitive Methodist Chapel by permission of Lois and Quentin Letts

3.   GRO HO 129/338/3/1/6 Attendance at Primitive Methodist Chapel 1851

4.   GRO D3187/1/4/1 Brinkworth Circuit Primitive Methodists, Stroudwater Branch, Register of Baptisms 1829–1949

5.   *Stroud News and Gloucester County Advertiser*, Spring 1947 'In search of a lost village: a visit to Dillay Bottom'

6. *Stroud Journal,* 1st April 1921 'Concerning tea party at the Primitive Methodist Chapel'

7. According to The Victoria County History (Pugh, *op. cit.* p.37) the chapel was in use until 1912. It clearly continued long after that date.

9

Wars and Depression:
First Half of the Twentieth Century

INTRODUCTION

The century began with the valleys in decline on account of the demise of the woollen industry in the Slad valleys as well as the poor state of agriculture. The population was sadly depleted and there was an air of decay. In 1901, according to the census, there were eighteen identified inhabited dwellings in the area but there were also eleven uninhabited or unoccupied dwellings, including Steanbridge House, which was changing hands about this time, Driftcombe Farm and Highwood Farm. The first half of the new century saw great changes but little improvement in the lives of the inhabitants. In part this was the consequence of world events, notably the First World War, the Great Depression and the Second World War. Changes in agriculture continued in this century, and reduced further the need for large cohorts of agricultural labour.

The year 1901 was a turning point in the history of the Slad Valley because it was the date of the break-up of the great estate of the Townsend family, which had dominated the valleys for about two centuries. In July 1901 the owner put the lands and houses up for auction by Bruton Knowles in a number of lots at the George Hotel in Stroud.[1] Suddenly the farms were occupied by their owners, not by tenants, and the social structure of the valleys changed almost overnight. The lots sold included:

> Steanbridge House, garden and some land bought by Mr S.G. Jones for £3,000;
>
> Steanbridge Farm (Mill) including farmhouse and outbuildings, tenant Mr R. Trotman, bought by Mr S.G. Jones for £700;
>
> Down Farm Estate bought by Mr R. Trotman, tenant, for £2,500 and lived in by him at 1901 census;
>
> Trillgate Farm, tenant Mr R. Trotman, bought by Mr Pimbury of The Edge for £1,025.

In addition there were a number of smaller lots. It seems that Snows Farm was sold to the Ayers family, who were its tenants, by prior arrangement.

Another change was the loss of the Primitive Methodist Chapel. At the beginning of the century it was well supported but, as time went on, attendances fell and services became less frequent. Many of the families who had worshipped at the Chapel for nearly a hundred years were no longer in the Valley and those who were left were too old to maintain it. It is thought that the commencement of the Second World War finally sealed its fate.

Agriculture had been going through a difficult time. Statistics for the whole of Gloucestershire give some indication of the extent of the problem. In 1872–81 the percentage of cultivated land under grains and pulses was 26.6%. By 1913–14 it was 16.7%.[2] The decline in arable continued to the 1930s. The area under wheat in Gloucestershire fell from over 47,000 acres in 1900 to some 25,000 in 1931. In the same period the acreage of barley fell from 28,000 to about 11,000.[3] The number of farm labourers in the county had declined by about 50% from 1851 to 1911.[4]

Sheep were still vitally important both in Gloucestershire as a whole and in these valleys though they were now of importance as a source of meat rather than wool. In 1900 there was more land in permanent pasture, either for grazing or for hay, than at any time since at least 1875. The photos of the Driftcombe Valley and of The Scrubs of about 1910 (35 and 55) show the great extent of pasture compared to the present time. Many of the fields of 1910 are now woodland.

During the First World War prices of agricultural produce more than doubled. Agriculture was badly disrupted as many of those in the valleys joined up and fought in France and further afield. One of those was Ernest Dickenson, the son of the farmer at Down Farm and father of Jim Dickenson. It was nevertheless possible during this period to make a profit. After the war government controls were relaxed or abandoned. Prices continued to rise for two years after the war but in 1922 plummeted to a little over half the levels of two years earlier.[5] Then came the depression which brought incomes to very low levels and some of the farmers incurred debts which took years to pay off.

Thus, at the beginning of the Second World War the area was still in a state of decay. The war helped to raise incomes but the state of the farms and the farmhouses was serious. During the war farmers had to contend with government direction and a severe shortage of labour, to some extent alleviated by the employment of land-girls. They did however have a guaranteed market for their produce. Moreover, food rationing and the fact that everyone had some employment, removed at last the spectre of starvation from the valleys.

During the war most of the population worked as agricultural or forestry workers. Some of the cottages were saved from collapse during the war by the influx of newcomers from the large cities who took refuge in the area. An increasing number found employment away from the valley and had a long walk to work, as a bus-conductress and a nurse, for example. Prices of some cottages were falling in this period. John Wright observed that 'in the early 1950s The Scrubs was the last stop before the workhouse'. This expresses his feelings of shock at the poverty and the hard lives lived around him, but in fact there was probably considerably less real poverty than in previous centuries. Expectations were rising but it was difficult to realise the aspirations.

The changes which had taken place produced other undesirable consequences. The discipline imposed by being known throughout the valleys and the rules for living an upright life, promulgated by the preachers of the Primitive Methodist Chapel, were no longer there and the standards of behaviour seemed to be in decline. More is certainly known of various transgressions!

LIFE ON THE FARMS

The way in which the farms were managed depended in large measure on the nature of the terrain. In particular, this determined the preferences for arable or pasture though the market situation for the produce, whether animal or vegetable, was obviously important too. Descriptions of the practices on Down Farm, and to a lesser extent Snows Farm and Sydenhams, give a picture of the still, by modern standards, very labour-intensive methods. The way of life, living close to the soil but enjoying life in a community with different personalities and temperaments, made for lively rivalry.

The largest farm sold at auction in 1901 was Down Farm (see photo 10), bought by Mr Robert Trotman for £2,500. He had previously been the tenant. He was quite a patrician figure, as his photo (13) shows. The farm was bought by Joseph Dickenson who, with his son, farmed there for around thirty-five years to 1947. Joseph Dickenson (see photos 15 and 16) was the son of the farmer at Rectory Farm in Bisley. As a young man he went into the grocery and coal merchanting business. He owned the Cotswold Stores in Stroud and, when he had made enough money, he bought Down Farm. He also eventually owned Detcombe Wood, Catswood and Longbridge Farm and a wood at Sheepscombe. In the farm he was supported by his son, Ernest, the father of Jim Dickenson. Ernest Dickenson lived with his family at Down Court. During the First World War he saw active service with General Allenby travelling over the Sinai desert. Curiously his son Jim, doing his military service, travelled over much the same ground in 1948–49 in the evacuation from Palestine. Ernest was a Special Constable in the Second World War, chosen partly because of his service in the First World War. During the first part of the war constables were on duty all night patrolling the villages. Jim, now of Lypiatt Lodge and the Farm Shop at Stancombe, worked at Down Farm as a boy from 1936 to 1945.

The rotation system from 1900 to the Second World War varied from one area and one farm to another, but it was generally similar to that on Down

Farm between the wars when the Dickenson family was farming there. In year one there was winter wheat (square head variety). This was followed in year two by barley or oats and in year three by swedes (Swedish turnips) as food for the sheep. In year four, and sometimes years five and six, 'small seeds' would be sown, usually a mixture of grass, white clover and often sainfoin (a grass fodder crop). Yields were very low. For winter wheat one ton an acre was good and in some years it would be less than half a ton. Frit-fly was a major pest, especially on oats, and it could almost wipe out the entire crop. Growing swedes was very labour-intensive because they had to be thinned and hoed by hand. It would take three persons days and days of work to hoe the field and then, according to the weather, the operation would have to be repeated as the weeds grew again. When the swedes were ready they were fed to the sheep on the field, but the sheep were not let loose on the field because they would have spoilt the crop. Instead the animals, perhaps fifty or sixty ewes, were confined in an area of the field by hurdles which were shifted to a new patch every day or so. The swedes were harvested and then, using a mangle cutter, were cut into pieces rather like chipped potatoes. To these were added hay, cut up through a chaff cutter, and also crushed oats. Keeping the sheep in the swede fields provided some good manure for the future crops. The grass crop was also for grazing. The sainfoin was especially good for sheep, acting as a sort of medicine. It might be that if there were a major problem with weeds the field would lie fallow for a year. Couch grass, docks and colt's foot had to be dug out by hand, a terrible job on a whole field.

Basic slag, which contains phosphates was, other than farm manure, the only fertiliser which was available. It was black and messy and had to be spread by hand. Later the Dickensons acquired a spreader. Mechanical aids were being developed but there were no tractors on Down Farm. Insecticides, as known today, had not been envisaged. As a consequence the labour required on farms was several times that employed today and the production of foodstuffs went on using traditional, hand methods.

Farm employees of the nineteenth and the first half of the twentieth century may be divided into three groups. The first was the skilled, trusted and respected worker. When referred to he would be called, for example, Carter Timbrell or Shepherd so and so. They would be better paid than the next group of employed agricultural labourer who did some skilled work but had less responsibility. The latter would do routine work, such as weeding or ditching. Lastly, there was the casual labourer, wanted at periods of urgent activity on the farm, especially at harvest or threshing time. The number of persons employed in Down Farm about 1900 was eight to nine.

Although Joseph Dickenson continued to own Down Farm until his death he passed its management over to his son Ernest in 1919. This was an unfortunate time to take over the reins of any agricultural business and the farm fell into debt as a result of the years of depression. It took until 1938–9 to clear the debt. Clearly during this time money was very short and the family just eked out an existence, working very hard to keep their heads above water. On occasion they had even to sell cattle to pay the wages. They always ate frugally. On the menu soon after lambing was lamb tail broth and on the 12th May, when the annual rook shoot took place, rook pie.

The Second World War brought much control from Government. The Ministry of Agriculture determined what crops should be grown and sent officials to enforce this. If the farmer did not do as bidden he could be evicted from the farm. Down Farm had to grow three to five acres of potatoes which, at a time when every process was done manually, required a lot of labour. The yield was five to six tons an acre. For this they had an allocation of fertiliser—ICI No 1. The lower part of Down Hill had always been ploughed but during the war the whole had to be ploughed, almost up to the trees on the top, locally known as 'the roundabout'. This could not be done with horses so the Ministry came and ploughed with a tractor and then set the crops. The farmer harvested them and marketed them. There was some resentment that the people who came from the Ministry and told them what to do were sometimes failed farmers. There was one who had gone bankrupt when managing his own farm but he received the OBE after the war for his agricultural work.

Sheep, rather than cattle, have always been the mainstay of animal husbandry in these valleys. Prior to the Second World War sheep were washed in the sheep dip by the bridge at Steanbridge the day before shearing to ensure the wool was clean. The sheep dip in the stream is still visible. Photos 19 and 20 of the sheep being dipped and their shearing show that there was a degree of mechanisation in the shearing process. The practice of dipping the sheep before shearing ceased during the war and was not restarted, presumably because labour was too expensive and other cleaning methods were available.

All through the Second World War working on Down Farm there were, in addition to Ernest Dickenson, only Jack Timbrell and Charlie Holford on a regular basis. Jack Timbrell was the Carter in charge of the horses (see photo 14). Charlie Holford had been the farmer at Chequers Farm, Bisley and then moved, first to Greencourt and later to Down Hill Cottage. While he lived at Greencourt he worked partly for Albert Skinner at Bisley Farm but he was a well-skilled thatcher and hedger and worked for farmers for some distance around, thatching their ricks whenever required. When he started working for the Dickensons at Down Farm he did more varied work and took over from Jack Timbrell ploughing when the need arose. It was then that he had the farm cottage on Down Hill. His son Philip went to Bisley School when they lived at Greencourt but, by the time he moved to Down Hill at age twelve, he took a bus from Slad to school at Uplands.

The harvest was a busy time and helpers were welcome. The first task was reaping the corn, then stacking the sheaves into stooks and, when they were dry, loading them on to wagons to take them to the rick. A skilled man had to supervise the building of the rick because if it was not well done it could collapse. At harvest two wagons were on the go. There was often one wagonful of sheaves which had not been unloaded the previous day, so the first job every morning was to unload those sheaves onto the rick. The other wagon would be in the field collecting the next load. There was a great need for labour when threshing. As many as seven or eight men were needed for the whole process, including taking the sheaves from the rick, cutting the bonds, feeding the drum, removing the grain as it came out of the machine and removing and stacking the straw.

Fortunately this part of the country was spared the experience of any major enemy action. The presence of Americans in the vicinity was a reminder of the stark realities and so also were the precautions which had to be taken everywhere, including the blackout, the need for Special Constables and Air Raid Wardens. A searchlight was located on Longridge Farm. There were some incidents. Norman Williams had a lucky escape on the Common when an enemy plane was strafing. He ran for cover and a bullet hit a tin roof. He was unhurt but a dog was killed. On another occasion Jim Dickenson saw a German plane being shot down from his vantage point on the top of Down Hill and saw the crew bale out with parachutes. The plane and the crew came down near Oakridge. Three crew survived; one was killed.

There were three working horses on Down Farm during the war, compared with about twelve some fifty years earlier. One, Boxer, was old but reliable and was used for special jobs. He was a much loved but wily old horse. When he was turning the cider mill he would work well until left alone, then he stopped until he was again observed. He had to be put down at the beginning of the war and this was done on the farm to avoid any possibility of his being ill-treated elsewhere. He was replaced by a young horse called Jolly. The two others, both Suffolk Punches, called Punch and Duke, were used to work the land, usually two at a time as seen in photos 17 and 18. Occasionally three horses were used at once, for example to pull a binder uphill. Punch was the quietest, even a bit lazy, but the other two had plenty of 'go'. Once when Jim Dickenson was riding home on Duke from Timmins, the blacksmith at Miserden, a group of Americans soldiers banged some tins and shouted 'Ride him cowboy'. This caused Duke to throw Jim off and bolt for home. Trudging back on foot, Jim was met by Jack Timbrell who was searching to see what had happened to him.[6] Horses could plough about an acre a day, whereas tractors could do ten acres a day. By the end of the war many farmers had tractors but at Down Farm they still used horses. They did, however, have some mechanical help. W.H. Berry came with steam engines (or steam tack as it was known) before the war. The fire in these engines was started with wood and then they burnt coal. Will Stevens did the threshing for them. He was the brother of Jack Stevens who farmed Rectory Farm, Cotswolds Farm and Fennels Farm. The first combine harvesters came into use during the war and Jack Stevens used a combine before the war was over.

With the on-going climate change, the harsh winters experienced from time to time since time immemorial are now a subject for some awe. The winter of 1940 was one such. The cold was so extreme that in freezing fog there were constant cracks, like the reports of a gun, as branch after branch of the frozen trees or whole trees broke and crashed to the ground. The local population had enough firewood for several winters to come. Jim Dickenson remembers that that was the year his father suffered a bout of malaria and Charlie Holford had to feed the animals. It was so slippery they had to crawl up Down Hill on hands and knees because it was impossible to walk upright. At Down Farm they kept only two cows to provide milk for home consumption. They made butter which was much in demand during the war and could be swapped for other things so they were not short of good food.

Cider was plentiful and the men were allocated a quart of cider daily. This had been made on the farm (see photo 12) by Jack Timbrell with apples from Peglers Orchard. It was Jim Dickenson's job to fetch the cider from the cellar, especially as his grandfather got more and more arthritic. He remembers his grandfather, who knew he would drink some if he had the chance, standing at the top of the cellar steps, saying 'Let me hear you whistle Lad'.[7] His grandfather used to give cider to a number of people, including Jimmy Bannen from Timbercombe. For many it was nearer for those walking from higher up the valley to cut off a corner and go across the fields to the yard of Down Farm, rather than going by the road. The Dickensons never minded people going across the fields as long as they did no damage. There were no 'keep out' notices on their farm at that time, though some other landowners did not welcome intruders. Jimmy Bannen, for example, was very protective of his land at Timbercombe and, on one occasion, when Jim Dickenson and young Doug Timbrell were blackberrying at Highwood, chased them away. They did not stop to argue!

Most people made some sort of country wine, especially dandelion wine. That made by the Pimbury family at Trillgate Farm was particularly memorable. At Down Court the lowest cottage down the hill was not inhabited and was used to keep feed and tools. It was also where the dandelion wine was made.

The family members all had to work hard but there was still time for some leisure activities. Farmer Dickenson used to play tennis before the First World War and he had a tennis court constructed on Down Hill. The boys played cricket on one of the fields. The young boys were out in their holidays from dawn to dusk playing and tracking animals. They had a continuing occupation teasing and infuriating the Ayers sisters at Snows Farm. On Sunday the family went to

Church in Slad, though sometimes Jim Dickenson would go with his friends to the Primitive Methodist Chapel. Every Sunday Ernest Dickenson and his family went for a walk somewhere in the valleys, often calling in on neighbours and perhaps having a glass of home-made wine.

At this time Down Court, once five cottages, was lived in by Ernest Dickenson and Jack Timbrell and their families (see photo 23). Charlie Holford lived at Down Cottage. Down Court, which was owned by Down Farm, had always been occupied almost entirely by those connected with farming and working at Down Farm. The only water supply was a sixty foot well, so every drop had to be wound out by hand. In the summer during dry spells it almost dried up, so Ernest Dickenson and Jack Timbrell used to carry drinking water from Down Farm house with a yoke across their shoulders, carrying two buckets at a time. The water had to be heated for the bath which, in the Dickenson family at Down Court, was taken once a week in the tin bath used by all the family, usually kept underneath the table. Jim had the first bath, then his mother and finally his father. The privy was up the garden and the journey there on a dark night was not a pleasant one. Clothes were washed once a week, boiled in the copper in the kitchen. Lighting was by oil lamps and candles, but the house was so draughty that when you went up to bed it was necessary to shield the flame with your hand because otherwise the flame would blow out. The cottage would be condemned in that condition today but then, that way of life was accepted because that was how most people lived. Needless to say there was no electricity and no telephone but there was a radio. That was run off accumulators changed once a week. It often ran out of power before it was time to collect the recharged one from the store. Around the middle of the century Down Court was no longer owned by Down Farm.

At the end of the war Jim Dickenson's father, Ernest, and his family left Down Farm and went to Abbey Farm at The Vatch. Ernest Dickenson had experienced great hardship after the First World War and had been very afraid that the depression of that period would be repeated after the Second World War. He and his wife did not want their son Jim to go through the same traumatic experience as they had. In the event the feared depression did not materialize.

At one time Snows Farm (see photos 25 and 26) had been farmed as part of Down Farm but the Ayers family changed that. They were in occupation from the middle of the nineteenth century to the early 1970s. In the early 1900s three Ayers brothers were working on the farm. A farm labourer lived at the house called Piedmont. In the 1930s and 1940s, and perhaps later, they were farming about 200 acres and had eight or nine cows. Their land included Down Barn Farm which was sold to George Butler soon after the Second World War. Norman Williams of Sydenhams used to rent some summer grazing from the Ayers. After the Second World War the family consisted of Osbourne, a bachelor, and three sisters. They were grandchildren of George and Marie who had moved there in the 1840s. Osbourne died of a heart attack in 1950. Florence had married and moved away but returned many years later when widowed. Mabel later went into a home. By 1963 there were two only: Grace, who had always run the farm and was very much in charge, and the widowed Florence (Flossie). They were both tall, rather formidable women who gave the impression that it would be unwise to cross them. Yet they were a delight to talk to when they were in a relaxed mood and the author remembers well sitting on the side of the path with Grace and speaking of their life and their farm. They rarely went far, although one of them said she had been to Bournemouth and that her sister had been to London, but neither town was liked and they returned within two days. When the sisters could no longer care for themselves, Rosie Bannen of Timbercombe went to live at Snows Farm for several years and looked after them. Their financial arrangements, including the remuneration for Rosie, was taken care of by their solicitor.

In addition to the usual farming activities at Snows Farm there were sidelines. For example, there were walnut trees behind the house and the nuts were picked and marketed. Osbourne, who was not primarily involved with the farming, had a business marketing rabbits, pheasants and other game. He used to set snares or use ferrets. He would often be out all night and sometimes Jim Dickenson went with him. Jim had to be very quiet. Osbourne took the rabbits from the traps as soon as they were caught because otherwise the foxes would have had them. He had an uncanny ability to locate the rabbit precisely when it had been killed by a ferret underground and he dug straight down to recover it. Ferreting or trapping were preferred to shooting rabbits because they avoided the cost of the cartridges and because all game without shot in them sold better at market. Osbourne sometimes used his gun which had a hole in the right-hand barrel. He took the hammer off and used only the left-hand barrel. Yet he managed to survive! He, or one of his sisters, took the bus to Stroud with prepared rabbits to sell, sometimes putting them on the train to be sold in London.

The Ayers and Dickensons did not get on. One of the Miss Ayers, Grace, had fancied Ernest, Jim Dickinson's father, and hence had no love for Jim's mother. They squabbled about anything and everything. When Jim's mother set a firethorn at Down Court, Grace accused her of copying the one at Snows farm. (The Snows Farm firethorn practically covered the house in the 1970s but was only half-way round fifty years ago. Sadly it is no longer there.)

As children, Jim Dickenson and his friends were always playing tricks on the Ayers family who had every right to be cross. The boys used to go nutting on the Ayers' land, trying hard not to get caught. On one occasion the Ayers posted themselves at intervals, one in the valley and one on each side of the valley, and the culprits had to escape by going all the way round to Dillay to avoid them. In spite of their pranks the Ayers went to Jim Dickenson's wedding.

John George remembers the Ayers sisters as being meticulous in the care of their property. They would keep the track to their house, long before it had any hard surface, free of weeds by laboriously hand weeding, and the sides of the road, now overgrown, were then beautifully kept. The Ayers had a vegetable garden with excellent crops. Every drop of water had to be carried to the vegetable and flower gardens from a spring running continuously into a trough in the kitchen.

In the old barn there is an ancient vertical unglazed window. Fern[8] says that it is reputed to have been brought from the Abbey of Gloucester after the dissolution of the monasteries. It is said that lepers were once housed in this barn and that food may have been passed in through this window. Fern also states that the barn was rebuilt about 1740 after a fire.

At The Scrubs the dominant farm was Sydenhams, run during most of the twentieth century by the Williams family (see photos 56 and 57). Henry Williams had lived there with his mother who worked the farm while her husband was working as a butler. Soon after 1900 Henry Williams rented Stancombe Ash Farm.

In 1936 Norman Williams was living as a tenant at Woodedge (see photos 60 and 61) on Scrubs Common where his son Roland was born. In that year he rented the 114 acres of Sydenhams farmland from Colonel Stokes, who had recently bought Sydenhams, and commenced farming, with only £300 to his name. At the same time it was arranged that Colonel Stokes would build a house for Norman Williams to rent and live in. This house, known as Sydenhams Farmhouse, is the only new house built in The Scrubs since the early nineteenth century and was constructed with great care. It was designed by Norman Jewson, one of the renowned Arts and Crafts architects, and built by a local builder, Freemans. Norman prospered with his farming and in 1954 he bought the farmland, thirty-seven acres of wood, the house and two cottages (Woodedge and Yew Tree Cottage) all for £10,500. Norman's wife (Roland's mother) did not want to live in the old house. Major General Escritt wanted to buy Sydenhams house and Norman sold it to him for £6,500. He sold timber from the woods for £1,400. He was proud of the deals he achieved.

Norman Williams was the linch-pin of the community. He admitted openly that he could hardly read or write and said 'that he couldn't do nothing else but farming'. Neither statement was taken by his friends at face value because he could certainly both read and write and was a first class business-man, but he enjoyed perpetuating the myth. When quite a young man he lost the use of an eye. He was cutting a cow's tail with sheep shears and the cow kicked so that the shears went into Norman's eye. He was a good farmer and treated his animals well, down to the last barn cat. He loved to talk over the problems he had met in his farming life and chuckle over the way he had managed to anticipate the market changes. He would cheerfully spend thousands on a new piece of equipment if it saved him some tax.

He was proud that he had 'hit the jackpot' in his property dealings. He claimed that he 'never put a foot wrong'. It was quite amazing in talking to him how he remembered the exact figures of every single one of his own transactions and also a good few of the deals of others. He was a very generous person. There are many still living round about who were helped by Norman Williams when in need. An evening spent with Norman was a jolly affair, well oiled by a continual supply of whisky.

The agriculture at Sydenhams Farm was similar to that at Down Farm. There were usually three cart horses. The last to go was Bill, still missed by those who remember him. There were three men working at Sydenhams in 1942 and also two land-girls at different times. The rotation of crops was the same and yields were similar to those at Down Farm. A major difference was that Norman Williams had a baby six foot combine in the late 1950s. Norman Williams was always prepared to mechanise. He had one of the first cars in the area, an open Austin 7. One day Roland, as a young boy, was watching the sheep as they followed the car. He fell out but escaped with only a few cuts and bruises. Roland remembers that car with some awe, even today. For eight years it was used over fields and for all sorts of jobs, such as delivering churns of milk to Stroud.

One of the sidelines of agriculture was the collection of stones from the fields for sale to the Council. They paid two shillings and sixpence a load but Norman Williams recalled that in doing this work he wore out two carts costing £10–20 each. Even in the 1960s and 1970s he was gathering stones with young lads running behind the tractor and throwing them onto the trailer for 10p an hour. There was then a good supply of lads from the cottages in the Valley, including the author's two boys.

Farming was a tough existence at that time for animals, people, and later, machines. The winter of 1940 is vividly remembered by those living at The Scrubs as well as at Down Farm. Mrs Hilda Ruther was married in the winter of 1940 and then lived at Yew Tree Cottage. Her husband was a farm worker. They went, after they were married, to stay for a few days with family at Berkeley. On their return they experienced the full fury of the winter. They arrived back in Stroud but had to walk from there. Trees were down and telephone cables lay across the roads. When they arrived at Sydenhams, where she worked, Colonel and Mrs Stokes gave them hot drinks and lunch before they battled on to their cottage. Yew Tree Cottage at that time was typical of many cottages with one room on the ground floor with a kitchen behind and a bedroom above. The privy was at the edge of the woods below. The winter of 1947 was also particularly hard. Farmers and all residents had to dig themselves out and then go over fields to some source of supplies.

Although the children in the Slad Valley from Steanbridge to Snows Farm went to school in Slad, those from Timbercombe went to school in Bisley. It was quite a walk up to Sydenhams and then on to Bisley. Bill Tombs remembers that if there had been a lot of rain, his father walked in front to shake off the water from the undergrowth so that the children did not get too wet. Because their orientation was to Bisley they were well known all along the route and the sense of community, then as now, seems to have been strong. Bill Tombs remembers that Mr Clark of Sydenhams brought a cake down to Timbercombe for his eighth birthday. It had eight cherries on it. He also recalls Norman's brother, Victor, while ploughing by the old common, asking, as he and his brothers passed, whether they wanted a Christmas Box. Of course they said yes and were promptly boxed on the ears. But he gave them half a crown too. When the hunt was out the children did not go to school because, they were told, the hounds might mistake them for a fox cub. Instead they opened the gates for the horses and, if they were lucky, got a sixpenny piece for their pains.

AT WAR WITH THE NEIGHBOURS

By the twentieth century the only farm, other than Sydenhams, in the Scrubs and the Driftcombe Valley was Driftcombe Farm at the head of the valley. It used to belong to Sydenhams but in 1924 the house and farm were bought from the Driver family by John Henry Grainger, and later by John Nathaniel Grainger. The farmer and his wife were known to everyone simply as Mr and Mrs Grainger. His son, known as Jack, worked in the goods depot in Stroud station. At that time Driftcombe was a farm of thirty-two acres.

Mr Grainger kept cows and sold dairy produce in Stroud. In addition, he marketed daffodils which he had planted on the bank opposite the house and grew watercress in beds below the house which he bundled up and sold in Stroud and the surrounding area. One old Slad resident remembers him selling watercress and butter in Slad. Norman Williams considered him a bad farmer. He tried to sell butter wrapped in old shirts but nobody would buy it. He asked the Ministry of Agriculture to grade his cattle but they couldn't or wouldn't because, they said, the cattle were likely to be dead next week. They did indeed die! Norman resented that Mr Grainger did not prevent his heifers from getting into nearby fields where Norman kept his bull. Mr Grainger had no bull of his own and there was no artificial insemination in those days! Mr Grainger sued Norman Williams because he claimed that the effluence from Norman's cowsheds was draining on to his land, which seemed unlikely knowing the distances involved. However, the action cost Norman £1,200. Although he was insured he could not claim the insurance because he had not involved the insurance company in the case.

Mr Grainger was a violent, formidable man by all accounts and did not like strangers at his farm. It is said that if someone unknown to him strayed too near he would be met by a shotgun pointing at him. Grainger's treatment of his wife was similarly disgraceful. She was desperate to get away from him and on one occasion begged for help from a farmer higher up the valley. She showed him that her breasts were covered in bruises and weals. She dressed in brown sacking. In her despair she would roam the valley singing songs of her husband's doings with other women, though it seems not without some sense of humour too. When he went out for the evening, she sang 'Ha Ha Ha, Hee Hee Hee, a dirty little harlot is waiting for thee'. But when she won a quarrel she sang Rule Britannia.

Mrs Daisy Bevan, of Driftcombe Cottage, grandmother of Sally Rees, told many stories about Mrs Grainger. Mrs Grainger said she didn't see why her husband should spend all her money on other women so she went and bought herself new corsets, or stays as she called them. She went along the road wearing them over her clothes, much to the horror of a man she met on the way.

There is no doubt that the Graingers were disliked, not only in the valley, but also in Bisley. Children used to play pranks if they thought they could get away with it. One trick was to mix the carbide from bicycle lamps in a tin with water to cause an explosion. Two or three bangs would bring Mr Grainger looking to see who had been shooting.

Mrs Grainger had a sad life and a macabre prelude to her burial. The Grainger's doctor and the Bisley undertaker were chatting in a pub at Bisley when Mr Grainger walked in and the doctor enquired after his wife.

'She has gone on.' he said.
'You mean she has died?' asked the doctor.
'Yes,' said Grainger, 'some days ago.'

Then it emerged that he had told no one, though he was 'going to do so'. All three men went down to Driftcombe in a Landrover and went up to Mrs Grainger's bedroom. As they approached, the rats flowed off the bed. Mr Grainger had wrapped the body in chicken wire, but to no avail. The rats had still been able to nibble at the body, especially where it was not covered up. The nose and ears had gone. The body was removed immediately. How long it would have remained there but for the chance meeting in the pub nobody knows.

It is perhaps not surprising that with the house having been witness to such horrors, at least two people have been frightened by ghostly experiences. Alan Lloyd of St Benedicts was doing some repairs to the roof of Driftcombe Farm house while Duncan Smith and his family were not in occupation. Suddenly, towards the end of the day, he heard someone calling 'Ned, Ned'. No one was about and the house was empty. Alan was terrified. He got off the roof by straddling the ladder and sliding down for maximum speed. Only later did he learn about the Graingers. There are some suggestions that Mr Grainger was Ned to his family and that Mrs Grainger was known as Nell but it has not been possible to confirm that. It seems that no one outside the family was on first name terms!

Some time later, in the winter of 1989, the artist, Carolyn White, was staying in the house for the winter. She was in the attic, which she used as her studio, putting the finishing touches to paintings of Nepal. It was dark outside, snowing and absolutely silent. She relates her experience, reliving memories of her feelings at the time:

> I sensed a presence behind me and turned suddenly from my painting. I saw the shape of a human figure shimmering in the air. Instinctively I knew it was a woman. I spoke out loud, asking her name. Needless to say she did not reply and I concluded that I was overtired. A few minutes later I again felt some disturbance and on turning saw the same apparition, this time a few feet to the left. She seemed in some distress and, realizing by this time that she was a ghost, I attempted to put her at her ease and asked her what she wanted. She disappeared.
>
> Much more alarming was an experience the following spring when, in the middle of the night, she seemed to pass over the foot of my bed. I heard, in a wailing voice, 'Ned, Ned'. In the morning I angrily phoned Duncan Smith and said 'why did you not warn me about the ghost?' Duncan, who had known of Alan Lloyd's experience, laughed and said that he thought the story might have alarmed me! Indeed it might, but less than finding out for myself.

Norman Williams bought Driftcombe house and farm in 1958 for £1,400. He then sold the timber for about the same amount. Grainger had no intention of selling it to Norman because they were not on good terms. Norman arranged for a friend to buy it and immediately sell it to him. Norman Williams then sold the farmhouse and some land to John Lawson Blackwell. Norman kept some of the land and, at that point, the so-called farm consisted of the house and a garden. Its later history is described in the next chapter.

If there had been a man such as Mr Grainger at Driftcombe Farm a century earlier, what would have happened? It is impossible to say. Indeed there may well have been such at that time. However, the tale of the Graingers illustrates only too well the state of the Valley in the mid twentieth century. There was, on the one hand, a traditional society with traditional, if sometimes elastic, codes of behaviour, and, on the other hand, the relative newcomers who had no roots in the area and whose behaviour was abhorrent to the majority of inhabitants.

A Traditional Family in the Valleys

The Mansells and the Timbrells and the Gardiners had been in the valleys in the nineteenth century and continued there until the middle of the twentieth century. It was to a large extent the long conversations with Mrs Lizzie Timbrell, née Mansell, which inspired the writing of this book. Meeting Mrs Timbrell, a wonderful old lady in a cottage at Down Court and talking to her about her garden and her life, are outstanding memories of the 1960s. Lizzie Timbrell was born in 1888 at Highwood Farm at the top of the Slad Valley. She said it was a nice house but, in spite of its name, it wasn't a farm, though it had been once. When she was a little girl the family moved first to Yew Tree Cottage at The Scrubs and later to St Benedicts Cottage. At that time the latter was a small cottage, just one-up and one-down, but there was another building in the garden and that is where she and her brothers and sisters, all nine of them, slept in bunk beds. Her father, with a 'long beard and a big belly' according to his grandson, was an itinerant hurdle maker, going from farm to farm to seek work and ply his trade. The family originally were of Huguenot origin and came from Brize Norton in Oxfordshire. They were regular attendees at the Primitive Methodist Chapel and the photo of the Easter Sunday tea party shows Lizzie Mansell in the front aged about ten. She was still a schoolgirl when she helped to knock down the old house, Piedmont. When she was older she was in service to the Driver family of Cirencester.

Lizzie Mansell married Jack Timbrell who had been born in Driftcombe Cottage, as had his father, Jonas (see photos 43 and 44). Both his father and mother worked on Sir John Dorrington's farm at Lypiatt. By 1901 the family had moved to Down Court and Jonas Timbrell worked for Down Farm. When Jack Timbrell left school he too worked at Down Farm. When he and Lizzie Mansell were married they moved to a cottage, part of what is now Down Cottage. They carried what little furniture they had from The Scrubs on their backs and then Jack Timbrell took a horse and cart as far as the stream and brought some more belongings from The Scrubs. The hill down to the stream is very steep but the old track went straight down from below St Benedicts and can still be seen bounded by wire fences on both sides. They crossed the Roman Bridge, which was wider then, with Mrs Timbrell's possessions and then went on to Snows Farm and round Down Mound to Down Cottage. Some time later they moved to Down Court. Jack Timbrell was employed at Down Farm, working first for Mr Trotman and then the Dickensons, for over fifty years until the 1940s. He was presented with a medal to mark his long service. After her husband's death in 1965 Mrs Timbrell continued to live at Down Court until she moved into sheltered housing in Stonehouse about 1968. She died in 1977, aged eighty-nine.

Many of Mrs Timbrell's brothers and sisters stayed in the area. It must have been a very close family life with so many relations of her family and her husband's family living within about a mile of each other, and they would have met anyway on Sundays at the Primitive Methodist Chapel. One of her sisters, Edith Helen, was born crippled and stayed at home at St Benedicts till she married. Edith was a great favourite of her father. When he got paid he put a coin in a hole in his work-bench and covered it over with putty and said that was for his Edith one day. On his death, when all the family possessions were being sorted out, Edith said she just wanted that work-bench. Unfortunately she never got it. Overnight it disappeared and no one could say who took it, but the culprit must have known it was worth having! By this time the family was living in Driftcombe Cottage. Edith ran away with her future husband, a Gardiner, whom she met at the Primitive Methodist Chapel and whose son Ivor still lives at The Camp. (The Gardiner family were, a long way back, of French origin.) Edith returned in 1919 and lived for fourteen years in Driftcombe Cottage where many of her children were born. In the early twentieth century there was a brother of Mrs Lizzie Timbrell at Driftcombe Farm.

A Pleasant Life at Steanbridge House

Steanbridge House (see photo 4) with a little nearby land, but of course without the great estate of previous centuries, was bought by Mr Samuel Gilbert Jones, referred to in *Cider with Rosie* as the Squire. He was from Hatherly in Gloucestershire but had been working in Burma. He wanted to return to his native country and to his native county. Samuel Jones was able to purchase the house and some surrounding land and buildings for £3,000. He also bought Steanbridge Farm.

Between the First and Second World Wars life at Steanbridge House was generally relaxed and pleasant. There were parties from time to time, often, in the summer, held outside in the beautiful garden. A special feature of the garden was the waterfall going down to the lake where there were two swans in residence. There was a special urn rising from the lake to hold food for the swans. The boys of the family used to fish in the lake and, as a boy, Commander Brian Jones, the great nephew of Samuel Gilbert Jones, landed his first catch there.

Laurie Lee describes the visit of the carol singers from the Choir to Steanbridge House:

> Our first call as usual was the house of the Squire, and we trouped nervously down his drive. For light we had candles in marmalade-jars suspended on loops of string, and they threw pale gleams on the towering snowdrifts that stood on each side of the drive. A blizzard was blowing, but we were well wrapped up, with Army puttees on our legs, woollen hats on our heads, and several scarves around our ears.
>
> As we approached the Big House across its white silent lawns, we too grew respectfully silent. The lake near by was stiff and black, the waterfall

frozen and still. We arranged ourselves shuffling around the big front door, then knocked and announced the Choir.

A maid bore the tidings of our arrival away into the echoing distances of the house, and while we waited we cleared our throats noisily. Then she came back, and the door was left ajar for us, and we were bidden to begin. We brought no music, the carols were in our heads. 'Let's give em "Wild Shepherds",' said Jack. We began in confusion, plunging into a wreckage of keys, of different words and tempo; but we gathered our strength; he who sang loudest took the rest of us with him, and the carol took shape if not sweetness.

This huge stone house, with its ivied walls, was always a mystery to us. What were those gables, those rooms and attics, those narrow windows veiled by the cedar trees. As we sang 'Wild Shepherds' we craned our necks, gaping into the lamplit hall which we had never entered; staring at the muskets and untenanted chairs, the great tapestries furred by dust—until suddenly, on the stairs, we saw the old Squire himself standing and listening with his head on one side.

He didn't move until we'd finished; then slowly he tottered towards us, dropped two coins in our box with a trembling hand, scratched his name on the book we carried, gave us each a long look with his moist blind eyes, then turned away in silence.

As though released from a spell we took a few sedate steps, then broke into a run for the gate. We didn't stop till we were out of the grounds. Impatient, at last, to discover the extent of his bounty, we squatted by the cow sheds, held our lanterns over the book and saw that he had written 'Two Shillings'. This was quite a good start. No one of any worth in the district would dare to give us less than the Squire.[9]

("Cider with Rosie" from *Cider with Rosie* by Laurie Lee (Copyyright © Laurie Lee 1959) is reproduced by permission of PFD (www.pfd.co.uk) on behalf of Laurie Lee (Estate)

In the Second World War the house was used as a home for invalids and a place to receive special evacuees, including the children of the Emperor of Abyssinia. Photo 4 shows the house as it was around 1920. The cedar tree on the left of the picture was unfortunately cut down by a subsequent owner. This so upset the gardener that he felt he could no longer work there and left to find other employment.

The house was inherited by Samuel Jones's nephew, Basil Jones in 1940. The tenants were allowed to buy their homes but they were sitting tenants and could remain as tenants as long as they wished. The properties were eventually sold by him. The house was at one time divided into two but is now back to its former glory as one house. The old stables have been converted into a modern dwelling, known as Cob House.

THE FIRST SECOND-HOMER OR A PROSELYTIZER?

One of those who bought cottages at this time was Bishop Herford of Mercia. He bought Greencourt, (then a group of three cottages, including August Cottage and Mullions), Driftcombe Cottage and some land and ruins in 1903 (see photos 35, 36 and 50). The deeds of Greencourt describe that part of the property as:

> All that cottage with the several pieces or parcels of arable or garden ground adjoining or near thrto with the several void and ruinous cottages thron site at Custom Scrubs otherwise Greencourt in the Parish of Bisley in the County of Gloucester then in the occupation of William Driver as tenant throf and for identification only and not by way of grant and restron delntd and edged pink in the plan drawn on now abstg press.

Curiously the deeds refer to a cottage in the singular and seem to use Greencourt to refer to an area rather than just a cottage or group of cottages. The photo, believed to be about 1910, shows all three cottages with separate front doors. The Bishop mortgaged the property once or twice but he continued to own it until his death in 1938.

Mrs Timbrell thought that the Bishop used all three cottages and that one contained a place for him to worship. This is confirmed by a report of the National Monuments Record of 1924 that the owner had said that the three cottages had been a monastery, called Driftcombe Cloisters but were now cottages.[10] It seems likely that his chapel was the cottage which is now Mullions because of the rather churchy pointed windows at the side (see photo 38) which were not there before his occupation. Photos 39 and 40 show a rather magnificent arch across the path. This arch was in existence during the Bishop's period of ownership and would have been a suitable access to the chapel. An arch is visible on the photo of Greencourt and the Scrubs of around 1910. It must have fallen down and been replaced because, by the 1960s, Sally Rees, as a little girl, remembers it as being on a smaller scale.

The Bishop was undoubtedly one of the characters of the valley—so unexpected in a remote valley in the Cotswolds. He may have wanted a country retreat, but it seems likely that one reason for the purchase of the cottages was to be near the Primitive Methodist Chapel and try to persuade the congregation to his own ideas. His story is told in Chapter 10.

CASUALTIES OF THE FIRST WORLD WAR

There were many casualties of the First World War in the valleys. So many had joined up to fight and many returned injured or did not return at all. At least two and probably more outsiders to the Valley came after the war hoping to ease the pain of their damaged bodies and, above all, lungs in the country air. The two we know a little about both lived at Woodbine Cottage (now Woodedge, see photo 60). One was a Mr Cox and the other Mr Benjamin Taylor. One of Benjamin Taylor's daughters, Kathleen, (see photo 40) later Mrs Richard, wrote down her memories of their moving to these valleys with her very sick father. She writes:[11]

> I don't recall the exact date, but it would be about 1920 or 1921 when we left Stafford to settle down in a little cottage, at the Scrubbs, near Bisley in the Cotswolds. This cottage had been rented to my parents as furnished accommodation and they had paid three months' rent in advance.
>
> One day Dad was trying to tidy the garden and a near-by cottage occupant came round and asked for the return of the barrow, which Dad was using. Apparently the previous occupant had only borrowed it. Then we found out that the table and chair had also only been loaned. This was only a minor problem compared with what came next. Within a week of arriving we had a letter saying that the owners had received 'notice to quit' and that we were to leave the cottage immediately.
>
> My parents heard of a little cottage that was available on Dilly Bank. The day arrived when we were to take the furniture to our new home, but the approach was difficult. We were able to walk through the woods to the cottage but our furniture had to be taken along the road and onto a cart track at the top of Dilly Bank.
>
> The only way to get the furniture to the cottage was to lower it down the bank, not an easy task and quite a struggle. Unfortunately, no sooner had the furniture been lowered down the bank than the owners of the cottage informed my parents that they had changed their minds about moving. They had been going through the process of divorce and it seems that they had 'decided to give it another try.'
>
> So there we were with the task of getting the furniture back up the hill again. The result of this occurrence was that we had to look at an awful (and I mean awful) 'one up, one down cottage' just below the Scrubbs. The rear of the building was built against the hillside with the result that the wall was always very damp. This dampness seemed to cause a plague of woodlice indoors. My mother would brush down the wall and collect shovels of these creatures to be disposed of. Now, where did she dispose them? I cannot recall.

There we existed for a short period until we heard of Woodbine Cottage. It was owned by Mrs Workman, who was recovering from a stroke. Arrangements were made for us to live at Woodbine Cottage with my parents looking after Mrs Workman. Mrs Workman died in about 1927 and the house passed on to my father, and there we remained until about 1929.

A Second World War Newcomer

Many of the occupants of the cottages during the Second World War had come to the area to get away from London or other large cities being heavily bombed by the German Luftwaffe. One of these was Mrs Daisy Bevan, who came from London and whose grand-daughter and great grandchildren still live in Driftcombe Cottage (see photos 49 and 50), the house she bought in 1941. The accommodation was then two-up and two-down. She saw it advertised in Dalton's Weekly and chose it from three cottages in the neighbourhood which were then available to buy. She paid £150. At the back of the cottage was a plantation of pine trees. She sold the timber for £155, which nicely paid for the cottage. When the floorboards were washed there was a strong smell of beer. It had been thought that they were salvaged from the ruined Old Ale House opposite but, as the cottage was described in 1938 as having a brewhouse, this alone may account for the smell of beer.[12] It is possible that it was run in conjunction with the alehouse. Outside the house there was a well twelve feet deep as well as a spring. There is a quarry at the back of the house but, whereas the stone used for the house is quite yellow, the stone in the quarry is white, which means that the stone for the house must have been brought from elsewhere.

Mrs Bevan lived in the house with her sons, Philip and Richard and daughter, Zola and later alone. In her later years Mrs Bevan rarely left the valley. Her son Philip was the postman and brought her all she needed from the outside world. She was once persuaded to walk as far as Greencourt for tea and that was a memorable occasion indeed, for she had everyone enthralled by her stories of life in The Scrubs. She had a wealth of information on the Valley and on the surrounding area. She once complained that the new village policeman was no good. On being pressed as to why, she said the trouble was he never told you anything that was going on. She lived there until her death in 1976 and left the cottage to her granddaughter Sally née Bevan, now Rees.

Marking Time for Fifty Years

The changes in the physical structure of the valleys in the first half of the twentieth century were, first, the gradual abandonment and ultimate collapse of many of the old cottages and, secondly, an increase in the area of woodland. Only one new cottage was built in the whole of this half-century. In many ways it was a period in which the valleys were digesting the changes of the previous fifty years, notably the loss of the woollen industry, the problems of agriculture and the decay and disappearance of population and dwellings. The depression of the 1930s and the two world wars made that process even more difficult. By the 1950s the valleys were almost holding their breath waiting for the dramatic changes of the next fifty years.

1. *Gloucester Journal* 1st June 1901 Advertisement for sale of Steanbridge, p.4 and 6th July 1901 'Important Sale of Property at Stroud'
2. Walton, John R. (2000) The Midlands in Paul Brassley and G.E. Mingay (eds) Chapter 5, Farming Regions in Collins, E.J.T. (ed) (2000) *The Agrarian History of England and Wales* (General Editor Joan Thirsk, former editor H.P.R. Finberg), Vol VII 1850–1914, Cambridge: CUP, p.393, Table 5.1
3. Page, William (ed.) (1907) *The Victoria History of the County of Gloucester,* Vol. II published for the University of London, Institute of Historical Research, reprinted Dawsons of Pall Mall 1972, p.243 and Ministry of Agriculture
4. Dewey, Peter (2000) in Chapter 12, Farm Labour, in Collins, E.J.T. (ed.) (2000) *The Agrarian History of England and Wales* (General Editor Joan Thirsk, former editor H.P.R. Finberg), Vol. VII 1850–1914, Cambridge: CUP, p.862, Fig. 12
5. Whetham, E.H. (ed.) (1978) *The Agrarian History of England and Wales* (General Editor Joan Thirsk, former editor H.P.R. Finberg), Vol. VIII 1914–1939, Cambridge: CUP, p.142
6. Thacker, Joy (1995) *Survival and Revival: Stroud during War and Recovery Years,* Stroud: Alan Sutton, p.191
7. Thacker, *op. cit.* p.55
8. Fern, Jim (1994) *Ferns in the Valley,* Evesham: Millvale, pp.9–10
9. Lee, Laurie (1959) *Cider with Rosie,* Hogarth Press, Penguin edition, 1962, pp.145–6
10. NMR Monument Report 114873 Alleged former Monastery, now cottages, NMR SO 80 NE 8, Grid Ref SO 8907 0790
11. Richard, Mrs Kathleen née Taylor, Memoirs, by permission of her son-in-law, Dave Smith
12. GRO D1405 2/153 Sale of properties after the death of the Revd Herford, Bishop of Mercia, 1939

The Unusual Bishop

One of the landlords of the Driftcombe Valley in the early 1900s was the Revd Ulric Vernon Herford, O.C.F. Bishop of Mercia (see photo 37). In 1903 he bought the three cottages at Greencourt as well as 'several pieces or parcels of arable or garden ground adjoining or near thrto with the several void and ruinous cottages.' These ruinous cottages included Driftcombe Cottage and the ruins nearby. The sum he paid was £130. A rather mysterious report to the National Monuments Record of 1924[1] states that the cottages at Greencourt had been called Dryftcombe Cloysters and was said by the owner (then Bishop Herford) to have been a monastery but that it was now cottages again. There is no doubt that it was the terrace of three bought by the Bishop to which the report refers because it mentions the date on one of them (August Cottage) of 1676.

Some of the persons living in the valley during his occupation were suspicious of his titles and he was thought to be 'not a proper bishop'. They were to some extent correct because, although he had been ordained as a Bishop, his titles and status would not have been recognized by the Church of England or any other mainstream church. His story is told by Georgius and Anson,[2] and in autobiographical notes.[3] His titles and status as described by Anson are: 'Ulric Vernon Herford, Mar Jacobus, Bishop of Mercia and Middlesex; Administrator of the Metropolitan See of India, Ceylon Milapur etc, of the Syro-Chaldean Church and of the Patriarchate of Babylon and the East; Founder of the Evangelical Catholic Communion.' Quite a formidable collection for a resident of the Driftcombe Valley some seventy years ago!

Ulric Vernon Herford was born in Manchester in 1866 of a learned Unitarian family. After university he was apparently oscillating between the Anglican and Unitarian churches but was ordained as a Presbyterian and became Minister of the Unitarian Chapel at Kings Lynn. After a number of posts, in 1898 he built a new red brick church in Percy Street, Oxford, which he called the Church of the Divine Love. The adjacent house became known as The Monastery for it was occupied by a few young men who led a quasi-Franciscan life. His dream was of a united Christendom in which 'the best and most precious elements of East and West, of Catholic and Protestant should be gathered together in one Evangelical Catholic Communion'. In 1901 he thought of making a pilgrimage to the Nestorian church in Persia, for he was now convinced that the Nestorian Church was 'the purest and most primitive Branch of the Holy Catholic and Apostolic Church'.[4] He explained in one of his publications that 'These Indian Syrian Christians, locally called Thomas Christians, were originally part of the great East Syrian Church which spread from Asia minor all over Persia, China and SW India, where S. Thomas is said to have established the Faith. It is said that in the eleventh century, when they had twenty five Metropolitan sees, the Nestorians exceeded the R. Catholics in numbers. Countless numbers were massacred by Jengiz Khan (1162–1227) or Timor (1336–1405)'.[5]

Instead of going to Persia, he contacted Mar Basilius Soares, Bishop of Trichur, a town on the Malabar coast of South India. The latter had the exotic title of 'Metropolitan of the Syro-Chaldean Church of India, Ceylon, Socotra and Messina'. His flock numbered no more than 8000. After further correspondence Herford finally set sail to Colombo in October 1902 on the German liner *Barbarossa* on his way to visit him. After a break of two days he crossed the straits to India.[6] His diary tells the story, day by day, of his journey, his meeting with his host, ordination and enthronement.[7] His two to three day journey to Dindigul by second class rail travel is vividly described, even down to the clothes and jewellery worn by men and women he saw on the way. At Dindigul he was met on the 21st November by his host and put up in a travellers' bungalow. He describes his host:

> He is somewhat tall and thin, and a little like Val Davis. Dark, of course, as he is Goanese, but not very. He is somewhat ambitious, I dare say, but energetic and self-controlled, I should think. He lives in what in England we would call a rather dilapidated cowshed, by the side of his church—a rather superior cowshed—in a village called Mutalapati, behind the Rock. He is strikingly free of any sign of 'eastern' graspingness—. He dresses in crimson or a white-trimmed with crimson-cassock and hood, and wears a large gold or silver Nestorian (Persian) cross. He lives entirely on gifts from his people, I understand.

In between discussions and meetings the Revd Herford was treated to some tourist visits, notably to a vast Siva temple. A few days later Herford was first ordained by Mar Basilus Soares and then on Sunday 30th November enthroned as Mar Jacobus, Bishop of Mercia and Middlesex (including the County of London). His enthronement is vividly portrayed in his diary:

At about a quarter to ten on Sunday morning we went in procession round the village. Mar Basilius wore his mitre, and father George, a very nice young Indo-Chaldean priest, who arrived on Saturday, walking before him carrying the crozier. Two gorgeous state umbrellas were held over our heads and a constable with a fixed bayonet walked on either side, which was very strange—a curious mingling of church and state. There was a very curious processional cross, with a little boy on either side bearing an unlighted taper; curious inverted heart–shaped standards surmounted by small crosses and small scarlet flags which men bore in front. Seven horns were blown on each side, and numerous drums, and exactly the same (as far as I could perceive) notes were played and cry raised as at the heathen funeral procession. In fact there was a triumphantly joyous din. Petards were fired off several times during the day. The village had been decked with leaves and wreaths and, at one place, in front of the church, there was a triumphal arch or canopy. They literally strewed their garments in the way—their long coloured broad bands about a yard wide and five or six long—taking them up from behind the procession, and running forward and laying them down again. I think also they carried branches, but I am not quite sure. I told you, did I not, how they 'fall down and worship' a priest in the most literal way, touching the ground with their heads frequently, reminding one of the N Testament phrase. The church bell-disks were also continuously beaten. We then entered the church by the west door, and the mass began. After the Creed the chief part of the consecration service was performed, questions and answers, reading of my Profession of Faith in which I was left perfectly free (in fact, Mar Basilius seems very glad to make use of my small store of theological knowledge) up to the annointing. Then the mass was finished and 'Benediction' given, and the ceremonies of the Staff, the Ring, and the Mitre completed. Then, fully vested, I went in procession, blessing the people, to the same joyous din, just round outside the church—the soldier constables one on each side as before. Then I came into the church again, and was seated in a chair in the middle of the church, while the people came and knelt and kissed my ring. I had to submit to it as is the custom. Some 160 men or more, about 50 women, and a dozen or so children came. I felt like the 'Little Duke' (xxii). This ended the service which had lasted about 2½ hours.

He stayed only two weeks amongst his new flock and was back in England on 1st January 1903.

Although there is in the diary what appears to be Herford's own account of his ordination and consecration, there have been and still are certain people who claim that he was an impostor from start to finish. This is because many of the documents produced are in his own handwriting and he signed for Mar Basilius on two of them. This may be because Mar Basilius was uneducated. The jury is still out on this matter.[8]

The Bishop had married in 1907 a woman of means, some years his senior. Mrs Herford shared her husband's enthusiasm for animal welfare and became joint secretary of the Oxford Anti-Vivisection Society. They maintained a large family of cats. The Herfords had no children. They led busy lives, participating enthusiastically in Oxford life and active in a number of societies. Bishop Herford was, it is said, a familiar and much-respected figure riding his bike round Oxford. Mrs Herford died in 1928.[9]

Mrs Herford remained an Anglican all her life. She had been known to advise candidates for ordination by her husband to 'stick with the Church of England'. Nevertheless, when she was needed by her husband she did as she was asked. There is a nice story of an occasion when the Bishop was ordaining a former Anglican curate, Revd W. Rowland Jones, which the latter recorded in his *Diary of a Misfit Priest* and is reported by Anson.[10] After Mr Jones had stayed overnight with the Bishop and his wife, Anson explains:

> The Bishop then conducted the ordinand to the little sacristy of the domestic oratory. Here was 'a mass of multi-coloured vestments', and 'layer after layer of white linen', not to mention 'many varieties of stoles and chasubles, which needed pins as well'. Before vesting Mar Jacobus shouted to his wife to bring more safety pins. The ceremony started by His Lordship pulling a small lever attached to the wall, 'which set something like the melodious chimes of Bruges reechoing through the chapel and the house'.
>
> Mrs Herford had already advised Mr Jones that, like herself, he ought to stick to the dear old Church of England, where there was 'at least no arguing, no fuss and no silly business', and where she got 'a bit of peace'. First came the ceremonies of baptism and confirmation with the holy oils smeared on generously. Before the ordination started Mrs Herford had to be summoned as a witness, because a certain Free Methodist deacon had failed to turn up, as he had promised to do. She sat at the back of the oratory and filled in the time by knitting.
>
> Addressing her episcopal husband she said: 'Do make it short, dear: I've got to get to the bakers early or I shall miss those lovely cakes'. But Mar Jacobus had no intention of curtailing the rite just for the sake of an extra good tea. Mr Jones continues: 'Mrs Herford was asked if she knew me, if she could vouch for my purity of character, if she had examined me in the Latin tongue, and if she had examined me in the certitude of my faith, and to all the questions she gave a vigorous affirmative. Altogether I had been

in her presence not more than an hour, and she had never once called me by my right name. Still—it was to be a valid ordination!'

'Can I go now?' came the piteous voice of the episcopal spouse.

The stentorian 'Yes' from the Bishop revealed his pent-up disturbance and set free his faithful wife who had readily sworn her soul away on my behalf.

Anson comments that

This long and elaborate series of ceremonies which took over two hours may have been typical of the clandestine ordinations carried out by the Bishop of Mercia. For which reason one cannot help feeling that his biographer was understating the case when he wrote:

'It is generally admitted by those who knew Bishop Herford that he was well liked, sincere and good hearted and undoubtedly well versed in his conviction and Faith. At the same time he struck some people as a very eccentric man, though not unkindly or spitefully so.'

The resident of the valley who felt that The Revd Herford was 'not a proper Bishop' turned out to be more right than he could have imagined.

It would be easy to assume that the reason the Bishop bought the cottages was that he wanted a retreat from his busy life. If so, he would have been the first second-homer in the valley, a feature of the 1960s and 1970s rather than the first half of the century. However, although that is a plausible explanation, it has never been a convincing one. He bought the property very soon after his return from India. In the 1920s he seems to have visited quite often, riding his bike from Oxford. There is a mystery concerning what exactly the terrace of three cottages owned by him was used for. It is possible that he did want to set up some monastic place there. Mrs Timbrell, who knew the valley so well, said that he had a chapel in one of the three cottages. It may well be that the Bishop had had one or two clergy, or would-be clergy, living in the cottages. This would have been entirely in keeping with his thinking. The Introduction by H.S.B. Mar Georgius, patriarch of Glastonbury, to the published extracts from the Bishop's diary states that:

It became abundantly clear to Mgr. Herford, after some years of work, and various attempts to form other local churches, which flourished for a time, and then petered out, that the prospects for establishing a large Evangelical Catholic Church were very small, and he accordingly changed the name of the organisation to The Evangelical Catholic Communion, partly because he thought the word 'Communion' less liable to a charge of schism than the word 'Church'; and partly because he thought he had greater scope by endeavouring to catholicise the Free Churches, and by that means to obtain control over a large number of Churches and Chapels of various Nonconformist denominations, which, through their Ministers, whom he would ordain, were to be affiliated to him. At the same time he did not neglect the opportunity to establish Evangelical Catholic Churches and Chapels where opportunity offered. Thus Vernon Herford can be said to be the founder of a sort of Nonconformist Oxford Movement.[11]

The observations by Mar Georgius above, suggest that the objective of purchasing cottages so close to the Primitive Methodist Chapel was not to obtain a second home as a rural retreat from his busy life, but as a means of spreading his own particular gospel amongst the Primitive Methodist community. This together with the fact that the house next to the Church in Oxford was known as The Monastery suggests that he may well have intended the terrace of three cottages to be a small monastery. It would also account for the churchy windows at Mullions (see photo 38) and for the rather grand stone arch across the path in front of the cottages (see photos 39 and 40). Norman Williams who, as a young boy in the 1920s, used to come and stay the night with him when he was in residence, remembered the chapel had a pulpit in it. For his company Norman was paid a shilling a night, an arrangement which today could attract criticism. In the mid-1930s the Bishop visited occasionally and he stayed in the middle of the three cottages. Philip Holford who lived next door at Greencourt with his parents remembered the Bishop (as he was always called) as rather a pernickety man. Sometimes the young Philip was called in to help, for example, to dry up after the dishes had been washed. In this case the cutlery had to be carefully held so that only the handles were touched with the hands, an idea foreign to small boys. By this time the cottage at the other end, now Mullions, was no longer a chapel but lived in as a cottage.

The Bishop was certainly one of the most colourful inhabitants of the valley and an extraordinary contrast to those who had lived there only twenty or so years earlier. The latter never travelled and probably had no knowledge of India or, if they did, only because The Queen was its Empress. Having learnt something of Bishop Herford, who apparently had a strong faith but bolstered by false ritual, one is glad, even relieved, that what looks like an attempt to attract the inhabitants of these valleys to his church did not succeed. This feeling is not based on theological arguments but rather concern that the Primitive Methodist Community, having conceived the idea to have their own place of worship, against all odds managed to buy the land, build the Chapel and run it for several generations, should not forfeit their control to an outsider.

The Bishop died in 1938, still owning property in the Driftcombe Valley. He was buried, clothed in episcopal vestments of Western shape, with mitre and crozier in Wolvercote Cemetery, Oxford.

1. NMR Monument Report 114873 Alleged former Monastery, now cottages, NMR SO 80 NE 8, Grid Ref SO 8907 0790
2. Anson, Peter F. (1964) 'Ulric Vernon Herford, Mar Jacobus, Bishop of Mercia and Middlesex; Administrator of the Metropolitan See of India, Ceylon Milapur etc. of the Syro-Chaldean Church and of the Patriarchate of Babylon and the East; Founder of the Evangelical Catholic Communion' in *Bishops at Large,* Chapter 5, London: Faber and Faber; and Georgius, H.S.B. Mar (ed.) (1954) *A Voyage into the Orient: being Extracts from the Diary of the Rt Revd Bishop Vernon Herford,* with Introduction, Footnotes and Appendices, Hove (Antwerp) Belgium: The Catholic Apostolic Church, typescript
3. Autobiographical Note on the Rt Revd Bishop Vernon Herford, issued with the S.U.P.P.C.A. Report for 1937 and Georgius, *op. cit. Diary*
4. Anson, *op. cit.* pp.130–31
5. Autobiographical Note, *op. cit.*
6. Anson, *op. cit.* pp.134–5
7. Georgius, *op. cit.* Diary, pp.8–19
8. Anson, *op. cit.* pp.136–7
9. Anson, *op. cit.* pp.142–3 and 152
10. Jones, Rowland W, *Diary of a Misfit Priest,* reported in Anson, *op. cit.* pp.146–8
11. Georgius, *op. cit.* Introduction, p.5

1. ROMULUS IN THE GUISE OF MARS

2. A LOCAL DEITY

These roman Votive tablets were found at The Scrubs in the early nineteenth century, close to the present cottage, Journeys End

3. STEANBRIDGE HOUSE MURAL 1815 TO 1830

4. STEANBRIDGE HOUSE 1920

Allowing for artist's licence and remembering that he had to draw from sketches, 100 years did not greatly change the house

5. LOWER STEANBRIDGE MILL MURAL 1815 TO 1830

6. STEANBRIDGE LAKE, FORMERLY MILLPOND, 2004

This mural at the Old Rectory, Bishop's Cleeve, is the only representation of the mill which has been found. It appears older than the Upper Steanbridge Mill

7. UPPER STEANBRIDGE MILL MURAL 1815 TO 1830

8. UPPER STEANBRIDGE MILL 1974

The mural at Bishop's Cleeve is of a 'business-like mill' recognisable today though the tall
buildings at the side have gone. Down Farm can be seen perched on the hill behind

CHA.S TOWNSEND ESQ.R

Homerton

Pub.d by T.Williams Stationers Court

9. CHARLES TOWNSEND 1731–1803, OWNER OF STEANBRIDGE ESTATE 1801–1803

The story of Charles Townsend is told in Chapter 6

10. DOWN FARM HOUSE 2004

Down Farm is the only farm in the area where the farmer still lives in the original farmhouse

11. CUB HUNT AT DOWN FARM 1982

12. OLD CIDER MILL AND PRESS AT DOWN FARM 2004

Prince Michael of Kent and Annette Xuereb Brennan preparing to hunt. The cider press remains as it was when used by the Dickenson family

13. ROBERT TROTMAN AT DOWN FARM ABOUT 1890

14. JACK TIMBRELL WITH JOLLY AT DOWN FARM

The Trotman family farmed at Down Farm for sixty years to 1909, buying it in 1901. Jack Timbrell, the carter, worked for Mr Trotman and later for Mr Dickenson, in total for more than fifty years

15. JOSEPH DICKENSON OF DOWN FARM ABOUT 1940

16. MRS JOSEPH DICKENSON ABOUT 1890

When the photo of Mrs Dickenson was taken, the family had not yet moved to Down Farm

17. ERNEST DICKENSON ON TOP OF A LOAD OF HAY
(WITH JACK TIMBRELL AND FRANK ELDRIDGE)

18. DRILLING ON DOWN FARM WITH JACK TIMBRELL AND JOSEPH DICKENSON

Horses were used for farm work at Down Farm for the whole occupancy of the
Dickenson family. The horses were much valued and are still remembered with affection
by Jim Dickenson

19. WASHING SHEEP BEFORE SHEARING AT THE BRIDGE AT STEANBRIDGE

20. MESSRS HALL AND LAINCHBURY SHEARING SHEEP AT DOWN FARM 1920S

The position of the sheep-dip can still be seen. The stream was dammed for the period of the dipping. Sheep-shearing was done with some mechanical help

21. TRILLGATE COTTAGE NORTH SIDE

22. TRILLGATE FARMHOUSE 2004

Trillgate Cottage may be the oldest in the valleys. No early photos have been found.
Trillgate Farmhouse was probably originally a single room downstairs and upstairs

23. DOWN COURT WITH JACK TIMBRELL ABOUT 1920

24. JACK AND LIZZIE TIMBRILL OUTSIDE DOWN COURT IN THE 1950S

Mrs Timbrell was the source of much information for this book. She and her husband
lived at Down Court, when it was two cottages, from the 1920s

25. SLAD VALLEY AND SNOWS FARM ABOUT 1910

26. SNOWS FARM 2004

Changes externally to Snows Farm were small in more than ninety years

27. SNOWS MILL RUIN 1996

28. SHEPHERDS COTTAGE RUIN 1974

Snows Mill (sometimes Down Mill) was at one time a flock mill and later a corn mill with a bakers shop attached. It was a ruin early in the twentieth century. Shepherds Cottage had not been lived in for about 100 years, but was used as a workshop. It was demolished for its stone

29. HIGHWOOD FARM ABOUT 1910

30. HIGHWOOD FARM RUINS 2004

This is the cottage where Lizzie Timbrell was born about twenty years before the first photo was taken. It is believed that the house was burnt down in the time of the Bannens. It is now a barn

31. TIMBERCOMBE ABOUT 1910

32. TIMBERCOMBE ABOUT 1992

Timbercombe was lived in by Rosie Bannen and her father and later by herself alone.
She was a great character and a friend of many who recall her home-made country wine,
her prolific cats, her many King Charles spaniels and, above all, her vivacity

33. ROSIE BANNEN IN HER SITTING ROOM AT TIMBERCOMBE ABOUT 1980

34. TIMBERCOMBE 2003

Rosie was very happy in her beloved cottage, despite no piped water or electricity, and
would be horrified to see it in its present state

35. GREENCOURT, AUGUST COTTAGE AND MULLIONS ABOUT 1910

36. GREENCOURT, AUGUST COTTAGE AND MULLIONS 2004

These photos show the change in the landscape and the cottage. St Benedicts well visible in 1910 is hidden behind the trees by 2004

38. MULLIONS 1965

37. REVEREND HERFORD, BISHOP OF MERCIA

Change was brought to the area by Bishop Herford who owned the terrace of three from 1903 to 1938. He used Mullions as a chapel and put in church-like windows on the west, previously blank walls

40. THE ARCHWAY BY MULLIONS LOOKING EAST
1920S

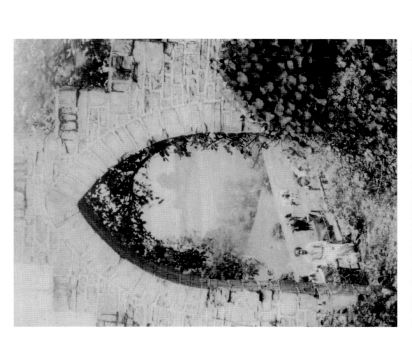

39. THE ARCHWAY BY MULLIONS LOOKING WEST 1915 TO 1922

The archway was built in the time of Bishop Herford, perhaps as an approach to the chapel in Mullions. The girl under the arch is Kathleen Taylor, later Mrs Richard—see Chapter 9

42 JIM DICKENSON AS A BABY ON THE ROMAN BRIDGE 1929

41. THE OLD SHOP RUIN WITH HANS AND PAT HOPF BEFORE THE
CHIMNEY FELL DOWN ABOUT 1969

Jim Dickenson is with his Aunt Edna and Betty Green

There is much speculation as to the business of the Old Sloop.

44. MRS JONAS TIMBRELL OUTSIDE DRIFTCOMBE
COTTAGE ABOUT 1900

43. MR JONAS TIMBRELL OUTSIDE DRIFTCOMBE COTTAGE
ABOUT 1900

These two lived in this cottage for forty or fifty years and their son Jack who worked as a carrer at Down Farm was born here. They were strong supporters of the Primitive Methodist Chapel

45. EASTER TEA PARTY AT THE PRIMITIVE METHODIST CHAPEL ABOUT 1900

46. CHAPEL ELDERS ABOUT 1900

Attendance for celebrations at the Primitive Methodist Chapel show its importance in the community. Mrs. Timbrell can be seen in the top picture, the tallest girl in the front row

47. FORMER PRIMITIVE METHODIST CHAPEL 1974

48. SCRUBS BOTTOM, FORMER CHAPEL 2004

The chapel was used as a house at the beginning of the Second World War. Successive owners have extended it.

49. DRIFTCOMBE COTTAGE AND OLD ALE HOUSE RUIN 1978

50. DRIFTCOMBE COTTAGE 2004

The ruins of the Old Ale House can be seen in the left of the gate in the 1978 photo.
There are some ruins still visible. This sixteenth- or seventeenth-century cottage has been
substantially extended

51. ST BENEDICTS 1962

52. ST BENEDICTS 2004

St Benedicts was a small cottage and, in addition, there was a single-room building nearby, identified as a cottage in that it had a fireplace. The house has been extended three times

53. SNOW AT THE SCRUBS 1985 WITH HANS HOPF

54. SUMMER IN A LANE IN THE DRIFTCOMBE VALLEY ABOUT 1980

There has been constant change in the seasons since time immemorial. Which way will it go now?

55. THE DRIFTCOMBE VALLEY ABOUT 1910

Driftcombe Cottage, the Old Ale House ruins and possibly Driftcombe Farm are visible. The trees have grown so much that none would be visible now from the same point.

56. SYDENHAMS FARM ABOUT 1920

57. SYDENHAMS 2004

Comparison of these two photos shows not only a very different use of Sydenhams but also some of the changes made to the house by Norman Jewson

58. THE SCUBS (HOUSE) AS TWO COTTAGES 1950S

59. THE SCRUBS (HOUSE) 2004

The present house combines two cottages, one of which has a date stone of 1814

60. WOODEDGE MID-1960S

61. WOODEDGE 2004

This cottage has, after successive extensions and improvements, changed from a two-roomed cottage in the seventeenth century to a spacious house

11

Dramatic Revival:
The Last Half Century

INTRODUCTION

In the last half century these valleys have experienced changes in the structure of the population, in the houses and other buildings, and even in the landscape itself, possibly as rapid and as striking as in any other period of their history.

Change got under way from the 1950s and the next two decades began one of the biggest revolutions in the history of the valleys. Increased prosperity in the country as a whole started a movement for town dwellers, particularly Londoners, to seek a cottage in the country for weekends and holidays or retirement. By that time the middle classes all had a car, so that the remoteness of the valleys became an attraction, not a deterrent, to buying a cottage.

In the 1950s and 1960s piped water was being brought to remote areas as part of Government policy and electricity and telephones could be connected up. Some of the cottages were in a bad state but in the 1960s it was possible to obtain grants to keep out the rain and install bathrooms. Some buyers bought a property, did it up and then sold at a considerable profit. One cottage, a two-up two-down, was bought in November 1961 for £275. Water and electricity were connected, a kitchen and bathroom installed and the redecorated cottage sold in May 1966 for £2,500. Most of the new residents and early weekenders lived simply in their cottages, making do with little equipment or furniture and being content with the available space. Guests were in those days put up on a bed on the floor or slept in a tent.

Some of the newcomers may not have realised what they were letting themselves in for by electing to live in a remote valley. Before mains water arrived cottagers relied on springs for drinking water, and tanks collecting water from the roof for everything else. These arrangements were not always reliable. In 1956 the spring in the field below Greencourt and the old Primitive Methodist Chapel dried up and the summer of 1959 was also a year of drought. There may have been water at the springs at Driftcombe Farm but Mr Grainger would have been unlikely to welcome anyone wanting to fill their buckets, except possibly

MAP 7

HOUSES 2004

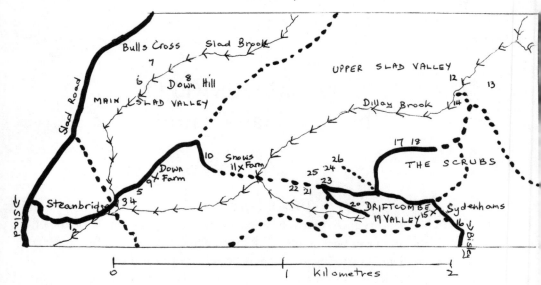

EXISTING HOUSES

X

EXISTING ROADS

━━━

SELECTED EXISTING TRACKS

●●●●

STREAMS

➤➤➤

Key

1	Steanbridge House	15	Sydenhams
2	Cob House	16	Sydenhams Farm House
3	Steanbridge Mill, Upper Steanbridge Mill and the Old Bakehouse	17	Woodedge
		18	Yew Tree Cottage
4	Steanbridge Cottage	19	Driftcombe Farm
5	Springfield Cottage	20	Driftcombe Cottage
6	Trillgate Cottage	21	Greencourt, August Cottage and Mullions
7	Trillgate Farm		
8	Down Cottage	22	Scrubs Bottom
9	Down Farm	23	St Benedicts
10	Down Court	24	Colombine Cottage
11	Snows Farm	25	Journeys End
12	Dillay Farm	26	The Scrubs
13	Beech Cottage		
14	Timbercombe		

with a shotgun. The nearest available drinking water was at The Wells at Bisley. In the days before everyone had a car, collection from there was not so easy. Not only the hot summers but also the cold winters were a major problem. In recent years there has not been much snow but until recently the cottagers expected to be snowed in at some time in the winter. In 1963 the valley was cut off for many weeks. Photo 53 shows drifts, cleared by a JCB in 1985. That was the year when the drifts round the corner on the road above Sydenhams were eleven to twelve feet deep and the valley was cut off for a week or so. Even after mains water was connected and electricity was available, there were still problems with power cuts of several days so that freezers could be a liability rather than an asset. Telephones were installed gradually with only shared lines available until into the seventies.

Those who lived in the valley learnt how to improvise and cope with their problems. In a snowy winter in the early 1960s one resident was expecting a baby any day. August Cottage had a large flagpole in the garden which was visible from the vicarage in Slad. An arrangement was made that, in case of emergency a flag would be raised and the vicar would know to send help post-haste.

By the 1980s the demand for cottages in the valleys was seemingly endless and was becoming the driving force in the economy of the valleys. This was largely due to an appreciation of life away from big cities, facilitated by greater affluence. As time went on the aspirations of the inhabitants and their access to finance changed. Existing cottages were extended. Many have been doubled or trebled in size in the last twenty years. In others expansion has been achieved by converting several cottages into one large house. Houses were furnished to a much higher standard. Prices are such that local people can no longer afford to live there. A small cottage once cost a few hundred pounds, even in the 1960s a few thousands. Now their improved and enlarged successors are hundreds of thousands and even a million pounds or more is becoming unsurprising.

If the houses which were there in the 1840s were still in existence, they would have participated in the prosperity, but by 2004 the number of cottages was much reduced. A comparison of the dwellings in Map 6 with those well over 100 years later in Map 7 reveals that the number of dwellings had halved from about fifty to twenty-six. Strict planning laws mean that, in the area as a whole, designated as an area of Outstanding Natural Beauty, these cannot be rebuilt and permission is not given for houses on new sites or the sites of previous houses. Substantially the number of dwellings is fixed, though the space available is not, because extensions have been permitted.

It is not possible to calculate with a high degree of precision the increase in property prices in the valley because so many alterations have been made to the houses. However, at a conservative guess, the price of a house that had not changed (if there were such a thing) has probably risen at least 100 times in the last forty years. From 1973 to 2004 prices have probably risen well over twenty times compared with prices for houses in the West Midlands of sixteen times and in the UK fourteen times.[1]

Farmers, and those concerned directly with agriculture, are in a minority in the valleys, although it is the existence of their land which makes the valley so attractive to newcomers. The occupation of farm labourer has almost died out. Indeed it is the old farm labourers' cottages, some of them once weavers' cottages, which are lived in by the new residents. Most of those living in the valley full-time or as weekenders have occupations carried on elsewhere. These include journalists, film directors, doctors and geologists. Some can carry on at least part of their professional activity from the valleys, facilitated by the revolution in communication, the telephone, the fax, and email. Probably even more important is the ease of travel. The car with fast roads has enabled visits to and from London or elsewhere to be speedy and relatively reliable. About a quarter of the residents also have a property in London, but although only a few years ago most of their time was spent in London, and the house in the valley was a weekend country cottage, now, for many, it is the house in the valley which is home and the London residence is a pied-á-terre to be used one or two days a week. This change has allowed the development of a more sociable community and one of the features of the valley is that it is as friendly a place as any village, in spite of the distances separating the cottages.

Not all the residents in the valleys are newcomers. One family in the valleys has connections in the valley for over sixty years. The tradition of handing down houses through the generations persists, with at least three being in the second or, in one case, third generation in 2004. Whereas 150 years ago most of the population barely moved out of their own or the neighbouring parishes, now most residents regularly go abroad for work or pleasure. At least five of the present owners were born abroad. There had been indications of change to come in the large houses in the valleys. The owners of Steanbridge House and Sydenhams had for long had army or similar connections external to the area. It was when the trickle of outsiders to the valleys became a torrent that the character of the population changed for ever.

Sadly the community is no longer based on local activities as the mainstay of life's existence, but on friendship between diverse and cosmopolitan residents. The time-traveller from the 1840s would be truly amazed. Looking around he would see the countryside covered in trees where he knew only pasture. He would see few sheep or cows. Some of the tracks he used he would find to be practically impassable, even fenced off, but some new ones covered in a hard topping. Where there were tiny cottages he would find large houses with gardens full of flowers rather than vegetables, and many of the cottages he knew would have disappeared.

On a work-day evening, when he would expect to see the labourers coming home from work in the fields and a few coming back from the mills down Steanbridge way, there would be nobody around. He would have anticipated seeing the handloom weavers taking a brief break from work for a meal. Instead some of the houses are empty and others inhabited by one or two persons instead of the six, seven or eight he was used to.

THE LOCAL RESIDENTS

Many of the inhabitants of the valleys by, say, 1970 earned their living outside Gloucestershire or, if they were retired, had done so. There were, however, some notable exceptions. One of these was Rosie Bannen, who was born in Ireland but was as much part of the valley as anyone could be. As a young girl she had come from Ireland to join her father, Jimmy Bannen. He was Irish but had served in the Boer War and the 1914–18 war, including the evacuation from the Dardanelles.[2] He had fled his country because of his involvement in the Irish rebellion of 1916. Had he returned, he faced arrest and possibly the firing squad. He worked as a timber cutter for Geoffrey Workman who owned several woods, including Highwood, and the Ryeford saw mill. Earlier, Jimmy Bannen and his daughter had, it is understood, lived in Highwood Farm but this had burnt down and is now a single storey shed used for storage (see photos). They moved to Timbercombe Cottage and Rosie lived there until her death in 1991 (see photos 31–33). In the time of Jimmy Bannen's occupation Timbercombe had the use of two fields and employed a lad.

Rosie was a sitting tenant. At least one of the owners of the cottage during Rosie Bannen's occupation wished her to leave. Various attempts were made by him or his agents to 'persuade' Rosie to leave the cottage or somehow to forfeit her right to continue as a tenant. Tractors were left with their engines running all night long; the track by which she had her coal delivered was blocked for long periods and the Social Services Department of the Council was told that the house was not fit to live in and that she should be rehoused. She was at one time offered 'a grace and favour' residence, that is, living rent-free, in which case she would have forfeited her security of tenure. Rosie was a resourceful and well-liked person. She remained in the cottage until her death, thanks to the assistance of Norman Williams, the local farmer, other neighbours, a sympathetic solicitor and the Catholic priest, Canon Tom Curtis-Hayward.

The cottage consisted of two rooms on the ground floor with a wooden staircase up the centre of the house and there was one large room upstairs. There was a lean-to at the back. It had barely been changed since it was built. A photo shows how it was heated by a range and open fire. There was no electricity and the water supply was a spring, with excellent quality water. A telephone was installed by Social Services after Rosie had a heart attack. She was a great character and was interested in all that went on. She used to get a lift to Bisley with the local postman to do her shopping and she usually visited the Bear Inn. She would also use the Bisley taxi service to go to Stroud. She kept a pair of shoes in Norman Williams' barn so that she could change from her wellington boots to go to Bisley or Stroud. When a casual visitor had thought she was just a country bumpkin who never went further than Stroud, she would say something like 'When I was in Turkey ...' or discuss the finer points of the Roman Villa at Fishbourne. When she went out of the Valley she took a lot of trouble with her dress and make-up and was rather elegant at parties.

Rosie kept about ten cats. One day she bought a pedigree King Charles Spaniel. It was mated with a Crufts champion and had four puppies. A business tycoon offered her £200 for one of the pups. 'If it's worth that much to him it's worth the same to me', she said and decided to keep them all. The cottage became rather overcrowded! She was extremely friendly to any passers-by and her friends were called in to have a glass of home-made parsnip or elderflower wine. Everyone who lived in the valleys or regularly walked there knew Rosie Bannen. She is much missed. Indeed she has almost become the personification of the good, simple life in this beautiful countryside.

After Rosie's death in 1991, the cottage was left empty and allowed to deteriorate. The owner refused to sell it for many years but finally sold to the family that owned the surrounding woods. Still it was allowed to deteriorate. The Welsh slate roof was removed.

If a planning application to build a Palladian mansion nearby had been granted, it would have been used as a store or perhaps even demolished.

Meanwhile it had been listed as an example of a traditional cottage worth preserving. In 2001–2 a planning application considerably to enlarge it was refused. It remains neglected and near derelict (see photo 34).

There are some less than happy tales to be told about other inhabitants. In the period after the Second World War St Benedicts Cottage was lived in by an ex-convict, his partner and her teenage daughter. He ill-treated the daughter and beat his partner, in spite of her loyalty to him while he was in prison, visiting regularly. The ex-convict was accused of attempting to rape Rosie Bannen at Timbercombe who woke in the middle of the night to find someone in her bedroom. She put up a fight and made such a noise that he ran off. As it happened, Rosie had been doing some painting with green paint. The next day a pair of trousers with green paint all over them was seen hanging up to dry on the washing line at St Benedicts. The owner of the trousers was arrested and went for trial at the Assizes in Gloucester. He asked to go to the toilet and escaped through the window. The county police notified the village policeman, who decided to keep watch on St Benedicts. It was winter. He began by waiting in the undergrowth but got cold so went and sat in the privy. At about 3 a.m.

the daughter needed to visit the privy and screamed when she found it occupied by the local policeman, fast asleep.

HOUSES FOR SALE

As the land from the smaller farms was consolidated into larger farms, the farm houses were no longer needed as such and were put on the market with a large garden and perhaps a paddock or a larger land-holding. At the same time the mechanization of agriculture meant that farm labourers were no longer occupying the cottages. In the 1950s and 1960s several properties came on the market at what now seem to be ridiculously low prices. This was the moment for people who lived in big cities, or perhaps abroad, to buy somewhere in beautiful, peaceful countryside, to live there or enjoy weekends or holidays.

One of the first cottages to be used in this way was The Scrubs, then two cottages. In 1951 it was bought by John Wright's mother in his name and she used it when he was working abroad as a civil engineer. In the late 1950s he bought the nearby Journeys End and in the 1970s Colombine Cottage. John Wright turned the two adjacent cottages into one (see photos 58 and 59) and lived there until his death in 2002, at that time the Valley's longest and oldest inhabitant. He had a distinguished war record and was decorated with the Military Cross for courage and inspiring leadership at Kohima in Burma. He was, in many ways, a very private person but was in his later years a delightful racconteur and an asset at any dinner table. He is greatly missed.

Another house bought in the early 1960s was Driftcombe Farm. After Norman Williams obtained it from the Graingers, he sold the house to a Mr Blackwell, who somehow managed to knock a hole in the back wall. The latter then sold it to Duncan Smith for £575. That year and again in 1965 and 1967 some further land was purchased by Duncan Smith from Norman Williams.

Duncan Smith, who did much to preserve and improve the house, died in 2003. He was a remarkable man, devoted to improving human welfare through care of the environment and the better conduct of international affairs. At the age of ninety, for example, he founded the Cirencester branch of the United Nations Association and was always working to move some project near to fruition, making full use of his powers of persuasion. He was at Fairford Air Base protesting at Britain going into the Iraq war one week before he died. He loved Driftcombe Farm and was continually planning improvements in the house or garden there. He wanted to build a Doric temple as a sitting area overlooking the Valley, one of the few of his ideas which was never realised. He did however manage to create a trout pond, fed by some of the springs on the bank opposite, and move the stream. His labour force consisted of his weekend guests, perhaps being roped in to a more active weekend than they had anticipated, and as many of his neighbours as he could persuade. In the 1960s and into the 1970s the road from St Benedicts to the bottom of the hill was concreted and maintained by the local community under the leadership of Duncan Smith. It was difficult to refuse to participate in the face of such unbridled enthusiasm, and his work parties were always great fun. His children and grandchildren use the cottage as they always did. It is sometimes let for holidays.

The stories about Driftcombe have become part of the Valley's stock of anecdotes as the activities of the Graingers, reported in the last chapter, bear evidence. Another tale concerns Rodney Smith, Duncan's son, who briefly and unwittingly harboured a man later accused of attacking Mrs Kilminster, who kept a store in Bisley, with an axe. In the early 1960s Rodney was working in the garden when a man came and started chatting to him. He was quite well dressed with a pair of snazzy jeans. As the conversation developed, it was arranged that the visitor would come the next day to do some work for Rodney. Then Rodney invited him in for tea. The visitor asked to make a telephone call and apparently rang up his girlfriend. A little later the telephone rang. Rodney answered. It was the police. They first asked whether he had anyone with him and Rodney said 'yes', and asked whether they wanted to speak to him. They first said 'no' but Rodney, who at that time had a good impression of his visitor, passed him the phone. It seemed he confirmed his identity and, when he put the receiver down said he must be going. 'See you tomorrow', he said. He then went off. Shortly after that the local constabulary and half a dozen locals armed with guns and any other suitable weapons arrived full of determination to catch Mrs Kilminster's attacker. Rodney's visitor, accused of the attack, was at large for two days but was eventually arrested. Mrs Kilminster was badly hurt but, in spite of her age, recovered in hospital.

In the early 1960s Mullions was lived in by Mrs Geary. She was the mother of David Geary, a BBC news-reader. She always dressed in the summer in flowery chiffon dresses with a large straw hat, rather of the Vita Sackville-West style. She is said to have tried to create the illusion to herself that her house was detached. She never took the shortest route to the road which went past the other two cottages in the terrace, but always went up the back way, pretending, it was said, that the other cottages were not there. An alternative explanation of that behaviour is that she was not wanting to disturb the other residents. She was fun to talk to, reminiscing about the Bloomsbury set, salons and debutantes' coming-out parties.

Another newcomer in the 1960s was Diana Lodge. She bought the ancient but half-derelict Trillgate Cottage in 1962 (see photo 21). She was another special person in the Valley and her life was one of immense diversity, determination and above all sincerity. She was born in 1906 in South Wales and trained at Bristol University as a school teacher. Against the advice of her father, she decided to pursue a life on the stage. When out of work between shows she became an artist's model, first for art schools, including St Martins and the Slade, and later at artists' own studios, including that of Duncan Grant, who painted many pictures of her. The rate was half a crown an hour. She met and later married Oliver Lodge, a poet and writer. Through him she became friends of the artists in the Bloomsbury Group. She lived with her husband in London and the Surrey countryside and during the Second World War in Canada and the USA. They returned to England in 1946 and stayed at a house near Painswick Beacon. Tragedy struck in 1955 with the death of her husband and of her son-in-law, leaving her daughter with three young children. For a while she went to Puerto Rico where a friend, Leopold Kohr, an Austrian economist and philosopher, was lecturing. When she came back her friends, Oliver and Denise Heywood, lent her a caravan and, while she was looking for a place to put it, she found Trillgate Cottage in a semi-ruined state. She put it into better order and lived there until her death in 1998, painting and involving herself in a number of charitable activities.

Diana was always involved in the quest for peace. She was in the Aldermaston March and had demonstrated in Stroud on behalf of Amnesty International. She had great humanity and, as a converted Catholic, raised funds to help their work for the poor, particularly in Latin America. She often exhibited her paintings with the proceeds of sales going to charities in El Salvador and other Central American states.[3]

Even in this peaceful Valley there was sometimes drama. In 1986 Diana Lodge heard a helicopter low over the Valley. She saw it through the trees and then it crashed with a frightening noise between the stream and her cottage. She rang 999 and ran, clutching a bottle of brandy, towards the helicopter. She saw two figures by the helicopter but then she fell and became a casualty herself. By good luck the pilot and observer, who had been inspecting power lines over the Slad Valley for the South West Electricity Board, were both unhurt except for a few cuts and bruises. Diana Lodge recovered, although it probably took her longer than the crash victims.[4]

After the 1960s there was a spate of second-homers especially in the Driftcombe Valley. They came to the old Primitive Methodist Chapel, now Scrubs Bottom; to Greencourt and later to August Cottage next door, a little later to St Benedicts and also to Woodedge. In the main valley they were in several houses, including Trillgate Farm.

TRANSFORMATION OF HOUSES AND COTTAGES

The ways in which the cottages have developed in the last forty years or so shows a considerable amount of ingenuity. The results are mixed. In a few cases the extension blends in to the old cottage. In other cases the house has completely changed in character from the original one-up, one-down or two-up, two-down. Whatever the style, there is no doubt about the substantial increase in the amount of accommodation. It is estimated that in 1900 two-thirds of cottages in these valleys had four rooms or less. In 2004 there was only one inhabited cottage in this category. It is estimated that in 1900 there were four houses with nine rooms or more and in 2004 the number in this category was probably as much as twelve or nearly half the total. In each case the kitchen is counted as a room.

One example of the transition is St Benedicts. The original two-room cottage is thought to have been built in the seventeenth century. About 1900 there was another shack-like building nearby. It had a front door, a window and a fireplace, probably at one time a separate cottage. In 1962 the cottage was bought by Alan and Jean Lloyd. It was owned by Henry Williams and negotiations as to the price went on at Stancombe Farm behind closely drawn curtains across the centre of the room so that everyone else was excluded. Henry Williams wanted £800 but Alan Lloyd said he couldn't afford that; it would have to be £600. But the owner insisted on £700. £100 was a great deal of money in 1962. Alan took his bank manager to see the house and kept him in the car until he had persuaded him to lend him the extra £100. Then he went back again to Stancombe and a deal was done and sealed by Henry Williams spitting on his hand before shaking hands with Alan. When the house was bought, it was found that tithes were owed to the Bishop of Gloucester. These were waived on application.

It was still basically one-up, one-down, with a front door which is now a window. By this time the other tiny cottage had only a corrugated iron roof and was used as a coal shed. Alan Lloyd linked the cottage and the old stone shed with clapboard. He extended the cottage and put in water, electricity and sanitation. There was also a green lean-to shed, probably built around the time of the First World War. Photo 35 of the area in 1910 shows the cottage much as in photo 51 of 1962 and may be compared with its present appearance in photo 52 after several further extensions.

Some of the changes made have combined cottages, notably two cottages at The Scrubs and the original five at Down Court, now one, though by the second half of the century there were only two separate residences there. On the other hand Steanbridge House old coach house is now a dwelling and Steanbridge Mill is now two or three dwellings.

Only one house has been built in the valleys in the last fifty years. Leslie Jelf of Down Farm built a bungalow below the farm house in the 1960s. This house, called Springfield Cottage, is the only cottage now attached to Down Farm. It is lived in by Tom George, the son of the farmer at Down Farm, who trains racehorses.

On the land near to Timbercombe where Rosie Bannen had lived, there was a proposal to build a large Palladian-style house with seven *en suite* bedrooms, large reception rooms and a grand staircase. There was to be a basement with a gun-room, laundry and garage for four cars. There was to be a large parking space outside. There was substantial local opposition to the proposal and the application for planning permission was turned down. A substantial hard-core track which detracts from the rural peace of the Valley had already been constructed. Fortunately it is now mellowing.

AGRICULTURE IN CRISIS

There has been a change in the ownership of farms in the last part of the twentieth century. The principal farm in the main valley is still Down Farm. There were other working farms in the area but their lands have been incorporated in the land of Down Farm or are used only occasionally for grazing. Those which are now part of Down Farm are Trillgate Farm and Steanbidge Farm as well as part of Snows Farm.

There have been major changes in the land formerly belonging to Snows Farm. After the death of the last of the Ayers, the farm was sold to a Mr Duddridge of Cheltenham who had retired from a profitable wholesale grocery business in the West Country. He was rarely resident. He gave some of the land up the valley to what is now the Gloucestershire Wildlife Trust. Some was bought by Down Farm and some sold with the farmhouse.

Higher up the valley is Dillay Farm on the north side of the Dillay Brook. In the mid 20th century it was owned and farmed by Mr Lionel Hancock who produced milk. He used to take it up to be collected on the road by Down Barn Farm, initially with a horse and cart and later by van. Unfortunately there was a disastrous accident. The milk cooling machinery broke down allowing some of the coolant to contaminate the milk. There was an outcry and the licence of the Hancocks to produce milk was withdrawn, in spite of the protests of their supporters. They switched to beef production but that was not profitable. They sold the farm to Mr Oliver, though Lionel Hancock's son, Tony, had an arrangement to graze the land. Mr Oliver died after the collapse on top of him of the wall of a well where he was working. Some years later his widow sold the house, sadly collapsing on the day of the removal and dying soon afterwards. The house was substantially extended and modernized. The surrounding woodland is largely used for breeding pheasants for shoots. The fields have always been grazing land but now it is very difficult to find anyone wanting to put sheep or cattle on it.

In The Scrubs Valley is Sydenhams Farm and, in addition, the land of Stancombe Ash Farm and Upper Southmead Farm both come into the Valley. Norman Williams had farmed Sydenhams for forty-six years. In 1982 Sydenhams farmland was sold because Norman Williams wished to concentrate on his late brother's farm at Stancombe Ash. Sydenhams Farm, comprising ninety-four acres, of which sixty-three were arable and thirty pasture, plus farm buildings, was sold by Norman Williams to David Melsome. Upper Southmead Farm and Stancombe

Ash Farm are both farmed by the Williams family, Norman's son Roland and his son, Martin.

There was little change in post-war agricultural practice until after 1960. In Down Farm there was still a rotation system of seven years. The major difference was that there would be two consecutive crops of wheat and barley rather than their changing every year. Then came a fashion for monoculture because, by that time, the availability of chemical fertilizers, weed-killers and pesticides meant that many of the problems of growing one crop continuously on the same piece of land could be overcome. Average yields increased enormously rising from twenty-five cwt. an acre in the 1960s to fifty cwt. in the 1970s and 1980s. This system was not satisfactory on the rather poor soil and gave rise to overloading of the land with chemicals, especially nitrates. There was a reaction against it and a return to more traditional cultivation methods with fewer chemicals.

Meanwhile the economics of agriculture were changing dramatically. Before the Common Market farmers sold their produce at the going price in the usual market situation. There were fluctuations due to the abundance or otherwise of the products but they were not extreme. There were acreage payments from Government for growing cereals so that the market was not entirely free. With the Common Agricultural Policy, prices for cereals doubled, or even more than doubled, and there was no longer a well-functioning market. Then prices plummeted and cereal production ceased to be profitable, even with the record yields. Bad weather in 1985 ruined the harvest on Down Farm and, with the prices of cereals having fallen heavily, Captain George decided to put more land down to pasture and increased the number of his ewes from 300 to 400.[5] At the same time prices of meat and dairy products fell overall. Farmers blame most of their problems on the actions of the European Union and of Government, as well as the buying power of supermarkets. The situation was worsened by the disasters of mad cow disease and foot and mouth.

Farmers in the main Slad Valley and farmers in the Scrubs Valley have reacted differently to this situation. The main farm in the Slad Valley, Down Farm, has abandoned arable production in favour of race horses. Captain George's son Thomas, following to some extent in his father's footsteps, has a business at Down Farm of training horses, initially for Point-to-Points and more recently for National Hunt racing. He employs about fifteen people. There is now no arable. The grassland is used for grazing and haymaking, mainly for horses. They still have some sheep and grazing is let to other farmers from further down the valley. Until recently it was rare to see cows on these fields but Hannah, one of Captain George's daughters, has introduced a herd of pedigree Dexter cattle, a small tough mountain breed. At The Scrubs, on the other hand, arable farming has increased. This has been made possible by the increasingly efficient agricultural machinery available. Compared with the era of horses rather than tractors, capacity to grow arable crops has increased manifold, from perhaps thirty acres with horses to 200 acres with modern equipment. Moreover yields have increased so that a first crop of wheat can yield three and a half tonnes an acre and barley three tonnes an acre. This represents a large increase over even the last twenty-five years. Prices however are very uncertain; for example, between October 2003 and April 2004 the price of milling wheat fell from £116 to £86 a tonne.

One of the new developments in The Scrubs Valley is the popularity of rape and, to a lesser extent, linseed, as major crops. Both these are what is known as a 'break crop' and both of them have the advantage of putting something back into the soil which is of value to subsequent crops. There are several possible rotations but a four-year rotation of rape, wheat, barley or set-aside, under which the land is uncultivated in exchange for a government subsidy, is a popular one. It is also possible to increase this to five years with two wheat crops following each other. Rape must not be grown more than once in four years because of the danger of disease.

The idea of a set-aside period when no crops are grown on one or several fields may appear at first sight to be reverting to a fallow year. In fact a serious difference is that when a field was left fallow, it was ploughed from time to time so that the ground was aerated and the weeds could not get too tight a hold. With set-aside the farmer is not allowed to do anything to the field. As a result there is little alternative but to use weed killer before cultivation can begin again. Fungicide usage for disease control has also increased in recent years. The Government has recently introduced a new arrangement called the Environmentally Sensitive Area (ESA) scheme. Under this plan no nitrogenous fertilizers may be applied to the ground and there must be no blanket spraying. In addition, mechanised cropping is forbidden in April, May and June. Broken down walls and fences must be repaired. The farmer is given financial incentives to fulfil these conditions, the amount of which varies according to previous use of the land. It is hoped that wild life will be allowed to regenerate under this scheme.

With the decrease in the numbers of sheep and cattle there is a problem in preventing   marginal, under-used, steep grazing land from becoming infested with brambles and bracken, or indeed, reverting to woodland. It is hard and costly to do so and farmers' willingness to continue to control the unwanted vegetation will depend, in the long run, on a prospect of better times ahead. Down Farm has a programme to continue to improve its pasture.

The Gloucestershire Wildlife Trust at Snows Farm is working to protect a particularly rare habitat of animals, insects and flora. The area is part of the Cotswold limestone grasslands which at one time covered nearly 40% of the Cotswolds. The development of modern technology, including the use of chemicals, has irretrievably spoilt most of these habitats. Fortunately, the land around Snows Farm was so steep that it could not be ploughed and the traditional grazing of sheep and cattle continued. This is very important to preserve the wildlife. Most of the sensitive, rarer wild flowers of limestone areas grow slowly and require high levels of sunlight. If grazing is discontinued, they are quickly swamped by vigorous grasses and scrub. Indeed the management of the reserve is complicated. Not only must it be grazed, but it must be rested for periods of time, because the continued presence of sheep or cattle allows a build-up of disease and pests, such as worms in sheep. That is why the land in the reserve is fenced into two parts each side of the stream to permit alternating grazing.

Among the wildlife there are over thirty butterfly species, including the Marbled White and Small Blue. There are rare Stinking Hellebores and Harts Tongue ferns and the Bee Orchid and, in the woods a wide selection of trees as well as bluebells in profusion, wood anemones and spurge laurel.

The activities of the Gloucestershire Wildlife Trust fit in well with the substantial and growing population of wild animals. The largest is the fallow deer but roe deer have been seen as well as muntjaks. Badgers are numerous and, at night, have on occasion been seen fighting, as though to the death, right outside the front door of a cottage. Foxes are there. Rabbits are back in force after their near extinction by myxomatosis and hares too are seen again. Smaller animals abound. Pheasants, though elegant, are becoming a pest. Having been bred for shooting in some estates, they roam over the whole area. Not everyone has total admiration for this abundance of wild life. Farmers do not like the damage to crops and believe that badgers are a source of tuberculosis in cattle. Tree lovers and foresters regard the grey squirrel as a pest for the damage they do in stripping the bark, especially of beech trees. Gardeners also dislike the damage to plants and the habit of badgers of digging up lawns and flower beds.

The challenges facing the productive continuation of the life of the valleys never cease to exist. It is arguable that a place which does not continuously change is somehow moribund. The valleys, in the last three centuries alone, have weathered the storms of the demise of the woollen industry, mechanization of agriculture, depopulation, and the decay and ruin of the built environment. They now face the challenge of the decline in agriculture. At the moment the future, as always, is unclear but the beauty of the hills and valleys, whether cultivated or not, clad in grass or trees, will survive and be an inspiration for the next 100 years to those who love the valley.

1. Nationwide Building Society, Index of house prices to 1st quarter 2004
2. *Stroud News and Gloucester County Advertiser*, Spring 1947 'In search of a lost village: a visit to Dillay Bottom'
3   Short biography of Diana Lodge, typescript, unsigned, March 1995
4. *The Slad Valley News* (1986) September, 'That Helicopter'
5. *The Slad Valley News* (1985) December

Gazetteer of Properties and their Inhabitants—Past and Present

Note on Content and Sources
All the sixty or so dwellings and mills which are in the Valley, or are known to have been there at one time, are included in this section of the book. They are divided into those still in existence and those which are ruins or sites of former buildings. The former are in alphabetical order of their present name and the latter are by regions as shown in Map 1.

The parish given after each building refers to the parishes before the reorganization of 1958. They thus tally with those in the tithe survey and the censuses. For a note on the reorganization see Appendix 2. Basic information is given under each entry, especially an indication of age and the salient features of the building, if known, and some data on the owner and occupiers. When the census is the source, age and occupation of the head of household are stated. For later entries it is rarely known which of the husband and wife or partners actually owns the house. Both have been included where known but this does not imply legal ownership. It has sometimes been difficult to piece together the history of each property and there has often been uncertainty as to precise dates or names. The author would be pleased to receive any additions or corrections.

It is unfortunately rarely possible to identify individual cottages from the censuses, only large named houses. Information has been included where possible. All the buildings are recorded on the appropriate maps.

Because most of the former mills have now become dwellings they are included with the houses. The mills mentioned are Snows Mill or Down Mill (ruin), Steanbridge Mill—Upper, Steanbridge Mill—Lower (demolished). There is also a note on the Vatch Mill which, although not within the area covered by this history, was of importance to those living and working in the valleys.

Primary sources of information are the tithe surveys of around 1840 and the censuses from 1841 to 1901 (for comment on these see Author's Note). Other sources are indicated by the list of references. Much information comes from residents, past or present, and from others well acquainted with the area. Most of the ages of the occupiers come from the censuses. The ages given in succeeding census do not always coincide with the census dates, presumably because of uncertainty as to the actual age of the persons concerned.

Key

O   Owned
Occ   Occupied

HOUSES AND FORMER MILLS IN EXISTENCE IN 2005

August Cottage (Bisley) is the middle cottage of a terrace of three (see photos 35 and 36). It was once called **Greencourt Two** and more recently **Driftcombe Cottage**. It has a date stone of 1676. It was owned, with other cottages nearby, by the clothier Nathaniel Samuel Marling (owner of The Vatch) and later by the owners of Sydenhams. The Revd Herford, Bishop of Mercia, bought it in 1903 with the other cottages in the row, Driftcombe Cottage, ruins and some land. It was used, with the two adjacent cottages of Greencourt and Mullions, by the Bishop as what he called a monastery, named Dryftcombe Cloysters, for a period prior to 1924.[1] When the three cottages were no longer a monastery, the Bishop resided in this cottage when he was staying in the Valley. Mrs Selby, who lived at Colombine Cottage, acted as caretaker while he was away. After the death of the Bishop in 1938, it was offered for sale by his executors with the other properties for a total sum of £150. It was described as a cottage containing one room downstairs and one bedroom. Mr Lane owned it for many years. He had been a tea planter in Ceylon but was living in Leamington Spa. It seems that August cottage was one of the earliest to be inhabited by those who had a main residence elsewhere, as both the Bishop and Mr Lane were in this category.

The water supply was a spring in the field below. In the 1960s there were two rooms downstairs with the staircase approached from the back between the two rooms. Electricity was connected in 1956 and mains water about 1963. The cottage was extended into the attic and with a new kitchen at the back in the 1970s.

DATES

1841	Nathaniel Samuel Marling O
1841	either John Niblett or Thomas Wall Occ
	Later Mr Mansell Occ
1903	and earlier George Partridge O
1903	Revd Herford, Bishop of Mercia O bought with several other cottages and ruins for £130. Owned to 1938
1920s	Mr and Mrs Gardiner (*née* Edith Mansell) Occ
1924	Mentioned in a NMR report as having been part of a monastery, now cottage

1936–38	and probably much earlier, the Revd Herford Occ
1940	Ainslie M Wadsworth O
1940s to 1961	Mr Lane O and Occ
1961–69	Roy and Eileen Hooper O and Occ
1969–75	Mr and Mrs Wiseman O and Occ
1976–91	Derek and Margaret Wild O and Occ
1991–92	Peter and Margaret Whalley (formerly Wild) O and Occ
1992–2003	Paul and Sarah Orchart O and Occ
2003	to present Anand Tucker and Sharon Maguire O and Occ

Beech Cottage is situated on the other side of the Slad Valley from Dillay. According to the tithe map, in the 1840s there was a group of three cottages there, each with a garden or small plot of land. Beech Cottage is the only survivor and the land includes that of the other cottages. The surviving cottage may have been built in the seventeenth or early eighteenth century. A major extension was built in the 1970s by Martin and Marilyn Dodds.

DATES

1841	John Minchin 75, agricultural labourer, wife and 4 children O and Occ
1950s	Johnny Coburn O and Occ. Wilfred and Annie Holbrook moved in to look after Mr Coburn and later the latter moved to a small cottage nearby.
1964	Richard and Rosemary Marsh Occ
Late 1960s	Margaret Garlick and later her husband, Mr Trotman
c. 1972	Martin and Marlyn Dodds O and Occ, built extension
1970s	Michael and Marlyn Leese O and Occ
1979	to present Colin and Gill Biscombe O and Occ

Cob House is the old stables of Steanbridge House. It was constructed in 1780 and converted to a dwelling in 1988. To the east of it is the former millpond of the Lower Steanbridge Mill.[2]

DATES

1985	Mr and Mrs John Falconer O and Occ
Present	Mrs Falconer O and Occ

Colombine Cottage (Bisley) is one of three cottages at The Scrubs on the headland overlooking the Slad valley. It was probably built in the early nineteenth century. This was always the smallest of the four cottages in this area and is still one-up one-down. The Holloways who are on the photo of the Primitive Methodist

Chapel tea party, lived in this cottage about 1900. In the 1930s it lived up to its name because the garden was a mass of Colombines. At that time and later it was occupied by Mr and Mrs Selby. Mrs Dickenson was a friend of Mrs Selby and used to take Jim Dickenson there when she visited. Mr Selby was a timber cutter by trade. He died from cancer fairly early in the war. They had no children. Mrs Selby eventually became mentally ill. Then it was bought by the Meezes. Mr Meeze had been to school in Slad with Laurie Lee and later worked at Morris Motors in Oxford. He and his wife used the cottage as a weekend retreat. He lived only six months into his retirement. He told his wife that if she wanted to sell she should give first refusal to John Wright. He bought the cottage in the 1970s, thus owning all three (formerly four) in the area. It was uninhabited for many years but improvements have been made and it is now lived in once again.

DATES

1841	John Harding 70, retired, and wife O and Occ
c. 1900	Holloways Occ. On photo of Primitive Methodist Chapel
1930s	Miss Cummins, who kept goats Occ
1940s and 1950s	Mr and Mrs Selby Occ
1960s	Mr and Mrs Meeze O and Occ
1970s–2002	John Wright O
2002	to present Lt Col Andrew and April Phillips O
2005	to present John Hopf Occ

Dillay Farm (Miserden) is in the Upper Slad Valley on the north side of the Dillay Brook. In 1838 it had an acreage of twenty-nine acres of which twenty-eight were pasture, an unusually high proportion for the area as a whole but normal in the higher parts of the Valley. Pasture has remained the dominant land use. In the mid-twentieth century the farm was owned by Lionel Hancock. His two sons, Tony and William, grazed the land for some time during the occupation of the next owner, Martin Oliver. The latter unfortunately was killed after the collapse on top of him of the side of a well which he was repairing. The house was substantially extended in the 1990s.

DATES

1838	John Partridge O
1838	George Wilkins, farm of 28 acres, Occ
1841	Daniel Shillam 25, yeoman, wife, 2 children and female servant Occ
1851	Joseph Woodfield 48, farmer of 50 acres, wife and 3 children Occ
1871	Joseph Woodfield 60, farmer, wife, child, 1 grandson and 1 servant Occ
1891	Alfred Ireland 52, farmer, son and his wife Occ
	Robert Trotman 41, farmer, wife and 2 children, niece and servant Occ

1901	Charles Driver 49, farmer and employer, wife, 5 children Occ
Pre-1923	A.H. Smith Occ[3]
1923–1942	Albert Hopkins, farmer of 48 acres, wife and children Occ. Timbercombe Cottage included in 1923 sale
1942	Farm bought from A.E. Filsell by E. Fawkes for £ 1300[4]
1946	George Hern, wife and two daughters Occ
1952	or earlier William Albert Parry O and Occ
1950s–1970	Lionel Douglas Hancock (son in law of Mr Parry) wife and two sons O and Occ
1970–97	Martin Oliver and Mrs Oliver O and Occ
1997	to present Rupert and Olivia Barrington O and Occ

Down Cottage (Miserden) is north of Downhill and has been called **Downhill** or **Down Hill Cottage**. It could also be **Duncombe Farm** shown in Bryant's map of Gloucestershire (1824). In the tithe survey there was one cottage and garden. There were however often three families living there and Mrs Timbrell referred to moving to one of the two cottages there in the early twentieth century. The original date of construction is not known. Prior to 1840 there were two houses owned by the Guardians of the Poor of the Stroud Union and Parish of Miserden. In 1840 Robert Lawrence Townsend bought both for £40 for the use of Joseph Watts.[5] There is, however, no evidence from the censuses that the latter lived there. It may be there were other cottages which Robert Townsend bought. However many dwellings there were on this site, the only survivor is Down Cottage. It was in a state of ruin in the 1960s but was rehabilitated as one house by the Pulvermachers in the 1970s.

DATES

1838	Tithe map shows one cottage, Daniel Selwin Occ
1838	Robert Lawrence Townsend O
1841	Daniel Selwin 70, cloth weaver, wife and housekeeper Occ
	William Say 45, agricultural labourer, wife and 5 children Occ
	Thomas Twinning 70, agricultural labourer and 1 child Occ
1851	Benjamin Birt 35, farm labourer, wife and 6 children Occ
	Daniel Selwin 80, retired weaver Occ
1861	John Davis 42, agricultural labourer, wife and 1 child Occ
	Samuel Smith 27, agricultural labourer, wife and visitor Occ
	Thomas Claridge 58, agricultural labourer, wife and 3 children (one in silk manufacture) Occ
1871	John Davis 58, agricultural labourer, wife and 1 son (coachman) Occ
	Thomas Claridge 68, agricultural labourer and Primitive Methodist preacher, wife and 1 daughter (wool weaver) Occ

	Samuel Smith 37, labourer, wife, 1 child and 1 lodger Occ
1891	Ann Davis 66, labourer Occ
	James Davis 46, general labourer, wife and 2 children Occ
	Joseph Witts 57, general labourer, wife, 1 child and lodger Occ
	Samuel Smith 56, general labourer, wife, 1 child and 1 lodger Occ
	Louisa Ireland 53, farm labourer, and 2 children Occ
1901	probably sold with Down Farm as workers' cottages
1901	James Davis 56, agricultural labourer, wife, 2 children and mother Occ
	John Joshua Flight 49, agricultural labourer, and 3 children Occ
Pre-1910	First of two houses, a general store Occ
c. 1910	after the general store, Jack and Lizzie Timbrell Occ
c. 1910	Second of two houses, a gamekeeper Occ
1938–49	Charlie Holford, former farmer at Chequers Occ
1938–49	Owned by owners of Down Farm
1960s	Ruined, Leslie Jelf O
1970s	Rehabilitated by Mr and Mrs Pulvermacher O and Occ
Later	(including 1981–84) Mr and Mrs Roger Hall Occ[6]
Later	two in between
1994–2000	James Holway and Sarah Woolley O and Occ
2000–03	John and Sarah Biggs O and Occ
2003	to present Paul Heatlie O and Occ

Down Court (Miserden) is south of Downhill (see photos 23 and 24). The building has housed workers of Down Farm. It is thought that at least part was built in the seventeenth century but the stone-work indicates that it was not all built at the same time. It was five cottages, though sometimes there were six households there. However by the 1920s it was just two cottages. By the 1960s it was altered with one cottage lived in by Mrs Timbrell, the source of so much information for this book. It became one house in the 1970s and was later extended and modernized.

DATES

1838	Robert Lawrence Townsend O
1838	Five cottages
	Samuel Brown, Richard Davies, Nathaniel Shovel,
	David Ireland and William Davies Occ
1841	Nathaniel Sewell 65, agricultural labourer, with sister Occ
	Samuel Brown 25, agricultural labourer, wife (wool carder) and 3 children Occ plus, in same house, Robert Mason 35, agricultural labourer and wife
	David Freeland 40, wool weaver, wife and 5 children of whom two, aged 6 and 15, wool carders Occ

William Davis 30, labourer, wife and 5 children Occ

Richard Davis 30, agricultural labourer, wife (wool carder) and 2 children Occ

John Hall 12, labourer Occ

1851	Robert Lawrence Townsend O

William Davis 43, journeyman/miller, wife and six children (signed Primitive Methodist Chapel deed) Occ

Thomas Faulkner 36, farm labourer, wife and 4 children Occ

Richard Davis 40, farm labourer, wife and three children (signed Primitive Methodist Chapel deed) Occ

Thomas Taylor 27, farm labourer with wife and two children Occ

James Terrell 27, farm labourer, with wife and 1 child Occ

1861	Abraham Ireland 28, agricultural labourer, wife and 1 child Occ

Thomas Beard 35, shepherd, wife, 4 children and visitor Occ

Richard Davis 50, labourer, wife and 5 children Occ

Joseph Davis 39, agricultural labourer, wife and 1 child Occ

Daniel Davis 81, gamekeeper, and wife Occ

Charles Woodward 39, agricultural labourer, wife and 6 children Occ

1871	Joseph Webb 34, shepherd, wife and 3 children Occ

Richard Davis 60, gardener, wife and 4 children Occ

Joseph Davis 47, agricultural labourer, wife and 2 children Occ

Charles Woodward 49, labourer, wife and 6 children Occ

Frederick Wooley 21, labourer, wife and 1 child Occ

1891	George Beard 39, shepherd, wife and 5 children Occ

John Cripps 54, agricultural labourer, 3 children Occ

William Cambridge 24, carter, wife and 2 children Occ

Caroline S. Restall 78, farmer with 3 children Occ

1901	Jonas Timbrell 62, agricultural labourer, wife and 2 children Occ

Charles Woodward 35, agricultural labourer, wife (tailoress), 5 children Occ

One uninhabited

1909–1920	Jonas Timbrell paid £1 2s 6p rent a quarter
1920s	two cottages:
	Down Farm O
	Jack (John Joseph) and Lizzie Timbrell and family Occ
	Shepherd Lainchbury Occ
1927–1946	Ernest Dickenson and family Occ
	Jack and Lizzie Timbrell and family Occ
Late 1950s & early 1960s	Dennis and Valerie Fisher Occ

1960s   Bernard Mills and Ann Mills (later Ann Smith) O and main Occ
                   Lizzie Timbrell one cottage Occ until about 1968
1994–5   Ann Spencer O and Occ
2002 to present   David and Heather Burwell O and Occ

Down Farm and House (Miserden) is in the main Slad Valley (see photos 10–12).
The present house was built in the eighteenth century on the site of an earlier house
and enlarged in the nineteenth century to become a substantial residence. In an
inventory for the sale of the farm house in 1810 it was described as having fourteen
bedchambers.[7] It has an elegant cellar and an old cider press. Down Farm was the
largest farm in the Steanbridge estate and has ever since been the largest farm in
the area. It was bought as a farm of 163 acres by Mr R. Trotman for £2,500 (see
photo 13) in 1901 when the Steanbridge Estate was sold at auction. The Trotman
family had previously been farming there as tenants and farmed there for a total of
about fifty years. It was sold in 1909 to Joseph Dickenson, who had the farm for
about thirty-five years. In the farm he was supported by his son Ernest, the father
of Jim Dickenson of the Farm Shop at Stancombe. The Dickensons were able to
retain the services of Mildred Robinson, who lived at Steanbridge Cottage, during
the war, when domestic servants were normally called up, by maintaining that she
worked on the farm, as indeed she did, looking after the chickens and helping on
the farm at times of specially hectic activity, such as threshing. About twenty cats
were kept on the farm, fed only bread and water. Otherwise the cats lived on the
mice and anything else they could catch. There was then a succession of owners
including Leslie Jelf, who was killed in an accident with a saw, and then the present
owner Captain John George. The farmland of Steanbridge Farm and of Trillgate
Farm was incorporated in Down Farm about twenty years ago. Some of the land
formerly belonging to Snows Farm is also now part of Down Farm. There is now
no arable but son, Tom George, trains racehorses. At one time the farm workers
lived at Down Court, including the farmer's son Ernest Dickenson.

DATES
1810   inventory for sale of farmhouse including about 25 acres.[8] It is not
                   known whether it was sold.
1838   Robert Lawrence Townsend, 162 acres of which 130 arable; included
                   Snows Farm and stretched as far as the Old Shop Ground O
1838   Robert Tuffley Occ. Occupied Snows Farm too
1841   Charles Gardner 25, yeoman, wife and 1 child and 3 servants Occ
1851   Charles Gardner 38, farmer of 250 acres and maltster; wife and 7
                   children, governess, servant and shepherd Occ
1861   Robert Trotman 55, farmer of 350 acres employing 5 men and 3 boys;
                   wife and 1 child, sister and servant Occ

1871	Robert Trotman 68, farmer of 400 acres employing 8 men and 1 woman; wife , son and servant Occ
1876	A new lease is drawn up from Robert Lawrence Townsend to Robert Trotman the younger for 220 acres and 4 cottages for 20 years and a rent of £263 per annum·[9] (see photo 13)
1877	Robert Lawrence Townsend dies succeeded by son of the same name
1886	Rent reduced to £210[10]
1891	Rent reduced to £130[11]
1901	Robert Trotman bought the farm from the owners of the Steanbridge estate for £2,500[12]
1901	Robert Trotman 51, farmer, wife, son, niece and servant O and Occ
1901–9	Robert Trotman O and Occ
30 June 1909	Farm auctioned at Stroud and bought by Mr Joseph Dickenson for £3,325[13] (see photos 15 and 16)
1909–1946	Joseph Dickenson, O and Occ with Ernest Dickenson also farming
1946	House and farm of 168½ acres sold to Mr G. Evans for £4,800, together with 200 acres of woodland for £1,275. Sold with the proviso that Mr. Joseph Dickenson (aged 85) could remain in the house until his death.[14]
1947–1967	Commander Hardinge, then Mr Cowmeadow followed by Fred Knight and Leslie Jelf
1967	to present Captain John George O and Occ

Downhill *see* **Down Cottage**

Driftcombe Cottage (Bisley) (see Photos 49, 50 and 55) is the last but one dwelling on the road in the Driftcombe valley. It was probably built in the early seventeenth century. It was home to members of the Timbrell and the Mansell families, both of whom played a prominent part in the Valley in the late nineteenth and early twentieth century. The Timbrells later moved to Down Court. In 1903 the cottage was bought by the Revd Herford, Bishop of Mercia, together with the three cottages in a row, now Greencourt, August Cottage and Mullions, and the ruined cottages behind Driftcombe Farm. He let this cottage. When he died in 1938 all the properties were offered for sale for a total price of £150. This cottage was described as 'a stone-built and tiled cottage containing living room, large pantry, two bedrooms, attic and brewhouse. The story of the Bishop is told in Chapter 10.

During the Second World War the cottage was bought by Mrs Daisy Bevan and her family who came to live in the Valley from London. When she died it was inherited by her granddaughter Sally. The accommodation was two-up and two-down. It was substantially extended in late twentieth century by Sally's husband,

Neil. He started by taking off the roof and replacing it in 1978 and had also to take down and rebuild the back wall. They were living abroad for some years, so work stopped for a while but they were able to move in 1992. Sally Rees, unlike her grandmother, finds she goes out several times a day to ferry her children to school and other events. The coming of the motor car, the steady fall in its price and a higher standard of living make that possible, though the situation is deteriorating due to the high price of petrol. Such reliance on the car would have been out of the question until well after the Second World War.

DATES

1840	Henry and William Davis O and Occ (also Ruins)
	Jonas Timbrell lived there as a young boy
1884	John (Jack, son of Jonas) Timbrell born there
1891	Jonas Timbrell 52, agricultural labourer, and three children Occ
1919–33	Ernest and Edith Helen Gardiner nee Mansell Occ.
1903–38	Revd Herford, Bishop of Mercia O. Bought with several other cottages and ruins for £130
1936–38	Mr Burrus and family Occ
1938	Mr Gardiner Occ at a rent of £6 per annum, the tenant paying the rates
1940–76	Daisy Bevan (and family in the early years) O and Occ
1976 to present	Neil and Sally Rees and family O and Occ

Driftcombe Farm (Bisley) is at the end of the road in the Driftcombe Valley. It was probably built in the early seventeenth century but it is believed that there may have been an earlier dwelling on the site. Signs of a building, believed to be Roman, have been found. It used to belong to Sydenhams but in 1924 the house and farm were bought from the Driver family by John Henry Grainger and it was later owned by John Nathaniel Grainger.[15] The farmer had a wife and a son known as Jack. It is not known what relation the earlier owner was. The farm was thirty-two acres. Mr Grainger was not liked in the area and Norman Williams regarded him as a bad farmer. When, in 1958, Mr Grainger wanted to sell, he would not sell to Norman Williams. A friend bought it on Norman's behalf and immediately sold it to him for £1,400. Norman then sold the timber for about the same amount. He sold the farmhouse and a garden to John Lawson Blackwell. Norman kept most of the land. In doing some maintenance work, John Blackwell damaged the back wall of the house and knocked down much of the barn. In 1962 Blackwell sold the house, which was in a bad state, to Duncan Smith, then of Hampstead, London, for £575.[16] That year and again in 1965 and 1967 some further land was purchased by Duncan Smith from Norman Williams. Duncan Smith needed to do much work on the house. When a lorry was delivering building materials it knocked into the wall of Driftcombe Cottage in the lane and damaged the outlet of the spring so that the spring no longer ran. Duncan also started digging out the bank behind the house thus damaging the footpath and the land belonging to Mrs Bevan. She took him to court to clarify the situation and try to prevent further damage. The farmhouse was repaired and the kitchen was added in the 1960s. It now belongs to Duncan Smith's children. It is sometimes let for holidays.

DATES

1746	Henry Stephens was on the Manorial Roll representing Driftcombe[17]
1841	Thomas Baker O
1841	Henry Davis Occ
1891	Joseph Partridge 82, farmer, and son Edwin, Refreshment-house Keeper Occ
1898	26 acres at Driftcombe sold for £250 following death of Henry Driver in 1895 and his wife Maria in 1897.[18] It may have been Driftcombe Farm
1901	Unoccupied
Early 1900s	One of Mansell family (brother of Mrs Lizzie Timbrell) Occ
Pre-1924	William Baker Driver and Frances Salina Driver O (also of Sydenhams)
1924	John Henry Grainger O and Occ
1943–58	John Nathaniel Grainger O and Occ
1958	Raymond Evered Woodhouse O
1958	Norman Theyer Williams O

HOUSE AND GARDEN ONLY
DATES

1958 or later	John Lawson Blackwell O and Occ
1962	Duncan Smith O and Occ
2003	Stefanie D'Orey, Rodney Smith and Jinny Cummins O
2003 to 2005	Guy and Kylie D'Orey Occ

Greencourt Cottage (Bisley) is at the eastern end of the terrace of three cottages once called **Greencourt One** (see photos 35, 36 and 40). It was built some time after 1676, probably early eighteenth century. The lintel over the front door would have been that of a large weaving window. The front door was adjacent to the next cottage. It was owned by the clothier, Nathaniel Samuel Marling, later by the owners of Sydenhams and from 1903 –1938 by the Revd Herford, Bishop of Mercia. He bought it with the other properties in the terrace, Driftcombe Cottage, ruins and some land (Deeds). It is reported in a NMR report of 1924[19] that the owner had said that the three cottages used to be a monastery, called

Dryftcombe Cloysters but that they were now cottages. After the death of the Bishop the cottage was offered for sale by his executors with the other properties. It was described as containing a living room, a very small sitting room and three bedrooms. All four cottages owned by the Bishop were put on the market for £150[20] but it is believed the final price was less.

Mrs Stott, who lived in the house during the Second World War, drove a lorry for Moreton C. Cullimore which was sometimes parked just above Down Court and sometimes at Sydenhams by the cart shed. Her husband was a sergeant in the army but they divorced about the end of the war. He had given Jim Dickenson a dagger which he said he had taken off the body of a dead soldier at Arnhem. Mrs Stott moved to Bisley and lived there until her death.

The back wall probably fell down in the nineteenth century as the stone there is different from that in the rest of the house and it is the only wall to have a slate damp-course. Slate would not have been transported until after the canals were built. The water supply was a spring in the field below. Electricity was available from about 1956 and mains water was connected in 1963. There was a stone staircase in the corner beside the fireplace in use until at least the early fifties. It meant that a coffin for Mrs Stott's father could not be removed from the bedroom by the staircase. It had to be taken out of the window. The stone staircase was removed in 1976 when the cottage was extended to the east.

DATES

1841	Nathaniel Samuel Marling O
1841	either John Niblett or Thomas Wall Occ
1903 and earlier	George Partridge of Sydenhams O
1903 and earlier	William Driver Occ
1903–40	Revd Herford, Bishop of Mercia O bought with several other cottages and ruins for £130. He died intestate in 1938
1924	NMR Report stating that the owner said that it had been, with the other two adjacent cottages, a monastery but that it was now a cottage[21]
1936–38	Charlie Holford and family Occ
1938	Mrs Mansell Occ at rent of £6 including rates[22]
1940	Ainslie M. Wadsworth O
1940–53	Joan Mary Stott O and Occ paid £75.
1953–55	Ethel May Baker O and Occ paid £375
1955–60	George Midway Charles Titley Landucci O paid £750
1960	Eugene Francis Kieff O paid £350
1960–66	William O'Nions O and Occ paid £275
1966–88	Hans and Patricia Hopf O and Occ
1988 to present	Patricia Hopf O and Occ

Journeys End (Bisley) is on the promontory overlooking the Slad valley. It was probably built in the early nineteenth century in an old quarry. It is thought that the discovery of some of the Roman votive tablets (see photos 1 and 2) was made in the course of construction of this cottage. In the 1930s and 1940s it was owned by Mr and Mrs Wren, an ex-policeman and his wife. Mrs Wren worked in Stroud and walked there and back every day. In the 1950s it was occupied by Mr and Mrs Lightfoot. She was the sister of Phillip Bevan of Driftcombe Cottage. They bought it for £50. When John Wright bought it in the late 1950s he repaired it and gave it some modern amenities. He lived in it while he was working on The Scrubs but it has been let for many years.

DATES

1841	Richard Davis O and Occ
1930s and 1940s	Mr and Mrs Wren O and Occ
1950s	Mr and Mrs Lightfoot O and Occ paid £50
Late 1950s	John Wright O
	Various tenants including:
	Simon (Ringo) Orton and Caroline Occ
1996–present	Fergus Macdonald Occ
2002 to present	Lt Col Andrew and April Phillips O

Lower Steanbridge Mill *see* Steanbridge Mill—Lower

Mullions (Bisley) is at the west end of the terrace of three and was once called **Greencourt Three** (see photos 35, 36, 39 and 40). It may have been built in 1676 as part of the same building as its neighbour August Cottage but it was probably a separate dwelling. The division between the cottages is a single brick wall. In about 1900 the door was in the front adjacent to August Cottage. There were no doors or windows on the west side of the cottage (see photo 55). In the 1840s it was owned by Nathaniel Samuel Marling and later by the owners of Sydenhams. From 1903 to 1938 it was owned by the Revd Herford, Bishop of Mercia, who had bought the whole terrace, as well as Driftcombe Cottage, ruins and land. Mrs Timbrell said that one of the three cottages in a row was turned into a chapel by him. If so it is possible that it was he who installed the pointed, rather churchy windows between 1910 (when the photo of all three cottages was taken) and 1920. In the early twentieth century there was an arch over the path (see photos 39 and 40). One can suppose that it was constructed as a suitable approach to the chapel. The new front door of the cottage and the attic windows were added later. It seems that the Bishop regarded the three cottages in a row as a monastery in the years prior to 1924, when it is reported in an NMR report[23] that the owner said it had been a monastery but was now cottages. Around 1924 Norman Williams used to spend the night at The Chapel (believed to be the present Mullions, rather than the Primitive Methodist Chapel) to keep the Bishop company. For this he was paid a shilling a night. All the property owned by the Bishop at the time of his death, Driftcombe Cottage and the three cottages in the terrace were put on the market for a total price of £150. Mullions was sold separately to Miss Gibson who lived in the cottage in the Second World War. She was a teacher and an artist. She was a friend of Jim Dickenson's mother and Jim still has two of her paintings. She once was bitten by an adder and had to walk all the way to Stroud to get an antidote. In the 1970s the cottage was lived in by Michael and Frances Horovitz, both well-known poets. Frances tragically died in 1983.

There was an arch over the path attached to the cottage in the late 1950s but it was not the same one as in the early part of the century. Perhaps the original one had collapsed and the stones had been reused. The kitchen was added in the 1960s by Alan and Gloria Peyton.

DATES

1841	Nathaniel Samuel Marling O
1903 and earlier	George Partridge O
1903	Revd Herford, Bishop of Mercia O bought with several other cottages and ruins for £130
1924	Report by owner that it had been part of a monastery and was now cottage[24]
1938 and in WWII	Miss Gibson O and Occ
Early 1960s–1965	Mrs Geary O and Occ
1965–70	Alan and Gloria Peyton O and Occ
1970 to present	Michael Horovitz O and Occ with Frances and/or Adam

The Old Bakehouse (Miserden) was once part of Upper Steanbridge Mill. It was in the living area of the mill but it had also at one time been a bakery. *See under* Steanbridge Mill—Upper.

St Benedicts (Bisley) is at the bend in the road down to the Driftcombe valley (see photos 35, 36 and 51, 52). No written record has been found of St Benedicts cottage before the 1840s, when the Davis family lived there, though the original one-up one-down was probably built in the seventeenth century. It had about one acre of pasture land. About 1900 there was another building nearby. It had a front door, a window and a fireplace, seemingly originally a separate cottage. There were also several outbuildings. According to Mrs Timbrell, the Ansloes in the Easter tea party photo lived at St Benedicts about 1900. The Mansells lived at St Benedicts after 1900 with nine children of whom Mrs Timbrell was one. The children slept in the second building in bunks. St Benedict is the patron saint of bakers and this cottage, at least sometimes, baked bread for other than its own residents, notably for the Easter Sunday tea party at the Primitive Methodist Chapel. The bread oven is there still.

According to Norman Williams, in the 1920s the cottage was sold for £25. It is possible that St Benedicts was the cottage referred to as having woodlice in the memoirs of Kathleen Taylor (see Chapter 9). In 1962 the cottage was bought by Alan and Jean Lloyd. It was sold in the 1970s to Lester Lowe, a bone surgeon. He was killed in a skiing accident and his wife sold to Hugh Padgham. He, in turn, in 1997 moved to Trillgate and sold the cottage to Kim McCrodden who extended it substantially, so that it has changed since the early sixties from a two-roomed house to a ten-roomed house.

DATES

1841	Isaac Davis O and Occ
c. 1900	Ansloe Occ
Early 1900s	William and Hanna Mansell and 9 children Occ
1920s	sold for £25
1950s	Mrs Cousins
1962 and earlier	Henry Williams (of Stancombe) O
1962 and earlier	Paul Francis Occ
1962–78	Alan and Jean Lloyd O and Occ paid £700
1978–83	Lester Lowe O and Occ
1983–97	Hugh Padgham O and Occ
1997 to present	Kim and Lynn McCrodden O and Occ

The Scrubs (Bisley) is the largest of those dwellings on the promontory overlooking the Slad Valley. It was probably built in the early nineteenth century. It was originally two cottages, one dated 1814. One cottage was one-up, one-down, and occupied by Miss Stevenson. She kept a donkey in the shed next door. The other was lived in during the Second World War by Mr and Mrs Gardiner. Mrs Gardiner, née Mansell, had lived as a child at St Benedicts further down the valley. Mr Gardiner gardened for Col Stokes of Sydenhams. In 1951 it was bought by John Wright's mother in his name and she used it when he was working abroad as a civil engineer. John Wright combined and extended the two cottages and lived there until his death in 2002. He left the cottage to his niece.

DATES

Early 20th century, including 1936–38	Miss Stevenson O and Occ of one cottage
Approx. same time	Dennis and Mrs Gardiner, (née Mansell) Occ of other cottage

1951	John Wright O and Occ
2002 to present	Lt Col Andrew and April Phillips O
2003–04	Major Charles Valdes-Scott Occ
2004 to present	Lt Col Andrew and April Phillips O and Occ

Scrubs Bottom (Bisley) (see photos 47 and 48) is the most westerly of all the remaining cottages in the Driftcombe Valley. It was formerly the **Primitive Methodist Chapel**, later known as **Beech Cottage** and later still **Piedmont Cottage**. It was built in 1840 after the land was bought for £5, collected mainly by those living in these valleys. The Chapel consisted of the west part of the present house. The Victoria County History says that the chapel was closed in 1912 but there is evidence that services continued there until the Second World War (see Chapter 8). In the photo of an Easter tea party about 1900 the windows seem to be blocked up. They were altered from pointed to oblong after 1912 by Miss Stevenson who lived at The Scrubs but arranged services at the Chapel.

In 1940 it was already occupied as a house. During the Second World War it was occupied by people of the name of Nicholas. In the middle fifties Alf James lived there. It was then called Beech Cottage. By arrangement with Norman Williams, he sometimes lived in this period at Yew Tree Cottage because life was too difficult in the Valley. In 1956, for example, the spring in the field below dried up and drinking water had to come from the Wells at Bisley.

The house was bought by the Kaners in the early 1960s. It was then known as Piedmont Cottage. Peter Kaner was a schoolmaster from North London, and it was mostly used as a weekend cottage, but for a year Peter Kaner was writing mathematics books and the family lived there all the time. During their occupation it consisted of one downstairs room (the old chapel) and two bedrooms above. It had no bathroom and the toilet outside was a chemical one.

It was then sold in 1975 to the Hortons who lived there permanently. They extended it, putting on the kitchen and rooms above. A bathroom was added. The work was done by John Horton and Alan Lloyd, formerly of St Benedicts Cottage. The Hortons emigrated to Australia. It was again substantially extended by Quentin Letts in 1999 and is now a large house.

DATES

1840	Land owned by Nathaniel Samuel Marling
1840	Land sold for £5 to build a chapel. For nearly a century it was the Primitive Methodist Chapel
1940	Edna Gardiner, daughter of Mr and Mrs Gardiner of The Scrubs, Occ
WWII	Mr Nicholas Occ. He was a schoolmaster at Bisley.

Late 1940s and early 1950s	Mr and Mrs Fletcher and six children Occ. He was a master at Stroud College.
Mid 1950s	Alf James Occ
1960s	Peter and Fleur Kaner O and Occ
1975	John Horton and Judith Eason O and Occ
1980s	Terry and Jan Britten O and Occ
1995–2004	Quentin and Lois Letts O and Occ
2004 to present	Quentin and Lois Letts O
2004 to present	tenants Occ

Snows Farm (Miserden) is in the main Slad Valley (see photos 25 and 26). It was built in the seventeenth century. The farm was part of Down Farm in 1839 but in the 1851 census it was said to be a farm of fifty acres and was rented by George Ayers, whose family were to farm there for about 130 years. It was otherwise the second most important farm in the main Slad Valley. Part of the land is now a reserve of the Gloucestershire Wildlife Trust. The remainder has become part of Down Farm. The house and some land are now separately owned. The barn has an old window of some note and is said to have a connection with lepers possibly housed in the barn. The outside of the house was used to film the second version of *Cider with Rosie*.

DATES

1838	Robert Lawrence Townsend O. Family probably owned the farm till 1901.
1838	Robert Tuffley Occ, farmed Down Farm too
1851	George Ayers 36, farmer of 50 acres, wife and 4 children Occ
1860	New lease from Robert Lawrence Townsend to George Ayers for Snows Farm and the water corn or grist mill and cottages for 21 years for a rent of £95 5s rising over seven years to £119 15s[25]
1860	George Ayers purchased timber from Down Wood and leased 39 acres of land.
1861	George Ayers 47, farmer of 100 acres employing 4 men and 2 boys, wife and 2 children Occ
1871	Nathaniel Ayers 29, farmer of 97 acres employing 2 men and 2 boys, and wife Occ
1877	Robert Lawrence Townsend died and was succeeded by his son of the same name
1891	Nathaniel Ayers 50, farmer of 97 acres, wife and 8 children Occ
1901	Believed the Ayers family bought the farm at the sale of the Steanbridge Estate
1901	Rose Ayers 51, farmer, and 6 children Occ

Early 1900s	three Ayers brothers worked on the farm
Mid-1900s	three Ayers sisters: Grace, Florence (Carey) and Mabel and brother Osbourne, grandchildren of George Ayers, O and Occ
1965	Grace Ayers and Florence Carey O and Occ
1972	Peter Duddridge O
1975	Peter Duddridge agreed that part of farm become Gloucestershire Wildlife Trust Nature reserve, remainder incorporated in Down Farm. House was let.
1989	Peter Duddridge made a gift to Gloucestershire Wildlife Trust of the land already in their management
1993 to present	Andrew and Lena Dickson house and some land O and Occ

Springfield Cottage (Miserden) This cottage was built by Leslie Jelf of Down Farm in the 1960s

DATE

Present	Tom George O and Occ

Steanbridge Cottage (Miserden) This cottage is close to the old Upper Steanbridge Mill. It was probably a one-up one-down cottage when it was built, maybe as early as the seventeenth century. It has been extended several times since then. On the occasion of excavation for one of the extensions it is said that an old Roman cistern was discovered.

It was probably once owned by the Townsend family as they owned the Mill next door and later all the property round about. It continued to be owned by the owners of Steanbridge Mill. It is likely that it was used in conjunction with the various activities at the mill or as an agricultural cottage. Before the Second World War it was lived in by the Robinson family. There were then three brothers: Harold, Victor and Ken and two sisters, Gertie and Mildred. Mildred was in service to Joseph Dickenson at Down Farm for many years until his death. Ken was the last surviving brother. He had at various times worked for the Ayers, Captain George and the Hancocks. The two sisters and Ken moved to Stroud where the women looked after Ken. He used to walk from Stroud to the valleys every day striding out with a piece of sacking round his shoulders. He would stop for no-one and didn't seem to hear any 'good mornings' or other greetings. He died in the 1990s.

DATES

Early 1900s	probably owned by owners of Upper Steanbridge Mill
1930s and probably much earlier	Ken Robinson and his sisters Occ

Early 1950s to early 1990s	Frank Green O
	Later sold to another owner
Late 1990s	Trevor and Catherine Carrelet (John George's daughter) O and Occ
2003 to present	Mr and Mrs Adrian Underwood O and Occ

Steanbridge House (Painswick) and Estate lie below Slad (see photos 3 and 4). The Townsend family (see Chapter 6) were slowly buying up land in the Slad Valley and enlarging their estate.[26] By 1840 the estate comprised almost the whole of the Slad Valley from Steanbridge to just below Dillay, including two mills, see Map 6. Part of the house at the back was built in the late sixteenth century. In the late eighteenth or early nineteenth century a two storey, five bay house was created, with a central Venetian window, a cornice and parapet. It seems that the Townsend family did not occupy the house for long after the death of Robert Lawrence Townsend in 1877 (see Chapter 6). The house and the estate were sold in a number of lots in 1901 and Samuel Gilbert Jones bought the house with some land for £3,000.[27] Samuel Gilbert Jones was the Squire referred to in *Cider with Rosie*.[28] When the house was sold in 1982, the agent's particulars stated that it included 18 acres with a lake, two cottages and excellent outbuildings. The Georgian and Elizabethan parts were, for a time, two separate dwellings. It is now one property again. The stable has also been converted to a dwelling and is known as Cob House.

DATES

Early 18th century	Henry Townsend and later William Townsend and another Henry were in the area. It is not known who acquired the house or when. Henry owned Lower Steanbridge Mill which was next to the house so that it is possible that it was he who owned the house at that time.
1766	Thomas Baylis O and Occ is reported as having built part of the house.[29]
Late 18th century	Theyer Townsend O bought Upper Steanbridge Mill and much land.
1801	Charles Townsend O, gunpowder merchant at Hackney, inherited from his brother.
1803	Robert Lawrence inherited land and estate and took name of Townsend O. Became Rector of Bishops Cleave and had murals painted there (see photos 3, 5 and 7). Renovated and enlarged Steanbridge House.
1815	House let, at least for part of the time to the Rookers Occ
1820	Mrs Smith Occ[30]

1830	Robert Lawrence Townsend died and was succeeded by son of the same name
1838	Robert Lawrence Townsend O and Occ. He also owned much land in the Slad Valley and in the side valley, see Map 6.
1839	House let to William Clissold
1841	Robert Lawrence Townsend 46, Army, wife, 2 children and 5 servants O and Occ
1861	Robert Lawrence Townsend 66, J.P., Army half pay, wife, visitor and 5 servants O and Occ
1871	Robert Lawrence Townsend 75, J.P., retired, landowner, cavalry, 5 servants O and Occ
1877	Robert Lawrence Townsend died and was succeeded by son of the same name
1891	John C. Collins 68, retired Surgeon Major in the Indian Army, wife born in Calcutta. Two children and four living-in servants Occ
1892	Robert Lawrence Townsend living in Cheltenham[31]
1901	Estate divided up and sold
1901	Samuel Gilbert Jones bought house with about forty-two acres of land for £3,000
1901	Unoccupied
1940	Basil Jones (nephew of Samuel) O
WWII–1966	Dr Phyllis Norton O and Occ Nursing home/Guest house and home for special evacuees. Dr Norton was a follower of Rudolf Steiner, social philosopher and educationalist.
1966–83	David and Dinah Naylor O and Occ
1983	Julian and Jane Newiss O and Occ
1983	House divided in two. Julian and Jane Newiss O and Occ; Toby and Ursula Falconer O and Occ
1991	two parts reunited. Julian and Jane Newiss O and Occ

Steanbridge Mill (Miserden) is the name of one of the houses which was part of the old Upper Steanbridge Mill. It was the west part of the mill and housed the machinery—see Steanbridge Mill—Upper for history.

Steanbridge Mill—Upper (Miserden) Sometimes, including in 1901 and as recently as 1979 but not necessarily continuously, called **Steanbridge Farm** (see photos 7 and 8). This was the Upper Steanbridge Mill, also once known as the **Jenny Mill**. It is said to be one of the first local mills to use the spinning jenny. It was probably built in the seventeenth or early eighteenth century. In 1781, when it was bought by Theyer Townsend, it was a fulling mill with two stocks and a gig. It had two gardens and forty-three acres of land. It was sold for £300. The deed refers to a mortgage due to Samuel Clutterbuck of £800 and the financial arrangements between these two parties dragged on for some years.[32] It was a small but important woollen mill well into the nineteenth century. It was later worked as a saw mill by one of the Ayers family, related to those at Snows Farm. They lived in the east part of the house. The stone or concrete pool in the front of the house is now a flower bed. It is said that at one time there was a baker in part of the mill. The old mill was converted to a farmhouse before 1882 but only the original residential east part was used. In the 1970s the west part of the building which had once housed the machinery, had been used to house animals and was in a near derelict state. It was transformed into a house by Alexander and Marion Kok. They used the detached stone and other materials lying around and obtained other old beams, doors and so on from other derelict buildings from as far away as London. The Koks lived in the renewed west part, called Steanbridge Mill, and sold the east part, then known as the Old Bakehouse, and a flat on the top floor, known as The Granary. At one time therefore the mill was three residences. It is now two, as the flat and the house beneath it are one property.

The farm was worked by the Close family, who were there in 1926,[33] and then Mr Hall. By the 1930s and all through the Second World War it was farmed by Mr Tomlinson. The land is now part of Down Farm. It is rumoured that in the 1970s cock fighting took place at the farm.

DATES

1763 and 1767	worked by John Pegler, clothier[34]
To 1774	worked by James Woodfield. His stock in trade was sold in 1774[35]
1781	bought by Theyer Townsend from John Pegler's executors for £300[36]
1815	Mr Driver Occ (see Chapter 8 for advertisement to let)
1838	Nathaniel Marling O. Worked by William Lay[37]
	Later worked by N. Partridge
1841	Henry Williams 30, clothworker, wife and 2 children Occ
1851	Jonathan Smith 46, farmer, wife and 1 child Occ
	Henry Baglin 24, milkman, wife and 2 children Occ
1861	John George Ayers 26, timber merchant, wife and 1 child Occ. There was a saw mill perhaps to late 1880s[38]
1861	George Goold 21, carter Occ
	Before 1882 converted to a farm house
1901	house and about 32 acres bought by Samuel Gilbert Jones for £700. It was owned by his family until the 1930s. Let to Mr Robert Trotman for the apportioned rent of £25 per annum[39]
1901	Edwin Franklin Occ 39, carter for farm, mother and sister
Around 1926	the Close family Occ, lived there and had a haulage business.

1928	House and 62 acre farm let by Marion Charlotte Jones, widow of Samuel Gilbert Jones to Charles William Hall for five years at £120 pa[40]
1934	let to Reginald Guy Tomlinson at £120 pa,[41] who lived and farmed there in WWII. He had a wife and daughter
	Later Titch Margesson O and Occ sold to Frank Green but continued to occupy for a time
Early 1950s to 1974	Frank Green O and Occ, farmed and lived in the house
1974–79	Alice Green (sister of Frank Green) O
1974–79	Michael and Angela Zajac Occ. Michael Zajac was relation of Frank Green
1979	Alexander and Marion Kok O and Occ of whole mill
Early 1980s	land sold to John George of Down Farm

The mill was then divided into three parts . These were: **Steanbridge Mill,** the west part where the machinery once was, **The Granary** and **The Old Bakehouse** below the Granary. The name of the Granary was later changed to **Upper Steanbridge Mill**

Steanbridge Mill (Miserden)
DATES

1979–85	Alexander and Marian Kok O and Occ
1985	Mr and Mrs Beevers O and Occ
Later	John and Bridget Williams O and Occ
Later	Mr and Mrs Mott Groom
1991 to present	John and Drucilla Fairgrieve O and Occ

Upper Steanbridge Mill (Miserden) formerly The Granary (see also Steanbridge Mill-Upper)
DATES

1980–82	Mrs A.S. Reeeves, mother of Marion Kok, O and Occ
1982–85	Myron Kok (brother of Alexander) O and Occ
1985–87	Myron Kok O
1985–87	Alexander Kok Occ
1987	Guy and Pamela Bentley O and Occ
Early 1990s to present	Trevor and Elizabeth Bentley O and Occ (see also The Old Bakehouse)
2004	for sale with the old Bakehouse

The Old Bakehouse (Miserden)

DATES

1980–85	Felix (brother of Alexander) and Anne Kok O and Occ
1985	Janice Hoare and Ms Williams) O and Occ
Early 1990s to present	Trevor and Elizabeth Bentley O (see also Upper Steanbridge Mill)
1994 to present	various tenants Occ
2004	for sale with Upper Steanbridge Mill

Sydenhams (Bisley) lies at the top of The Scrubs/Driftcombe Valley (see photos 56 and 57). Sydenhams was a Lesser Manor House in the Middle Ages. Its lands were in Bisley Parish mainly on the higher ground on The Scrubs and in the Driftcombe Valley. The house and the farm, particularly the arable land, are now split up, but in the first part of the twentieth century Sydenhams was only marginally smaller than Down Farm in the main Slad Valley.

Part of the present house dates from the thirteenth or fourteenth century, and has small windows of that period, one lighting a stone newell staircase. It has gables and mullioned windows. The gate-posts in the wall in front of the house are mediæval. The house was enlarged to the south-west in the early seventeenth century.[42] The house was thoroughly repaired by William Clarke from about 1930. Much of the work was done by Norman Jewson, an architect of the Arts and Crafts Movement. Clarke replaced the corrugated iron roofing on the barns with stone tiles. Drinking water was still collected from Bisley Wells, though during his occupation piped water was brought by gravitation from springs, enabling two bathrooms and central heating to be installed.[43] There was no gas or electricity. Outside the house the farmyard was in a mess, with animals all around. When Colonel Stokes bought the farm in 1936 he built a 300 foot well to avoid going to the Wells at Bisley for drinking water. He also installed an electricity generator. He was always a helpful person and it was he who built Sydenhams Farm House for Norman Williams who was renting the farmland. General Escritt, who had been in the Control Commission in Germany after the Second World War, bought Sydenhams in the early 1950s and was succeeded by the Cradock Watsons who lived in the house for some twenty years. When Geoffrey died, Gay Cradock Watson sold the house and moved to Yew Tree Cottage. Sydenhams was modernized further by Charles and Ute Howard with more bathrooms and other changes. They lived there for about ten years, selling in 1998 to Peter and Julia Barton, who have completed the work, making tasteful use of the barns without spoiling the period external appearance. Although the farmlands of Sydenhams were often let to tenants, they were in the same ownership as the house until 1954 when Norman Williams bought the land. Some woodland and pasture below Sydenhams belong to the owners of the house and some of this land was part of

Driftcombe Farm bought by Norman Williams from the Graingers. The property now comprises about 60 acres.

Unfortunately the old deeds of Sydenhams are lost. Some history can be pieced together from a number of sources as recorded below.

DATES

1302	Path to Sydenhams mentioned in the charter of William de la Pere[44]
1304	William of Sydenham was juror at the inquisition of Edmund Mortimer[45]
1377/8	Charter mentioned—see below
Before 1546	John Smallbrugo held a virgate of Sydenhams for twenty shillings and one penny a year
1546	William Smallbridge inherited virgate of Sydenhams from his father, John, and wife of John is granted a tenancy
1608	Sydenhams belonged to Thomas Smart who claimed to hold it by a charter of 1377 or 1378[46]
1620	James Burrows or Burrowe O and Occ, left it to his wife for life, and for the remainder of the term for which he held it to his sons. It is surmised that the family later left Sydenhams and entered the wool trade[47]
1632	John Gardener of Sydenhams, Yeoman[48]
Pre-1641	Richard Gardiner and Ann Gardiner with 73 acres[49]
1641	Samuel Sevill bought Sydenhams. It continued in the Sevill family through at least six generations to after 1810. Successive generations of the family were named either Samuel or William. Various transactions by the family included adding bits of land to the estate from time to time until 1810[50]
1810	William Sevill mortgaged Sydenhams to William Parker, a wealthy clothier from Chalford, for £4000 plus the payment of interest. It seems that Parker foreclosed because the ownership passed to William Baker. He was a relation of William Parker and had inherited from him, probably through Thomas Baker, the great nephew of William Parker[51]
1841	William Baker, 96 acres of which 45 arable O
1841	Charles Wright 35, farmer, wife and 5 children Occ
1851	Giles Driver 26, farmer of 100 acres, wife and 1 child Occ. Driver family probably owned it till 1927.
1861	Giles Driver 37, farmer of 100 acres employing 3 men and 2 boys, wife, 5 children and 1 servant Occ
1871	Giles Driver 48, farmer of 100 acres employing 1 labourer, wife and 5 children Occ

1891	George Partridge 50, farmer, 5 children and 1 farm servant Occ
1901	George Partridge 60, farmer, wife and 3 children Occ
Later	Norman Williams' grandmother, also young son Henry William Occ. Norman's grandfather was butler, probably at Edgeworth.
1920s (probably 1927)	William Lionel Clarke O bought from W.B. Driver and J.B. Driver
1936	Colonel Herbert Bland Stokes, house and 70 acres pasture, 45 of arable and 45 woodland O and Occ. Asking price had been £6,500
1936	Norman Williams rented farmland.
1954	Norman Williams, O bought farmland, 37 acres of wood, the house and two cottages. He paid £10,500. His wife (Roland and Jean's mother) did not want to live in the big old house
1954	Major General Frederick Knowles Escritt, house only O and Occ, paid £6,500
1960s	Geoffrey and Gay Cradock Watson, O and Occ, house bought for £14,000
c.1988	Charles and Ute Howard O and Occ, house bought from Mrs Cradock Watson
1998 to present	Peter and Julia Barton O and Occ

Sydenhams Farmland (Bisley) As house to 1936
DATES

1936	Norman Williams Occ
1954	Norman Williams O and Occ
1982	David Melsome O and Occ
1982	by agreement Barn sold to Geoffrey Cradock Watson

Sydenhams Farm House (Bisley) is above Sydenhams on the other side of the road. This is one of two twentieth century houses in the valleys. It was built in 1936 by Colonel Stokes for Norman Williams and, to make it more convenient, he diverted some electricity from his own generator at Sydenhams to this new house. The house was largely designed by Norman Jewson. Its form is the traditional L-plan with stone mullioned windows and leaded casements. The front doorway, with its angled porch hood, has a door to Jewson's design with ironmongery made by Alfred Bucknell of Waterlane. Internally the principal feature is the staircase. This is typical of Jewson's work with ogee tops to the newell posts and fielded shaped balusters which are derived from Gimson's furniture.[52] Norman Williams first rented the property and then bought it in 1954.

DATES

1936–54	Colonel Herbert Bland Stokes O
1937–54	Norman Williams Occ
1954–c.1975	Norman Williams O and Occ
c.1975–77	Anne Bluck O and Occ
1977–86	Dr Jim Hartwell and Mavis Hartwell O and Occ paid £32,000
1986 to present	John and Meg Weston Smith O and Occ

Timbercombe Cottage (Bisley) is in the Upper Slad Valley (see photos 31–34). It was formerly known as **Glovers Cottage**. This cottage was built in the nineteenth century and is unusual in that it is still much as it was constructed. It is now listed as an example of a two-up two-down dwelling. The Bannen family are thought to have moved there when their house at Highwood caught fire. Unfortunately, it has not been lived in since Rosie Bannen died. Planning applications have been turned down on the grounds that they altered the original cottage too much. It is in a poor state of repair.

DATES

14th century	Tymbercombe woods and family name Tymbercombe are referred to in documents.
1841/2	Timbercombe Cottage not on the tithe map or in apportionments
1891	probably one of three households mentioned in census (see Site and Ruins at Timbercombe below)
1901	(Timbercombe House) Francis Charles Driver 26, engine driver of steam roller, wife and 2 children Occ
1923	House owned by owners of Dillay Farm
1927	Frank Tombs and family, including young son Bill Tombs Occ
1932–36	approx. Frederick Hopkins, wife and children Occ
1936	Jimmy Bannen Occ with two fields and one lad
Later to 1991	Rosie Bannen Occ
1990s	Mr Heaven O
2002 to present	believed Green family through Offshore company O

Trillgate Cottage (Miserden) is to the east of Down Hill (see photo 21). It was probably built in the fourteenth or fifteenth century and was known as **The Nap** or **Knap** into the nineteenth century. It has old beams and large stone fireplace with chamfered sides. The edges of the beams are charred, suggesting that it was once a larger house, perhaps a manor.[53] It was bought by Diana Lodge with the surrounding land for £850 in 1962. She lived there until her death in 1998.

DATES

1838	The Nap was more than one cottage and garden
1838	Robert Lawrence Townsend O
1838	John Bendall, agricultural labourer Occ
	Nathaniel Hillman, stone mason Occ
	Edward Franklin, agricultural labourer Occ
	William Churches, cloth weaver Occ
1841	Edward Franklin 65, agricultural labourer, wife and 1 child Occ
	Nathaniel Hillman 65, stonemason, with wife Occ
	John Bendall 40, agricultural labourer, wife and 3 children Occ
	William Churches 75, cloth weaver, wife and 1 other Occ
1851	Nathaniel Hillman 75, stonemason, wife Occ
1861	Edward Franklin 84, agricultural labourer, son, daughter-in-law and 2 grandsons Occ
	William Masters 24, carter and wife Occ
1871	Peter Bickens 30, labourer, wife and 2 children Occ
	Abraham Ireland 38, labourer, wife and 3 children Occ
	Samuel Franklin 51, labourer, wife, 5 children and 1 boarder Occ
	Thomas Restall 52, farmer of 30 acres, wife and 3 children Occ
1891	Mary Franklin 53, widow and 3 children Occ
In WWII	Frank Eldridge Occ
1962	Diana Lodge O and Occ
1998 to present	Colin Lodge O

Trillgate House and Farm (Painswick) is just below Bulls Cross (see photo 22). It appears on a 1820 manuscript map of Painswick as **Thril Yat** and also on Greenwoods map of 1824. Built in the seventeenth century, it has a fireplace with arms. It seems originally to have been one room downstairs and one upstairs, both of grand proportions with large and beautiful mullion windows. It has been extended on both sides, probably in the nineteenth century. It was occupied by the Trotman family for over thirty years, the farm sometimes being run by women of the family. The farm was bought by a Mr James Pimbury of The Edge for £1,025 at the auction of the Steanbridge estate in 1901.[54] It was let at that time to Mr R. Trotman at a rent of £45. At the same auction Mr R. Trotman had bought Down Farm where he had been a tenant and it is likely that he later bought Trillgate Farm. In the 1980s the farmland was sold to Captain John George. The house and large terraced garden are now owned separately from the farmland.

DATES

1680	Date on fireplace
1820	Robert Lawrence Townsend O

1820	Mrs Tuffley house and 56 acres Occ and Widow Tuffley 33 acres Occ[55]
1839	Robert Lawrence Townsend O
1839	Robert Trotman Occ, farmer of 80 acres of which 60 arable
1841	Robert Trotman 65, farmer, 4 children and 1 servant Occ
1851	Edward Trotman 50, yeoman of 100 acres employing 2 men and a boy Occ
1861	Hannah Trotman 63, farmer of 100 acres employing 2 men and 1 boy in partnership with sister, 1 servant Occ
1871	Hannah Trotman 73, independent, and 2 sisters Occ
1876	Robert Trotman transferred the lease of the farm to his son Robert Trotman the younger, and his sister Hannah Trotman who had been living and farming there for some years. The new lease was for 118 acres, house and buildings and three cottages for a period of 20 years at a rent of £144 per annum.[56] The three cottages were inhabited by Abraham Ireland, Widow Dickenson and Ephraim Claridges.
1877	Robert Lawrence Townsend dies and his son of the same name inherits.
1880	Hannah Trotman dies, Robert Trotman has lease[57]
1886	Rent reduced to £106 per annum[58]
1891	Rent reduced to £70 per annum[59]
1901	Farm of 88 acres sold to Mr James Pimbury of The Edge for £1,025. Farm rented by Robert Trotman at the apportioned rent of £45[60]
Later	Cook family Occ, believed did alterations[61]
Before and during WWII, including 1926 Mr Pimbury Occ	
Later	Mr Fletcher
1965	Alan and Ivy Sinkinson Occ[62]
1980s	Roy Randall O and later another owner
1980s	farm sold to Captain John George of Down Farm
1990s house	David Bill O and Occ
1997 to present	Hugh Padgham and Cath Kidston O and Occ

Upper Steanbridge Mill (Miserden) is one of the three houses which was part of the old Upper Steanbridge Mill. It is the east part of the old mill and is L shaped, see Steanbridge Mill-Upper for history.

Woodedge (Bisley) is on the north of the Old Common (see photos 60 and 61). It was formerly known as **Woodbine Cottage**. It was probably built in the early seventeenth century as one-up one-down with staircase in the corner of the room and was extended at least twice in the mid-1900s. When considering the dwellings as they are now, it is tempting to regard them as having always been one-family houses. This is far from the truth. After 1918 Woodedge, then still small, housed at least two unrelated families and, in addition, a Mr Cox, who had been gassed in the First World War, lived in a make-shift lean-to with his family. He had been a shoemaker in Birmingham but after the war, on doctor's orders, had to live in country air. He worked for Colonel Stokes. Another neighbour from 1921 was Mr Benjamin Taylor who had also been gassed in the First World War and was living in the country away from pollution. At that time Mrs Workman, who was recovering from a stroke, owned the cottage. Arrangements were made for the Taylor family to live at Woodbine Cottage looking after Mrs Workman. When she died about 1927 the house passed to the Taylors.[63] They kept pigs, goats and chickens.

In 1936 Norman Williams lived at Woodedge. His son, Roland, was born there in 1937. Later there were a number of tenants of the cottage while ownership resided mainly with the owners of Sydenhams. From 1954 to 1967 it was owned by Norman Williams. When he sold it to Geoffrey Cradock Watson, the sale was subject to Lionel and Elsie Parker, the parents of Norman's first wife, living there rent-free for life. Then, after a number of occupants, it was sold to Jo and Annette Xuereb Brennan. Over several years the cottage was extended and improved and is now a seven-roomed house.

DATES

1841	Isaac Gardner O and Occ
1920s	Mr Cox Occ part only
1921–27	Mrs Workman O and Occ and Benjamin and Isabel Taylor and 2 children Occ
1927–29	Benjamin and Isabel Taylor O and Occ
1936	Colonel Stokes O
1936–37	Norman T Williams Occ, Roland Williams born there
1954	Norman Williams O
1967	Geoffrey Cradock Watson O. He paid £8,500 including some land below Sydenhams.[64] The arrangement was subject to Lionel and Elsie Parker, parents of Norman Williams' first wife, occupying it rent free
Later	Mr and Mrs Blake Occ
1982 to present	Joseph and Annette Xuereb Brennan O and Occ

Yew Tree Cottage (Bisley) is on the north of the Old Common. It was built in 1823–4 by Bisley Parish as an overflow for paupers of the Bisley Workhouse. It is assumed that it fell into disuse as a poor law house after the Poor Law Amendment Act of 1834.[65] In 1841 it was still owned by the Parish Officers of Bisley and occupied by Widow Driver. At one time it was owned by Norman Williams' grandmother and was largely in the ownership of the owner of Sydenhams.

DATES

1841	Parish Officers of Bisley
1841	Widow Driver Occ
Late 1890s	William and Hanna Mansell and family Occ
1936–38	Harry Jefferies Occ. He worked for Norman Williams and did a milk round. He was killed in WWII. His parents farmed at Catswood.
Later	grandmother of Norman Williams O and subsequent owners of Sydenhams
1940–41	Mr and Mrs Ruther Occ, son Brian, born there
Later	Miss Stevenson moved there from The Scrubs
1954	Norman Williams O
1965	Geoffrey Cradock Watson O, bought for £3500
1970s	Tony and Pat Nicholson Occ
1980s	Gay Cradock Watson O and Occ
1995 to present	Roger and Audrey Harding O and Occ

KNOWN RUINS AND SITES BY AREA
The areas are shown on Map 1

The Scrubs
Site East of Yew Tree Cottage (Bisley) On tithe map and in apportionments. No remains can now be seen. Thomas Dickerson lived in a cottage above Timbercombe. It was unusual for a cottage to be owned by another cottager.

DATES

1841	Thomas Dickerson O
1841	Mary Hunt Occ

Site on Far Side of Common (Bisley) is on the tithe map and in apportionments. No remains can now be seen.

DATE

1841	William Dickerson O and Occ

Site up the road from Colombine Cottage (Bisley)
In addition to the cottages in this area which are still standing, there was a long narrow building believed to be only about eight feet from back to front. Its roof

can just be seen on the early 1900s photo. It was probably a storage building though it could have been a cottage at one time.

Site of Mediæval Village east of Sydenhams (Bisley)

This is recorded in the National Monuments Record.[66]

Site of possible Temple at or near present Journeys End (Bisley)

Votive tablets have been found here.[67]

Driftcombe Valley

Ruin of Old Ale House (Bisley) The building has been a ruin since around 1900 (see photo 49). The name and location of the Old Ale House has been passed down by word of mouth. In 1974 it was possible to see where the rooms had been but now all that remains are a few stones, visible on the photo of Driftcombe Cottage. Around 1840, the cottage and the field in which it is are referred to as 'Reddings and houses' and they were occupied by Robert May. He was eighty years old and retired. In 1851 there was another Robert May living in Driftcombe Valley, though not necessarily at the Old Ale House, with wife and children. In 1861 he was still there. In 1851 he was described as an agricultural labourer but in 1861, by which time he was sixty-three, he was described as innkeeper. Mrs Timbrell said her husband remembered the Old Ale House and said that around 1890 it was open only on Sundays. The ale or beer was delivered by donkey. They would also have brewed their own beer. There are still hop plants growing on the site of the building. In 1891 Edwin Partridge lived at Driftcombe Farm and described himself as a refreshment-house keeper. He may have been connected with the Old Ale House. Opposite the Old Ale House is Driftcombe Cottage, where in 1938 a part was described as a brewhouse. This too may have had a connection with the Old Ale House.

DATES

1841	Robert Lawrence Townsend O
1841	Robert May, probably aged 80, Occ
1851 and 1861	Another Robert May there or nearby Occ

Ruins of Two Houses behind Driftcombe Farm (Bisley) Very little is known about them except that according to the Tithe map of 1840, they and Driftcombe Cottage were owned and occupied by Henry and William Davis. William Davis lived in one of them with his family including four children and Henry Davis lived in the other. The latter had a wife and one child. These families do not seem to have been living there in 1851. There are large bay trees in what would have been their front gardens. Mrs Timbrell said she remembered people living in the cottages so that would mean they were still there say 1895 to 1900. She said the cottages were owned by Mr Driver of Cirencester. They were later owned by George Partridge of Sydenhams. When they were bought from him by Revd Herford, Bishop of Mercia in 1903 they were described as ruined. They probably fell into disuse around 1900.

DATES

1841	Henry and William Davis O and Occ (also Driftcombe Cottage)
Later	Mr Driver of Cirencester O
1903 and earlier	George Partridge of Sydenhams O
1903	Revd Herford, Bishop of Mercia O (already in ruins) bought with several other cottages and ruins for £130
1938	Revd Herford dies
Present	site belongs to Driftcombe Cottage

Ruins below St Benedicts (Bisley) Ruined early in twentieth century. In the woods above the garage near to Greencourt and below St Benedicts there are still ruins. Curiously no house is marked on the tithe map of about 1840. Mrs Timbrell said that there were two houses there of which one was lived in by the preacher on the Easter tea party photo about 1900 (see Chapter 8). The house can, with imagination, be seen in the trees on The Scrubs photo 35 of about 1910. Some of the stones were used in the renovation of St Benedicts in the early 1960s.

DATES

1842	not on tithe map
c. 1900	two houses

Site of Piedmont House and Farm (Bisley) Once known as **Jordans**. The house was probably in existence in the seventeenth century. An early reference to Piedmont is found in the Bisley school records. There was a boy in 1756 at the Blue Boys School referred to as David the son of David (or Daniel) Bucher of Pidemount. However on 5th May he was turned out for 'not keeping the school'.[68] Also in 1756, Piedmont was described as the largest of a group of eight cottages recorded in Custom Scrubs and Nottingham Scrubs.[69] Piedmont is referred to in a late eighteenth century paper among the deeds of Lypiatt where it is spelt Pidemont.[70] In 1788 Theyer Townsend bought the farm of a little under fifty acres for £700.[71]

Piedmont Farm in 1841 was on the south slopes of the Slad Brook. Unusually, almost all of its seventy-nine acres was pasture. It was farmed by Charles Gardner, who later farmed Down Farm. The land he rented included the place in Stonedge field where Piedmont House stood and also Piedmont Orchard which was below the old Primitive Methodist Chapel now Scrubs Bottom.

The house is marked on the tithe map but it is not numbered and therefore not in the apportionments. The site of the house lies north of the hedge that goes down to the Roman Bridge just a few yards below the five-barred gate. In the former rubbish dump by the hunting gate there was a ten foot well. Some thirty years ago it was possible to trace the boundaries of the garden of Piedmont by standing at Snows Farm and looking across, but the trees and undergrowth have grown so that is no longer possible. In the wall nearby is dressed stone which presumably came from the house. The house would once have been on the track going down to the Roman Bridge, which is now enclosed between two fences and overgrown. Charles Gardner, who farmed Piedmont Farm, did not live in Piedmont House which, for a well-to-do farmer, would have been too modest a dwelling. By the standards of cottagers, however, it was a big house of about four rooms, as remembered by Lizzie Timbrell. In 1841 it was inhabited by a farm labourer, Henry May. This may be the Henry May who was party to the inventory for the land for the Primitive Methodist Chapel. He was described as a labourer from Custom Scrubs. He could not sign his name and simply made a mark. It was later owned by Snows Farm.

Mrs Timbrell helped to knock the house down when she was a schoolgirl, say 1895–1900. She helped load the stone into a cart. It was to be used in construction of a house for one of the Winterbotham family of clothiers.

There has been much local discussion as to the origin of the name Piedmont and precisely the area to which the name referred. It had over time a number of different spellings. See also Appendix 2 on Place Names.

DATE	
1756	referred to in documents
End 18th century	referred to in deeds of Lypiatt Place
Before 1788	occupiers included Walter West and John Woosfall Occ
1788 and earlier	Thomas Baghott and Thomas Baghott Delabere O (with over 40 acres)
1788	Theyer Townsend of Steanbridge O
1841	house, Henry May 40, agricultural labourer, wife, 3 children and 1 servant Occ
1841	farmland, Charles Gardner Occ
1861	John Woolley 40, carter, wife (agricultural labourer), 1 child and visitor Occ
Pre-1895	Ayers family O and farm labourer Occ
Between 1895 and 1900	house knocked down

Main Slad Valley

Ruin of Snows Mill (Bisley) also known as **Down Mill,** for example, in census of 1841. It is shown in 1823–4 on Bryant's Map of Gloucestershire as Snows Mill (see photo 27). It lies below and to the south of Snows Farm. Its date of construction is not known. It was said to have been a flock mill at one time and later a corn mill. It was bought by Theyer Townsend, probably in 1792. One of the occupiers of Down Court in 1851 was described as a miller. In 1860 it was leased to George Ayer with Snows Farm as the 'water, corn or grist mill with the cottage garden and appurtenances'. In the late nineteenth century while it was a corn mill there was also a baker's shop there. All that remains now is the depression of the mill pond and a wall, about 3 foot high, linked presumably to the mill machinery.

DATES

1780	Elizabeth Rogers of Arlingham
1792	date probably acquired by the Townsend family. It was a corn mill.
1841	George Harding 20, miller, and Henry Minching 25, agricultural labourer Occ
1860	leased with Snows Farm by George Ayers from Robert Lawrence Townsend[72]
Late 19th century	mill and a baker's shop
Before 1960s	buildings had disappeared.

Ruin on Down Hill (Miserden) once known as **Shepherd's Cottage**. The date of construction is unknown but probably seventeenth century (see photo 28 of 1974 and note well-crafted windows). The cottage was originally one-up, one-down with the stairs in the back corner beside the fireplace as was usual. It fell into disuse as a cottage by the early 1900s. It was used by Mr Mansell of St Benedicts to make hurdles during the winter. It was also once used to make harnesses for horses. The photo of the ruined house taken in 1974 presented a problem because when the author tried to find it again nearly thirty years later it could not be found. Finally a few stones were discovered and it was confirmed by the person who helped to knock it down that it was indeed what had been known as Shepherd's Cottage. Much of the stone, although not the windows, was reused at Down Farm.

DATES

1838	Robert Lawrence Townsend O
1838	Thomas Ireland Occ
Late 19th century	used as a barn

Early 20th century	used by Mr Mansell to make hurdles in the winter. It had also been used to make harnesses for horses.
1974	a ruin (see photo)
Later	Stone removed for use at Down Farm
2002	just a small heap of rubble

Site of Detcombe (Painswick) is behind Down Hill and below Bulls Cross. In 1820 it was described as cottages and gardens (in the plural). There was one cottage and garden on the tithe map but in the census of 1851 there were three inhabited cottages and two uninhabited dwellings. The cottage referred to in Laurie Lee's *Cider with Rosie*[73] as Hangmans House where Laurie Lee used to play as a child was situated at Detcombe,or Deadcombe Bottom, as he called it. It is understood that it was possible to see where cottages had been until the 1960s or even later, but no trace of any cottages there has now been found.

DATES

1820	Robert Lawrence Townsend O
1820	Jane Cooke, Thomas Verender, John Burdock and Henry Merchant Occ[74]
1839	Robert Lawrence Townsend O
1839	Paul King Occ
1841	Thomas Birt 35, gardener, wife (woollen clothworker) Occ
	Jane King 75, woollen spinner Occ
	Nathaniel Cook 40, agricultural labourer, wife and 4 children Occ
	John Burdock 55, agricultural labourer, wife and 1 child Occ
1851	William Clapham 57, farm labourer, wife, 1 child and visitor Occ
	Ann Murdock 30, charwoman, daughter and sister Occ
	Jonas Woodward 66, agricultural labourer, wife and 2 children Occ
1861	Joseph Partridge 52, agricultural labourer, wife and 4 children Occ
1871	John Partridge 27, farmer of 6 acres, wife (cloth worker), 3 children and visitor Occ

Site of Cottage on Down Common (Miserden) Very little is known of this cottage or cottages, situated where the path through the wood, in which the Old Shop ruins are to be found, now comes out onto arable fields. In 1851 two uninhabited cottages were mentioned under the heading of Down Common. There is still some sign of a former building: a flat piece of land and a large heap of stones.

Site of Cottage in Down Wood (Miserden) In the census of 1841 Down Wood is mentioned as having one dwelling lived in by George Hawkins, agricultural labourer with wife and five children. The location is not known.

Site of Possible Roman Building

Signs of a Roman building have been found below and between Snows Farm and Down Farm.[75]

Site of a Tenement called Sidenham and another (unnamed) in area near Piedmont and Timbercombe

An indenture of 1788[76] identifies these two sites as well as that of Stonedge House as being no longer there.

Site of Steanbridge Mill—Lower (Painswick) also known as the Weaving Mill or The Slad Mill (see photo 5). This mill was in existence in the early seventeenth century. It was a woollen mill until at least 1854. It is depicted to the right of Steanbridge House in the murals painted between 1815 and 1830 at Bishop's Cleeve Old Rectory as a typical Cotswold, very domestic style building, two-storey with mullion windows. It was still standing in 1895 but has since been demolished. The mill pond lies between the present house called Steanbridge Mill and Steanbridge House. It is referred to in *Cider with Rosie*, especially in connection with the suicide of Miss Flynn.[77]

DATES

1608	probably worked by Richard Webb when he owned the water-course to his mill[78]
Early 18th century	owned by Henry Townsend and later William Townsend
1815	Mr Driver Occ
1820	Robert Lawrence Townsend O
1820	BenjaminWood tenant[79]
1830	Robert Lawrence Townsend Junior O
1836	leased to Nathaniel Samuel Marling
1849	Mathew Lister making cloth at Slad Mill
1854	Marling sublet it to Horatio Collier. It is described as a fulling mill with 3 stocks and 2 large water wheels. It was fed from a leat which came from a pond higher up the valley. Lease included four racks on Rack Hill.
1895	still standing but later demolished.

Upper Slad Valley

Ruin of Highwood Farm (Bisley) was a small farm but it was only a house by 1891 when Lizzie Timbrell (née Mansell) was born there. Photo 33 of about 1910 shows a pleasant house. It is thought that Rosie Bannen and her father lived there in the early 1930s before they moved to Timbercombe Cottage but that there was a fire and it became derelict (see photo 34). The remaining ground floor is used as a barn.

DATES

1841	Thomas Bishop 75, farmer of 40 acres, wife Occ
1851	Thomas Bishop 87, farmer of 40 acres, wife, lodger and servant Occ
1891	William Mansell 39, carpenter, wife and 3 children Occ
1901	uninhabited
Early 1930s	Jimmy Bannen and daughter Rosie probably lived there
c.1937	derelict
2004	a shed

Ruin of Old Shop (Miserden) (see photo 41). The Old Shop was already old in 1838 and the area where it was situated was called the Old Shop Ground. Its use or uses are the subject of much handed-down anecdotes and speculation. They include gin and prostitution, a bake-house, a retail shop, a cloth workshop and a farriers. It may have been all of them in its history. There is now very little left but a photo of the ruin in the 1960s shows it before the chimney fell down.

DATES

1841	Daniel Davis 60, labourer, wife and 3 children Occ
1851	William Dickenson 43, farm labourer, wife and 2 children, farm labourer Occ
1861	William Dickenson 52, farm labourer, wife and 1 child Occ
1871	William Dickenson 63, farm labourer, wife Occ
1926	Shown on the ordnance survey map as 'in ruins'

Site of Stonedge House (Bisley) Stonedge House is mentioned in a deed of 1708 and was already in existence in the seventeenth century.[80] Its exact site is not known but there is a flat piece of ground below Stonedge Wood which seems a likely site and, at one time, there was some dressed stone in a field wall there. In a deed of 1788[81] there is a reference to where Stonedge House formerly stood. It must have been fairly important to have been mentioned by name and was probably recently demolished. It is possible that a cottage was later built on that site. Lizzie Timbrell used to play as a child in a ruin which they called Suicide Cottage because of what had once happened there. This may have been built on the site of Stonedge.

Site and Ruins at Timbercombe (Bisley) Timbercombe is mentioned in fourteenth century documents onwards, often simply referring to the manorial woods.[82] Timbercombe seems to have been fairly important in the eighteenth century, It was part of a marriage settlement in 1700.[83] In 1706 or 1707 there was a conveyance of a house and land in Tymbercombe referring to a messuage called **Lynnetts** with garden and two barns with close called Overbottom ½ acre, lately planted with fruit trees.[84] There is a will of William Sewell of Timbercombe, yeoman, dated 25 March 1708 who left to his son William Sewell 'his two pieces of arable and pasture land, called the two Gratton Grounds, presently mortgaged for £40 lying below the house called Stonedge House and if dead to other children …'[85] (Gratton and Stonedge are in lands of Piedmont see above). A document of 1732 lists a ground called Timbercombe in Fee of the Manor of Sturmye's Court as being held by the Feoffees of Bisley and let from then on in yearly tenancies.[86]

There is one cottage at Timbercombe still in existence (see above). In addition, it is still possible to see the location of the walls of two or possibly three cottages situated on the steep path from the old Scrubs Common. These may have been the cottages under the name Timbercombe in 1891. Mrs Timbrell remembered them being inhabited around 1900. Later Mrs Timbrell's brothers (Mansells) bought the more derelict one with an orchard.

DATES

1354	Walter Tymbercombe arranges for his son to remain on his land[87]
Between 1361 and 1398	Johannes Trymbercombe was on the Pannella Comitatas for the Hundred of Bisley (Hundredum de Byseleye)[88]
Time of Henry VI	was part of Overcourt Manor and mentioned in connection with the sale of faggots.
1450–51	mentioned in Ministers accounts 29 Henry VI[89]
1547	land again referred to in documents[90]
1700	part of a marriage settlement
1706 or 07	Conveyance of house and land
1708	Will of William Sewell, yeoman, left Gratton Grounds to son
1732	Timbercombe in Fee to the Manor of Sturmye's Court, held by the Feoffees of Bisley and let from then on in yearly tenancies.
1841	Houses and gardens not on tithe map
1891	Three Timbercombe dwellings mentioned: Timbercombe House, Enoch Driver 72, retired farmer Occ Timbercombe Cottage, Joseph Hunt 52, general labourer, and wife Occ Timbercombe Cottage, Charles Woodward 25, agricultural labourer, wife and 4 sons (3 illegitimate) Occ

One of these three may be the Timbercombe Cottage which is still in existence, see above.

Site and Ruins at Nottingham Scrubs (Bisley)

Higher up the Valley from Timbercombe and opposite Dillay Farm there were three cottages marked on the tithe map. One is now Beech Cottage (see above). The second is no longer visible but there is a ruin of the third which would have been a one-up, one-down cottage. The last two were in 1841 owned and occupied by the same person.

DATES (Cottage 2)

1841   Moses Hunt 45, agricultural labourer, wife, 4 children and one lodger O and Occ

1851   Moses Hunt 56, agricultural labourer, wife, 2 children and 2 lodgers (under heading of Scrubs) Occ

1861   Moses Hunt 67, agricultural labourer, son, son's wife and 3 children (under heading of Nottingham Scrubs) Occ

DATE (Cottage 3)

1841   Moses Hunt O and Occ

Site and ruins east of Dillay Farm on the same side of the stream (Miserden)

A cottage and garden is marked on the tithe map for Miserden and in the apportionments.

DATES

1838   John Partridge O

1838   James Ireland and William Nicholls Occ

Dillay Bottom (Miserden)

Dillay Farm, Timbercombe, Highwood Farm and cottages at Nottingham Scrubs and perhaps the cottage east of Dillay have been known as Dillay Bottom. An article in the *Stroud News and Gloucester County Advertiser* in 1947[91] described them as a lost village and says that the locals living there at the time said that there had been a pub and a shop. Indeed the community may have extended further up the valley, though the higher up the more likely that the connection of the population was to Camp or Bisley rather than to Dillay.

Special note on The Vatch

The Vatch is not included in the area covered by this book. It was however important to the Valley because many of the cloth workers from the area would have walked to work in The Vatch. They would have become embroiled in the unrest which sometimes erupted. For that reason a note on The Vatch is included here. The Vatch was once known as Veyseys or a name with similar spelling. There was at least one mill at The Vatch as early as the thirteenth century.

Later there were at least three mills at The Vatch. One was a paper mill called Hermitage Mill, but also sometimes Vatch Mill. There were two mills which were woollen mills for most of their existence: the main Vatch Mill and Upper Vatch Mill.

The main Vatch Mill lay at the junction of the Slad stream and a small stream that enters it. The pond is still there. It was a grist mill at the end of the sixteenth century. In 1592 the Lord of the Manor sold it to Thomas Clissold and that family owned it for much of the seventeenth and eighteenth centuries. It was probably a fulling mill early in the seventeenth century. By 1820 Nathaniel Marling was in occupation and he told the factory inspectors that it was burnt down and rebuilt in 1827. No record has been found as to whether the fire was connected to the unrest at the mill which had turned very ugly in the weavers' riots of 1825. The industry was in recession after the prosperity of the Napoleonic wars; the introduction of machinery, especially the flying shuttle, had pushed the hand loom weavers in particular into dire poverty. The riots were specifically about the payment for work done. The riots were widespread in the Frome valleys and there were riots at The Vatch which caused much damage. When the mill was rebuilt, it contained three steam engines which produced 66 hp and two water wheels of 12 hp each. In 1838 Marling installed six power looms in the mill, in addition to the fifty-five hand looms which he already had there. In the Vatch Mill every process of cloth manufacture was carried out.[92]

In 1862 the Vatch Mill employed 300–400 persons.[93] According to a funeral note of Robert Hastings, who died in 1908 having been owner of the Vatch Mills from 1863, he employed 400–500 persons at The Vatch, drawn from a wide area including The Scrubs. Senior local residents of Slad in 1957 described the Vatch Mill as having had 600 or so workers.[94]

The Vatch Mill was demolished during the 1890s. When the chimney fell a bystander was killed.[95]

Upstream from there was the Upper Vatch Mill which was run in tandem with the main mill for much of the time. For much of its life it was a fulling mill, although the Victoria County History reports that it was at one time a paper mill.[96] In the 1830s it was owned and occupied by Nathaniel Samuel Marling. Replies to the factory inspectors in 1834 state that at Upper Vatch Mill, rebuilt in 1830, the ground floors were used for fulling by water power and the upper floors were used for hand weaving.

DATES
The Vatch Mill
1517   Thomas Solan (or Zelam) Occ

1592	Lord of the Manor sold as a grist mill, known as Fetch Mill
1592	Thomas Clissold O till at least 1612[97] (Pugh 1976 p 127)
1656	Mrs Clissold, widow, and another Thomas Clissold[98] (Pugh 1976 p.127) O
Early 17th century	probably a fulling mill
1724	another Thomas Clissold O
1768	advertised for letting (Pugh 1976 p127)
1811	Henry Wyatt Occ till at least 1822
1820	Mr Mason O
1820	Nathaniel Samuel Marling Occ
1825	Weavers' riots
1827	Rebuilt after a fire
1830s	Nathaniel Samuel Marling O and Occ
1838	Marling installed 6 power looms in addition to the existing 55 hand looms
1842 to at least 1856	William Fluck O and Occ
1863 to c.1877	Robert Hastings O and Occ
1877	Mill for sale
1901	had been demolished. Bystander killed by falling of demolished chimney

Upper Vatch Mill

1776	Francis Chapman Occ, paper mill
1794	William Ward Occ, paper mill
1822	Edward Mason O and Occ, fulling mill
1830 to at least 1840	Nathaniel Samuel Marling O and Occ
1882	disused
1901	had been demolished

1. NMR Monument Report 114873 Alleged former Monastery, now cottages, NMR SO 80 NE 8, Grid Ref SO 8907 0790

2. Verey, David and Brooks, Alan (1999) *Gloucestershire: The Cotswolds*, Buildings of England Series, London: Penguin

3. Gloucestershire Records Office (GRO) D2299/7449 Bruton Knowles Lists: Dillay Farm,1923

4. GRO D2299/7449 see 3 above

5. GRO D2056/6 Purchase by Robert Lawrence Townsend from the Overseers of the Poor of Miserdine of two cottages on Downhill 1840

6. *The Slad Valley News* (1981) September and *The Slad Valley News* (1984) June

7.   GRO D2080/77 Inventory and Sale of property at Down Farm, 1810
8.   GRO D2080/77 see 7 above
9.   GRO D1815 Townsend (Location 7.79.3) Documents relating to the Townsend family and estates and leases for Down Farm, Trillgate Farm and Snows Farm, 19th century
10. GRO D1815 Townsend (Location 7.79.3) see 9 above
11. GRO D1815 Townsend (Location 7.79.3) see 9 above
12. *Gloucester Journal* 6th July 1901 'Important Sale of Property at Stroud'
13. GRO D2299/8469 Bruton Knowles Lists Down Farm 1946 and *Gloucester Journal* 3rd July 1909 Report on the sale of Down Farm on 30th June 1909
14. GRO D2299/8469 Bruton Knowles Lists Down Farm 1946
15. Deeds relating to Driftcombe Farm by permission of the late Rodney Smith
16. Deeds relating to Driftcombe Farm see 15 above
17. GRO D745 M6, Bisley Manor Court Records
18. GRO D1241, Box 29, vol 5 Inland Revenue Estate Duty documents, 1879–1902
19. National Monument Report 114873 Alleged former Monastery, now cottages, NMR SO 80 NE 8, Grid Ref SO 8907 0790
20. GRO D1405 2/153 Sale of properties after the death of the Revd Herford, Bishop of Mercia, 1939
21. National Monument Report 114873 see 19 above
22. GRO D1405 2/153 see 20 above
23. National Monuments Report 114873 see 19 above
24. National Monuments Report 114873 see 19 above
25. GRO D1815 Townsend (Location 7.79.3) see 9 above
26. GRO D2056/1–7 Various indentures for purchase of land and buildings in the Valley
27. *Gloucester Journal* 6th July 1901 'Important Sale of Property at Stroud'
28. Lee, Laurie (1959) *Cider with Rosie,* Hogarth Press, Penguin edition, 1962
29. *Stroud News and Journal,* 27th May 1971
30. GRO P244a M1 1/5 Painswick Parish Map of 1820 and references
31. GRO D1815 Townsend (Location 7.79.3) see 9 above
32. GRO D2056/7 Sale of Steanbridge Mill to Theyer Townsend in 1781 and arrangement over a mortgage involving Samuel Clutterbuck 1791 and other documents
33. *Stroud News and Journal,* 27th May 1971
34. Pugh, R. B. (ed.) (1976) *The Victoria History of the County of Gloucestershire,* Vol. XI, published for the University of London, Institute of Historical Research by OUP, p.53
35. *Gloucester Journal* 7th February 1774 Sale of stock in trade of James Woodfield
36. GRO D2056/7 see 32 above
37. Pugh, R. B. (ed.) (1976), *op. cit.* p.53

38. Census and Hyett, F. A. (1957) *Glimpses of the History of Painswick,* Gloucester: The British Publishing Co Ltd, p.78

39. *Gloucester Journal* 6th July 1901 see 27 above

40. GRO D2299/5386 Bruton Knowles Lists Steanbridge Farm 1928

41. GRO D2299/5386 see 40 above

42. Verey, David and Brooks, Alan (1999), *op. cit.*

43. GRO D2299/5938 Bruton Knowles Lists Sydenhams, 1936

44. Rudd, Mary A (1937) *Historical Records of Bisley*, Published privately, Edn 1977, Alan Sutton, p.84

45. Rudd, Mary A. (1937), *op. cit.* p.84

46. Pugh, R. B. (ed.) (1976), *op. cit.* p.7

47. Rudd, Mary A. (1937), *op. cit.* p.85

48. GRO D269B/T10 Deed of 1632 relating to property in Over Lyppiat

49. GRO D1388/III/10 Schedule of deeds relating to Sydenhams 1641–1810

50. GRO D1388/III/10 see 49 above

51. Oakridge Historical Research Group, 'Watercombe House: A history of ownership' undated

52. Hill, Michael (1987) unpublished note on Sydenhams Farmhouse. By permission of Mrs M. Weston Smith

53. *The Slad Valley News* (1986) September

54. *Gloucester Journal* 6th July 1901 see 27 above

55. GRO P244a M1 1/5 Painswick Parish Map of 1820 and references

56. GRO D1815 Townsend (Location 7.79.3) see 9 above

57. GRO D1815 Townsend (Location 7.79.3) see 9 above

58. GRO D1815 Townsend (Location 7.79.3) see 9 above

59. GRO D1815 Townsend (Location 7.79.3) see 9 above

60. *Gloucester Journal* 6th July 1901 see 27 above

61. Pugh, R. B. (ed.) (1976), *op. cit.* p.65

62. *The Slad Valley News* (2004) Autumn, '1965 Electoral Register'

63. Richard, Mrs Kathleen née Taylor by permission of her son-in-law, Dave Smith

64. Deeds relating to Woodedge—by permission of Jo and Annette Xuereb Brennan

65. Pugh, R. B. (ed.) (1976), *op. cit.* p.31 and Letter from County Archivist to J. Duce Esq, 25.8.1987 in GRO

66. NMR Monument Report 114916 Deserted Mediaeval Village at Sydenhams, NMR SO 80 NE 39, Grid Ref SO 898 078

67. NMR Monuments Report 114865 Three Roman altars found at Custom Scrubs indicating a possible temple site, NMR SO80 NE4, Grid Ref SO 8907 0802

68. GRO D149 R39 Bisley Blue Boy School records 1754–1761

69. Pugh, R. B. (ed.) (1976), *op. cit.* p.7

70. Rudd, Mary A. (1937), *op. cit.* p.85

71. GRO D2056/2 Indenture and Bargain and Sale for Piedmount House and Land, 7th September 1788
72. GRO D1815 Townsend (Location 7.79.3) see 9 above
73. Lee, Laurie (1959), *op. cit.* p.35
74. GRO P244a M1 1/5 see 30 above
75. NMR Monument Report 114887 Possible Site of Roman Building NMR SO 80 NE 16, Grid Ref SO 882 081
76. GRO D2056/2 see 71 above
77. Lee, Laurie (1959), *op. cit.* pp.94–104
78. Tann, Jennifer (1967) *Gloucestershire Woollen Mills*, Newton Abbott: David and Charles, p.215; GRO P244a M1 1/5 Painswick Parish Map of 1820 and references
79. Rudd, Mary A (1937), *op. cit.* p.111
80. GRO D2056/2 see 71 above
81. GRO D2819 Box 16 Victoria County History Notes on the Parish of Bisley
82. GRO D149/T12 Documents relating to Timbercombe 1701–1707
83. GRO D149/T13 Documents relating to Timbercombe 1701–1707
84. Rudd, Mary A. (1937), *op. cit.* p.111
85. Rudd, Mary A. (1937), *op. cit.* p.199
86. Page, William (ed.) (1907) *The Victoria History of the County of Gloucester*, Vol. II published for the University of London, Institute of Historical Research, reprinted Dawsons of Pall Mall 1972, p130
87. Kimball, Elisabeth Guernsey (ed.) (1940) 'Gloucestershire Peace Rolls 1361–98', *Transactions of the Bristol and Gloucestershire Archaeological Society*, Vol. 62
88. Rudd, Mary A. (1937), *op. cit.* p.399
89. Rudd, Mary A. (1937), *op. cit.* p.399
90. *Stroud News and Gloucester County Advertiser*, Spring 1947 'In search of a lost village: a visit to Dillay Bottom'
91. Davies, Gwladys (*c.*1905) 'Mills of the Slad Valley' typescript in Gloucestershire Local Studies Library
92. *Gloucester Journal* 10th May 1862 Employment at Vatch Mill
93. Crump L. M. (ed.) (undated) 'The Slad; The Story of our Village in Living Memory 1850–1957', Typescript
94. Beard, Howard (1997) *Painswick, Sheepscombe, Slad and Edge,* Archive Photograph Series, Chalford: Chalford Publishing Co.
95. Pugh, R. B. (ed.) (1976), *op. cit.* p.127
96. Pugh, R. B. (ed.) (1976), *op. cit.* p.127
97. Pugh, R. B. (ed.) (1976), *op. cit.* p.127

Appendix 1

Processes of the Woollen Industry in the Stroud Valleys

Various types of cloth were produced in the Stroud valleys, and therefore the processes varied. The most famous cloth was a dense smooth broadcloth in which no individual threads were visible. The processes for its production are different from those of some other cloths, notably worsted, especially in that it required fulling, a process by which the woven cloth was shrunk. Another difference is that the broad loom required two persons to do the weaving until the introduction of the flying shuttle. Another cloth produced locally, including in these valleys, was cassimere or kerseymere for which a patent was taken out by Francis Yerbury in 1766. The main processes involved in production were as follows:

Scribbling, Combing and Carding: There were several stages in the preparation of the wool for spinning and weaving. The fresh wool was washed, often on the sheep before shearing, and dried. Then the fleeces were pulled apart and sorted and for some cloths, notably Spanish medley, the wool was then dyed. To make the wool easier to manage at the spinning and weaving stages, some sort of oil or grease was applied and extraneous matter was removed by a process known as scribbling. After that, there was a difference in the way short and long staple wool was treated. For long staple wool, intended for the production of worsted, combing was the next task, mainly undertaken by artisans in Cirencester and Tetbury. For the short staple wool, intended for broadcloth, a card with spikes on it smoothed and prepared it for spinning. These processes were carried out by hand in the workers' homes, usually by women and children, but were eventually transferred to factories. Carding machines were introduced into Gloucestershire by a Stroud millwright called Stephen Price in the early nineteenth century. He produced them in Acre Street in Stroud. They helped to perfect the finish of the fine wool used for Stroud district cloth. The scribbling process was mechanised about the same time.

Spinning: The process by which the wool is drawn out to a single continuous thread is known as spinning. As with carding, it was traditionally a home occupation undertaken by women and children. The 'spinning jenny', which was invented by John Hargreaves and patented in 1770, enabled several spindles to be worked at one time. It could be used either in houses or in mills. Some of the first recorded spinning jennies in the Stroud area were worked in the Stroud Market House in the 1790s. One of the mills in the area of this book was called the Jenny Mill. In 1838 William Playne, a major Stroud clothier, commented how the spinning jenny, in improving the quality of the thread, had greatly increased the productivity of weavers. However by 1840 Playne had stopped using the jenny and switched to the mule with even greater productivity. Twenty years later the mule was established in factories worked by steam (Mackintosh 1993a).[1] The spinning of wool for cassimere was different from that for broadcloth, with different proportions of wool for warp and weft and another type of twist.

Sizing and Warp Winding: The spun thread was treated with a sort of weak glue to make it easier to weave smoothly and then wound into lengths suitable for looms, known as chains, for the warp.

Weaving: Cloth is produced on a loom by weaving weft threads through the warp threads. Broad looms originally needed two persons to work the loom but the introduction of the flying shuttle enabled one person to weave the broadcloth. The flying shuttle was introduced into the Stroud valleys by Nathaniel Watts at Wallbridge Mill in the 1790s.[2] Cassimeres were woven on a narrow loom with a two and two twill weave.

Weaving was the last of the cloth-making processes to go into factories. At first the hand looms were introduced in to factories so that, from about 1800, the hand loom weavers may have worked either at home or in factories. The law of that time was that no weaver could have more than two looms. In 1802 there were no looms in factories in Stroud,[3] although there were some in nearby areas and they increased in the first decades of the nineteenth century. By 1840 most of the manufacturers in the county had installed looms in their mills. At Vatch Mill, by 1838 there were fifty-five hand looms and six power looms. Power looms were probably introduced from around 1830. Initially they used water power but later steam power or a combination of the two.

Mending and Burling: Menders checked for any broken threads. This was followed by burling which is the process whereby small bits of vegetable matter and any knots are removed from the woven cloth with tweezers. These tasks were carried out mainly in the home with the weaving and presumably later moved to the factory.

Scouring and Fulling: When the cloth was woven it was beaten using originally stale urine for its ammonia content, to remove the oil and size used in spinning and weaving. It was then ready for fulling, sometimes known as tucking. This process was a special feature of the production of broadcloth. Using a little water and fuller's earth or later, soap, the cloth was hammered for about twelve hours or much more, according to the quality of the wool and the cloth required, to shrink and thicken it. At one time this process was undertaken using human feet stamping in large pans but it was mechanised as early as the twelfth century and machines were recorded in Gloucestershire about 1270. Fulling was the earliest of the woollen industry processes to be taken into factories. Two wooden hammers called stocks were raised and lowered alternately using water power. This needed skilled supervision to ensure that the shrinking was even. Cassimeres were fulled less heavily than broadcloth. Vatch Mill was probably a fulling mill by the early seventeenth century.[4] Between 1840 and 1850 a milling machine started to supersede the old fulling process.

Roughing or Gigging: After fulling, the nap of the cloth was raised. This was done by hand using teasles but a machine called a gig was invented in the sixteenth century using teasles attached to rollers. There was opposition by the cloth-workers to gig mills because they greatly reduced the labour required. In the 1550s a law was passed making gig mills illegal, except in Gloucestershire where gig mills were already well established and developed further in the seventeenth century. It is said that clothiers in other parts of the country did not generally favour gig mills because they thought that their use disguised imperfections in the cloth. Nevertheless other areas sent their cloth to Gloucestershire to be gigged.

Shearing: This is a very skilled process by which the knap raised by the teazles is removed and the cloth made smooth. An improved machine for shearing, using a rotary action, was introduced by Lewis brothers of Brimscombe around 1815.[5]

Dyeing: Traditional broadcloth was sent to London or abroad undyed or was dyed in the piece, that is, at the end of the whole process. For some cloths dying was done in the wool at the start of the process. Dyeing was a specialist activity housed in separate sheds rather than in the clothiers' mills. Dyed cloth was dried and stretched on tenter racks in the fields or occasionally in a special building. The Stroud cloth was traditionally red, though other colours were produced. A painting of about 1760 in the Stroud Museum shows the red cloth in the fields in the Stroud valleys.

1.   Mackintosh, Ian D (1993) 'The Playnes and Industrial Change', Typescript, Jan 1993
2.   Loosley, John (1993) *The Stroudwater Riots of 1825*, Stroud, Glos: The Stroud Museum Association, p.2
3.   Tann, Jennifer (1967) *Gloucestershire Woollen Mills*, Newton Abbott: David and Charles, p.48
4.   Tann, Jennifer (1967), *op. cit.* p.213
5.   Mackintosh, Ian D. *op. cit.*

Appendix 2

Place Names

There are three problems with place names: how they are spelt, what they mean and exactly what they refer to. Some important names which feature in this book will be discussed in alphabetical order. Changes in house names are mentioned under the entry for the property.

Custom Scrubs (sometimes Custom Scrubbs)
Custom Scrubs is the name given to an area, largely synonymous with the old Common in the Scrubs. The name denotes that there were certain rights of the inhabitants, such as gathering of wood and possibly grazing of cattle or pigs. It was used in the census of 1841 but after that date was replaced in many documents by The Scrubs.

Driftcombe
Driftcombe is the name of a former farm, now a house, in the valley below Sydenhams. It is also the name of a cottage near Driftcombe Farm. Until recently August Cottage was also known as Driftcombe Cottage.

In the census of 1851 it refers to eleven cottages believed to be those lowest down in the valley along the track from Driftcombe Farm to the Primitive Methodist Chapel and probably taking in St Benedicts Cottage and Piedmont. It is used in this sense in this book to describe that area (see Map 1).

In Bryant's map of 1823–4 it is spelt Drifcomb

Miserden Parish
Miserden parish until 1958 included most of the Slad Valley as far as Steanbridge. In 1958 most of this rather thin tongue of land relatively far from Miserden village became part of Painswick Parish, but a part was included in Bisley Parish. The Victoria County History continues to use the old parish to describe the area because most of their interest is in the period prior to 1958. Similarly, in the Gazetteer in this book the old parishes are retained.

Painswick Parish
See entry under Miserden Parish

Piedmont

There has been some confusion as to the origin of the name Piedmont and on the house and land to which it refers. The name has variously been spelt as Pidemont or Pidemount

The most precise description of the area or property covered by the term Piedmont is that contained in the tithe map and apportionments of about 1840. The seventy-nine acres of farmland of Piedmont stretched from Piedmont Orchard (below the Primitive Methodist Chapel) along the south side of the Slad Valley (see Map 6). Piedmont Farm had been sold to Theyer Townsend in 1788.[1] At that time the boundaries were not the same as in 1840 and the farm was then less than fifty acres. At some time before 1788 it was known as **Jordans**.

Piedmont Farm house was on the flat piece of ground below the gate next to the old track going down from the Driftcombe Valley to the 'Roman Bridge'. Until a few years ago it had been possible to identify the site looking across from Snows Farm but the vegetation is now too dense to see it (see Map 5). In the tithe map the square marking the location of this house did not have against it 'house and garden' as would be expected and it is not numbered and therefore not in the apportionments. However, in the first inch to the mile Ordnance Survey map of 1828, the name Piedmont refers to the house as shown on the tithe map. In the 1851 census there is no specific mention of Piedmont. It would have been included in the houses under The Scrubs or Driftcombe. After the house was knocked down about 1900, the map-makers didn't seem to know what the name referred to and moved it along to find some buildings, ending up near to the terrace of three houses. Because of the position of the name Piedmont on the recent Ordnance Survey maps, the whole area of the Driftcombe Valley has, in the last forty years or so, often been described by the name Piedmont. Indeed there was a signpost, Piedmont, to the Valley.

Its location may be described as part of the Driftcombe group of dwellings or as part of The Scrubs. Here it is included in the former because that is the present access and because the land extended well to the west of The Scrubs.

There has been frequent surmise as to the origin of the name Piedmont including its possible connection with Huguenot weavers but no evidence has been found to support the suggestion that there were Huguenots in the Valley. Jim Dickinson uses the handed-down pronunciation of 'pied', as in multi-coloured, and 'mount'. The house known as Piedmont included a barn and stables.

The Scrubs (sometimes Scrubbs)

The Scrubs has two meanings. The first covers the whole of the side valley of the Slad Valley from Sydenhams down to the cottages at the bottom of the valley also known as Driftcombe and recently as Piedmont. This is the modern usage and the postal address of all the houses in that area is 'The Scrubs'. It is used in this sense in the title of this book. The old usage denoted the area of the former Custom Scrubs or the old Common and the area and houses and cottages round about. It was used in the 1841 and 1851 censuses and later in this way. It is used in this book to denote that area at the approximate level of Sydenhams as shown in Map 1. It is also the name of a house on the promontory overlooking the main Slad Valley.

Steanbridge

Steanbridge is the name of a hamlet below Slad which is reputed to be the oldest part of Slad. The name may be derived from stan, or sometimes staen, the Old English word for stone, and bridge. This refers to the bridge across the Slad Brook which goes back at least to1353. In 1778 it was recorded in the Bisley Vestry minutes[2] that a 'staenbridge is to be built between the parish of Painswick and the parish of Bisley it is agreed that it shall be paid out of the poor rate.'

On the other hand, in 1820 the place was referred to as Steevensbridge.[3] Whatever the origin of Steanbridge, it is the name of a house below Slad and of former mills in the area, namely Upper and Lower Steanbridge Mills.

Sydenhams

Sydenhams is sometimes spelt Sidenham, Syddenham, Sydnams or Sidnams.

The name refers to the house and its land and also to the farm which was once part of the same property.

1.   GRO D2056/2 Indenture and Bargain and Sale for Piedmount House and Land, 7th September 1788
2.   GRO P47 VE 2/2 Bisley Vestry Minutes Book 1774–1806
3.   GRO D269B/T10 Deed of 1632 relating to property in Over Lypiatt

Appendix 3

Glossary and Measures

Assart: A piece of land, often irregular in shape, fenced for cultivation or for construction of a dwelling. The term is usually applied to the mediæval period.

Baulk: A ridge left unploughed between furrows.

Bordar: A term frequently found in the Domesday Book meaning a smallholder who farmed 'assarted land on the edge of settlements'.

Bovate: The amount of land an ox could plough in a year varying from 10 to 18 acres.

Broadcloth: Cloth up to two yards wide. The term came to mean quality thick cloth that had been fulled so that individual threads were not visible (see Appendix 1).

Burling: Removal of small bits of vegetable matter and knots from the cloth after weaving (see Appendix 1).

Carding: Smoothing of short staple wool, using a card with spikes, before spinning (see Appendix 1).

Cassimere: A special fine woollen cloth (see Appendix 1 and Chapter 5).

Chain: Thread used for the warp in weaving.

Copy holder: A tenant holding a copy of the entry in the rolls of the Manorial Court Baron which recorded his or her possession of a holding on agreed terms.

Core: A piece of flint from which flakes or blades have been removed.

Cottar: The term used in the Domesday Book and other mediæval records for cottagers.

Crop mark: Differentiation in the colour or growth of crops which indicates the plans, below ground, of former structures.

Customary tenant: A tenant holding his land according to custom rather than the will of the Lord of the Manor.

Demesne: Land retained by the Lord for his own use and on which the peasants were required to do a certain number of days work.

Dredge: Grain from a sowing of barley and oats mixed.

Ell: See 'Measures' below.

Fallow: Arable land which is left unploughed for a year in order to recuperate.

Freebench: The custom on some manors whereby the widow of a copyholder retained between a third and all (usually in practice a half or more) of her late husband's land until her death or remarriage.

Freeman: A man who is free, that is, neither a slave nor a serf.

Fulling: Banging of cloth with hammers, known as stocks, in a little water and fullers earth or soap to shrink and thicken it (see Appendix 1).

Gig: A machine for raising the nap on cloth with teazels (see Appendix 1).

Grist: Corn for grinding.

Heriot: A payment (often the best beast) from an incoming tenant to the Lord of the Manor.

Homager: One of twelve jurors of a manor court.

Journeyman: An artisan who works for someone else and, in the case of the weaving industry, does not have his own loom.

Kerseymore: As cassimere, a superfine woollen cloth.

Lynchet: Bank of earth between the ploughed strips of ground in the open fields of the mediæval manorial system.

Master Weaver: A skilled weaver who owns his own loom or looms.

Messuage: A term used in deeds to signify a dwelling house and the surrounding property including out-buildings.

Mule: A machine to spin wool (see Appendix 1).

Open fields: The widespread system whereby the agricultural land of a parish was farmed in large fields divided into strips.

Oppida: Tracts of countryside enclosed by banks; from first millennium BC.

Rack: An instrument for stretching. Used for the stands, called tenter racks, to hang the dyed cloth to dry and stretch.

Sainfoin: One of the grasses introduced in the second quarter of the seventeenth century as a fodder crop.

Scribbling: Removal of unwanted matter from wool (see Appendix 1).

Serf: Unfree peasant of the Middle Ages.

Shearing: Final removal of any stray threads from cloth so that it is totally smooth (see Appendix 1).

Sizing: Treatment of the spun thread by a type of weak glue (See Appendix 1).

Slinging: Embezzlement of cloth or materials.

Stock: Wooden hammer used to beat cloth in the process of fulling in the manufacture of broadcloth (see Appendix 1).

Tenement: Originally the term referred to any rented property, especially those smaller than farms but larger than the properties of cottagers. Its modern meaning of working-class flats in towns is Victorian in origin.

Tenter rack: See rack.

Tucking: Same as fulling (see Appendix 1).

Tyning: A term used, often in the naming of fields, to denote that the area had been enclosed.

Villein: The unfree tenant of manorial land under the feudal system.

Virgate: A standard holding of arable land in the Middle Ages of up to 30 acres spread amongst the open fields of a manor. The actual measure varied from place to place and over time.

Warp: Threads stretched lengthwise in a loom to be crossed by the weft.

Weft: threads woven across the warp.

Yardland: Similar to a virgate.

Measures
Land area
Pole: Measure of 30¼ sq yards. 40 poles = 1 rood.
Rood: Measure of ¼ acre=1210 square yards = 40 poles.
Acre: 4,840 square yards = 4 roods.

Capacity and weight
Bushel: A measure of capacity for corn, fruit, liquid etc. of about 8 gallons in Britain. The capacity of a bushel was very variable from place to place and commodity to commodity. The conversion of the bushel measure of crop yields to weight varies according to the quality of the crop. Variations of at least 10% were commonplace. Guidelines are as follows: 1 bushel of wheat = 57lb; 1 bushel of rye = 55lb; 1 bushel of barley = 49 lb; 1 bushel of oats = 38lb. These are the conversions used in this book.[1]

Peck: A quarter of a bushel.

Length
Ell: About 45 inches.

1.   John, A.H. (1989) Statistical Appendix, Weights and Measures, p.1124 in Mingay, G.E. and Higgs, J.W.Y. (eds) (1989) *The Agrarian History of England and Wales* (General

Editor Joan Thirsk, former editor H.P.R. Finberg), Vol. VI, 1750–1850, Cambridge: CUP, Statistical Appendix-Weights and Measures; and Harrison, Giles V., 1985 'Agricultural Weights and Measures' Appendix 1, pp.815–25 in Thirsk, Joan (ed.) (1985) *The Agrarian History of England and Wales* (General Editor Joan Thirsk, former editor H.P.R. Finberg), Vol. V.2, 1640–1750, Cambridge: CUP, Appendix 1

Subject Index

This index covers subjects and concepts discussed in the main text of the book, including appendices 1 and 2 but not 3 (on glossary and measures) which is an index in itself.

Index of Personal Names

NOTE

Names of those mentioned in the main text are included as well as those in the Gazetteer. Names in the references are not included except where the source is specifically mentioned in the text. There are many more inhabitants of the valley than listed in the Gazeteer but it has not been possible to identify the houses in which they lived.

First names are given when they are known. Listing of several first names under one surname implies that they are of the same family but it is likely that many listed separately are also related to others of the same name. However spelling was not always accurate, especially in the censuses and consequently some apparently different names may be of the same family or even be the same person.